OUR GRANDMOTHERS,
OUR MOTHERS,
OURSELVES

A CENTURY OF WOMEN'S LIVES

Our Grandmothers, Our Mothers, Ourselves

A Century of Women's Lives

Editor: Charmian Cannon

Contributors: Irene Brent
Charmian Cannon
Renee Engstad
Marj Fleming
Mary Hill
Joan Hutten
Sima Kruks
Josephine Negro
Elizabeth Parrish
Patricia Smith
Estella J. Ward

Third Age Press
London 2001

Third Age Press

ISBN 1 898576 27 0
Second edition 2001

Third Age Press Ltd, 2001
Third Age Press, 6 Parkside Gardens
London SW19 5EY
Managing Editor Dianne Norton

© Ogomos
First published in 2000 by Ogomos ISBN 0-953 8 926-0-3

The quotations from T S Eliot are taken from *Four Quartets,
Collected Poems 1909 - 1962*. They are reproduced by kind
permission of Faber and Faber Ltd.

Cover design by Estella J Ward. Art Work by Mel-Art Graphics,
158 Regents Park Road, London NW1 8XN.
Printed and bound in Great Britain by Intype.

To younger women and girls,
particularly those
in the next generations
of our families

This edition is also dedicated
to the memory
of dear Sima
who died on August 10th 2000

A guide to our small galaxy

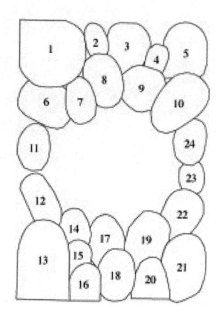

Key to the front cover

1. Joan & Patricia's Mother
2. Jo's Mother
3. Mary
4. Jo
5. Renee's Grandma
6. Patricia
7. Joan
8. Elizabeth
9. Sima's Mother-in-law
10. Sima
11. Joan & Patricia's Mother
12. Marj's Mother
13. Charmian's Mother
14. Marj
15. Charmian
16. Charmian's Grandma
17. Estella's Paternal Grandma
18. Charmian
19. Estella's Maternal Grandma
20. Estella
21. Estella's Mother
22. Irene's Grandma
23. Irene
24. Sima

CONTENTS

FOREWORD

Charmian

This book was written by a group of women who have been meeting regularly over the last few years at a London branch of the University of the Third Age. We have traced the history of 20th century women as it is embodied in the lives of our grandmothers, our mothers, and ourselves. All of us have contributed, orally and in writing, through discussion and argument; and by listening to each other.

In the early days of the project we presented some of our material to a regional women's history conference called *Women's Voices* and were amazed at the interest it evoked among younger women. That recognition of the importance of what we were doing was an element in our decision to prepare the book.

Our purpose is twofold: to explore how our work developed because of the light it sheds on how adults learn; and to show the value of doing history by tracing the course of personal lives. We do not claim to be representative of all older women in this country (what U3A group could be?), but the three generations have seen enormous changes in the opportunities and experiences open to women, and we come from diverse class and cultural backgrounds. When some of our grandmothers were young the first debate in parliament on women's suffrage took place. Our mothers were born between 1880 and 1904, either in Britain or other parts of Europe. When they were growing up in this country they still could not vote. It was not until after the Second World War that women were admitted to degrees at the University of Cambridge, and only in 1955 whilst we were all working, that equal pay was agreed for nurses and teachers.

We started the exploration of our memories in 1995 when our ages ranged from 63 to 78. We have grown a bit older since then and reached the millenium, so we have explored a century of women's lives. It is time we put together all this knowledge for others to share. We hope that readers in our age group will find that our experiences evoke memories for them; and that younger readers may feel inspired to ask their mothers and grandmothers about their pasts before they are lost forever.

The Editor

ACKNOWLEDGMENTS

Embarking on the publication of a book based on the writing of eleven women is daunting, especially when they have no experience of such an exercise, and are relatively inexperienced in computer technology. It is difficult to know where to begin our acknowledgments because we owe so much to so many people for their support. After the first women's history conference we contributed to, Christine Zmroczek of Roehampton College said: 'You should write a book', thus consolidating an idea already in our minds. At a later stage Gwen Parrish gave us the benefit of her experience in producing books based on U3A writing, and read and commented on the draft. Other people who have read successive drafts and helped us shape the book, arc Janet Hadley, journalist and friend of the editor; Maureen Forrest, who joined the U3A group too late to be part of the project, but whose comments were most helpful; and Jon Cannon, also experienced in journalism. His perspective on family life was not too different from his mother's! The group is indebted to Cyril Cannon, the editor's husband, who read and proof-read the book and suggested it would not be complete without a chapter about food! He made valuable comments on the text, and from his background in printing, made the editor aware of the importance of punctuation, and meticulous attention to typographical presentation. He is not to blame for the remaining mistakes. Martin Lethbridge of Mel-Art has patiently responded to numerous requests and taken the book through the design stage.

The editor would also like to acknowledge the debt she owes to Dorothy Sheridan and Al Thomson of Sussex University, who taught the Life History Certificate at Sussex which introduced her to the theoretical perspectives underlying the book. Her project for the course provided part of its original impetus.

Mary Hill has given constant support and advice as Assistant Editor; Estella Ward has been a talented and committed Art Editor. Together with Sima Kruks and Elizabeth Parrish, they have met many times as members of the publication committee to steer the work through successive stages. All the contributors have been most patient in rewriting their original drafts, and responding to telephone calls about obscure details. The typing skills acquired by Renee and Mary in their early office careers have proved invaluable. Everyone has read the book and often made careful comments and corrections; they have shown remarkable faith in the outcome.

Our debt to the U3A is evident throughout.

Charmian Cannon, Editor.

Out and About

This is a 'quadracycle' with a small rear wheel to give stability – 'especially fashionable for women & elderly gentlemen' around 1880

Charmian's great aunt & her husband enjoying a cycle ride

Estella's family & others – trip to Brighton about 1922

PART ONE: THE LIFE HISTORIES

Chapter 1

How We Did It:
The Life History of our Project

Charmian

The setting for our work was a course entitled *The Hidden History of Women* taught at the U3A in London, during the academic year 1994-5. Numbers were small and fluctuating and there was not a great level of participation (Joan has pointed out that some students come to the U3A and sit and listen passively or even occasionally have a quiet snooze). The course leader was Mary, who has remained a central member of our group. We started again in 1995, mostly with different students, and after two or three weeks decided to switch over to a different approach, looking at women's history through talking about the lives of our mothers and grandmothers.

It seemed a pity just to let all these memories disappear into the air of the classroom and we felt we could do more with them. Charmian had heard about oral history as a growing interest among people tracing their family backgrounds, and she volunteered to take notes from members' contributions and attempt some analysis.

It was soon obvious that her notes were going to be inadequate records. We experimented with tape recording, but with eleven women participating, interrupting and asking questions it was far too confusing. We then agreed to provide written back-up material to supplement our spoken accounts. So from the beginning we were using both spoken and written 'stories'. This really took off. Everyone became fascinated by the divergent experiences of our forebears, and it became difficult to stop the flow of talk.

At the time some of us felt that recounting our mothers' and grandmothers' stories was rather self-indulgent unless we put them into a historical context, particularly as we had come together to study women's history. We attempted to get students to read and comment on short pieces of background material. This was successful occasionally, but did not really develop, and was felt by some to distract from the main purpose of the group.

When we had all contributed, Charmian took several sessions to report back our work from a sociological perspective. We began to see the significance of doing this. It was still about our families in relation to one another, and themes emerged which we developed for a conference at the end of the academic year.

After one year the nature of the group had fundamentally changed. It was no longer a taught course with one knowledgeable leader and others asking occasional questions. Mary had never been happy with this, and it was thanks to her willingness to 'let things happen' that the project was able to develop. Because of Charmian's role in reporting back she became, for a short while only, a kind of teacher. But we were all deeply involved and it became apparent that what we were doing was becoming quite a serious project.

During this early period we evolved ethical guidelines about confidentiality and so on, although we didn't call them anything so grand. First, we decided that anything said in the meetings must remain confidential to the group; this helped us feel free to express ourselves. At the same time we agreed that no one should be pressured into talking about anything they didn't want to. This was an important assurance at first, though our attitude to self-revelation became more relaxed later. Secondly, we agreed that written contributions could be made more widely available with the permission of the author. All written materials were kept together in what we proudly called the 'archive', for future reference.

During the second year we moved from discussing our foremothers to taking turns to report on our own life histories, which were even more enthralling! Then we took topics which we felt we wanted to expand on, such as education, war, work, and family, and which different members volunteered to lead. We also discussed among other things, feminism, singleness, and the social context of retirement. Many of these discussions and the writings that accompanied them have become the basis for the sections in this book.

Through all this the group relationships became more and more democratic, though not smoothly. In fact it became rather 'a free for all' at times. Mary and Charmian used to issue notes for future plans which were discussed and sometimes ignored. We experimented with different kinds of organisation: rotating chairwomen with different attitudes to the job, takers of minutes. Through a mixture of frustration and tolerance we began to settle, discovering techniques for making people shut up or encouraging the reticent. These didn't always work and anarchy was usually just around the corner, specially when we started working on the book.

However, we kept going through it all and there were several milestones which helped to bind us together. The first of these was our joint presentation at a conference on women's history in May 1996, the significance of which has already been mentioned. Working to prepare for this gave us a heightened sense of purpose. We found talents we hadn't suspected. Estella was a wonder at drawing graphs and maps for the overhead projector. Jo produced a time chart, Mary made an overall plan. We rehearsed, six of us spoke, and our contribution was warmly received. We had arrived in the world of professional women's history, which was a new one for many of us.

The next milestone was our first Christmas party in one of our homes. 'Bring your own' parties have become a recurring feature, allowing us to recognise that we still have private lives outside the telling of them.

At the end of the second year of our work we decided we should stop before we ran out of steam. But we were very reluctant to break it up. Some of the group decided to pursue further themes in women's history with Mary, and are still doing so at the time of writing, taking turns to prepare presentations. We all committed ourselves to making this book, an idea which had been brewing during our second year. This of course involved regular meetings, the occasional party, and lots of opportunities for creative anarchy.

What do we know and how do we know it?

As we systemised our work we found it raised many issues about the nature of memory. If we had pretensions to calling it a research project we had to be sure we knew what we were doing. The life history approach relies upon memory with all its patchiness, its avoidance or distortion of traumatic events. We found that it telescopes time so that childhood for instance evokes an unspecific aura of happiness or misery, enlivened by occasional vivid incidents such as this one recalled by Jo: 'My sister and I played Mummies and Daddies by throwing a doll's teaset across the room. Can't remember parents in fact behaving in this way!'

Our stories overlap as we recall memories of grandmothers and mothers from a child's point of view and then draw away to reflect on them as adults. Accounts have tended to fade away as we reached 'retirement' and we had to make an explicit commitment to include material about our present lives when we were writing our life stories. Speculating on why this was so, we thought it was partly because we were focussing on 'history' and partly because the recognised aspects of a life, such as schooling, marriage, family, and work, are past. Life in retirement is more difficult to pin down, though it seems to be just as busy. Maybe too, life as one lives it is always formless because we have had no time to stand back and give it a shape. Or is it, as Jo thinks, that we have become victims of society's ageism and consider our old age of no consequence?

Memory is not just a personal matter either. 'Family history was handed down,' says Elizabeth. Much of what we think we know is passed on in this way, and altered in the telling. Jo describes what she writes as being often based on 'family legends'. Did they really happen like that?' she wonders. Three-generational life stories are likely to be particularly crowded with myths and anecdotes passed down between members. As Patricia comments: 'The other generations were not able to speak for themselves. We did the selecting of the memories.' Joan is explicit: 'I cherish the story of my grandfather walking fifteen miles overnight to hear a preacher he enjoyed. He stayed to the evening service and walked back through the next night.'

Our memories are also suffused with myths from the wider society - what might be called 'cultural myths', which reach us through reading, television, story telling, gossip. Entangled in our stories are popular memories of European persecution, economic depression and two world wars, some of which happened before we were born. Sima writes of the emigration of her Jewish grandparents from East Europe in 1885. 'At that time pogroms were raging all over Russian-held territory and refugees were pouring into this country.' This is probably right historically, as pogroms increased after the assassination of the Tsar in 1882. But both political and economic motives are usually elements in any mass migration, and every immigrant community carries a dramatic piece of folklore about its arrival from the home country.

Elizabeth, writing about her grandmother in Wales, evokes the notion of community which is part of nostalgia for a rural past. 'The women in the community were very close, often visiting each other to reminisce about their lives. In this way social and family history was handed down. In times of crisis everyone rallied round to help.'

Are there any more dependable sources we can use to widen and confirm our stories? Some of us have tried to address the question of the sources of our family 'knowledge' and these accounts appear at the beginning of our life histories. Charmian feels overwhelmed by family documents, Irene has her mother's autobiography written for the benefit of her children. At the other extreme are those who through family trauma or disruption have no records at all. Some members of the group have been moved to try to find out more through talking with relations. Joan and Patricia are sisters who give different interpretations of events, and we have enjoyed listening to them argue about incidents in their childhood. Mary had singularly uncommunicative parents but has been able to fill in parts of her family life by talking to her siblings, and her niece has now become interested as well.

Mothers and Daughters

Our work has involved re-examining our relationship with our mothers. Many women have tried to write about their mothers and found that the intensity of feeling in the relationship makes it a complex process. They may be incredibly supportive or restrictive or both, but our mothers' presence and personality affects us even after we are adult, and after they have died. We had an interesting session discussing this, starting from Elizabeth telling us about Nancy Friday's book *My Mother Myself*. We remembered phrases which we have used to our children as echoes of those our mothers had used to us, even if we had vowed to bring them up differently: 'You may be laughing now, but it will all end in tears!' 'No child of mine is going to...'

Even at our advanced age we are not 'free' of our mothers; but we have found the process of reflection a means of working through family relationships. Fathers were significant too, and often made the most important decisions affecting both our own lives and those of our mothers. The dominance of fathers is, of course, supported by law and custom as we trace back through the generations, but is often tempered by the personalities of both parents.

When we read back our life histories for the purposes of this book, we found that, in spite of the significance of mothers and the strong feelings they evoke, in some cases they remain rather hazy figures. There are two elements in our accounts: the historical, as we compare the experience of three generations and relate it to the circumstances of the time; and the personal, in which we try to trace the influence of one generation on the behaviour of the next. This has been much more difficult to tease out, and much more subject to emotional blocks.

How did we present ourselves in our histories?

People compose their stories in ways which are acceptable in their culture. An idyllic, sunlit voyage of discovery, or alternatively an indomitable struggle against adversity: 'From abject poverty to gold taps', as Patricia puts it. There are elements of all these in our histories. Jo presents her life as a determined struggle to escape her mother's fate: 'At the age of twelve I remember looking at my mother and vowing I was never going to allow myself to be in her position'.

We found that a useful way of making sense of our lives was through the idea of 'turning points'. For Estella, winning a scholarship to grammar school was such a turning point. 'All the things I had read about in fictional schoolgirls' books became reality. The life I began to lead with my new school friends was in sharp contrast to that of the East End street arab I had been.' Her reading became a meaningful part of her life.

People also tell different stories for different audiences. We were a particular audience and although there were only small differences of status or education between us, we must have felt uncertain of each other at the beginning, which will have affected our presentation of ourselves. However, as trust grew we listened with more attention and hesitant accounts grew in confidence, a process helped by starting with our grannies rather than ourselves. As one of us said: 'A good thing which has come out of this for me, is the realisation that others share the same experiences. I am not alone.' Mary points out that the same process was experienced by members of feminist consciousness-raising groups in the 1970s.

Talking and writing

What will you confide to a group of friends you have come to trust? What difference does it make to recount memories on the telephone, as happened occasionally? What will you write down for the group when you've had time to have second thoughts?

When we turned talking into writing, our stories became less spontaneous, more ordered, more distanced. Some of us found writing less embarrassing than speaking when dealing with sensitive matters. On the other hand our later discussions about intimate relationships and attitudes to sex, are confined to unrecorded talk and we have discussed reasons for this more fully in the chapter on the family. The greatest challenge comes when you know strangers will read what you have written. Gaining confidence that a wider readership was interested in what we were doing and deciding to publish, we found ourselves looking at our work in a different light.

We have tried to introduce some order into our stories by providing a chronological sequence of life's stages. But there were tremendous differences in the way we each approached the task; in the detail we reveal, and in our willingness to talk about traumatic experiences such as bereavement or divorce. We have all shaped our stories in ways acceptable to ourselves.

So there are many elements involved in what we have done. If the boundary between objective 'facts' and subjective responses is always blurred, then life history work is intensely subjective. But its value is that it has given us a chance to reflect on our lives in the context of history. We would all agree with Rousseau in his *Confessions:'I have one...faithful guide...the chain of feelings which have marked the development of my being...I may make factual omissions, transpositions, mistakes about dates, but I cannot be wrong about what I have felt.'*

Chapter 2

Introducing our own Life Histories:
Convergence from Diversity

Jo

'Men make their own history but...they do not make it under circumstances chosen by themselves but under circumstances directly encountered, given, and transmitted from the past.' [Women too!] Karl Marx

At the early meetings of our group we had no idea of the extent of diversity we would find in our histories. To the outsider we appeared a homogeneous gathering of elderly women, although in fact we cover a wide age range. Irene and Sima, born towards the end of the First World War, were in their mid-teens in 1932, when Marj and Elizabeth were young babies.

Our life experiences, and those of our mothers and grandmothers, between them span the whole of this century and extend back into the previous one. Naturally these were profoundly affected by the 'circumstances directly encountered, given, and transmitted from the past.' Although these are personal stories and won't often refer directly to the public affairs of the century, this does not mean that the women telling the stories were unaware of social and political developments, and how these opened up opportunities for the current generation or imposed limitations on our foremothers. For example, it was the Depression of the 1930s - launched with the stock market collapse four months after her birth - that blighted Jo's childhood; and which drove Elizabeth's mother to leave her strong social support network in Wales as the family moved to London in search of work.

The significance of these age differences, however, is most apparent in the diversity of our experiences during the Second World War. Being of school age during the war contributed to the scrappy nature of Jo's education, while the child Elizabeth was sent to live with her grandmother in Wales; Renee and Estella were evacuated with their schools. Others in the group were already adult when the war started, or became so during it. This meant that Mary and Patricia were able to escape boring jobs for opportunities to travel and develop new skills in the services; Sima took on a specialised job previously the preserve of men; and Irene got married having arrived in this country in 1939 as a refugee. There is no doubt that whatever our age, the war was a major event. We are the generation which still talks about 'before' and 'after' the war rather than seeing it as a piece of history.

The geographical diversity between us became obvious when we started sharing the histories of our grandmothers. Most of them could never have known each other because they came from all parts of the United Kingdom and beyond. Of our twenty grandmothers half were born in continental Europe. They were part of the rich cultural mix from which the UK and London in particular has greatly gained. All but one of the women of non-UK origin were Jewish, mostly coming from Eastern Europe in the late 19th or early 20th century. Our parents, and in some cases ourselves, have moved within the United Kingdom as work patterns demanded, forming part of the general shift of population from rural to urban living that has been a feature of Britain since the 18th century. Now we have converged on London which has always acted as a magnet to the adventurous, the enterprising or the desperate.

This group of elderly women has in addition a diverse range of religious backgrounds. As already noted there was a large Jewish element, though not all were practising Jews. Among the Christian families, also not necessarily practising, there was a mixture of Catholics, and various kinds of Protestant nonconformity. We wonder about the significance of there being nobody from a Church of England background among us. Even in the solid middle class families there is little sign of the 'Establishment'.

Although by the time we met as a group we could all be described as 'middle class' there was in many of our family origins a strong working-class element. When we discussed it there was an initial resistance to the idea of seeing ourselves in class terms. But actually we didn't have any difficulty in categorising ourselves or our parents and grandparents by class, though actually there are complications in assigning class to women. Class in families is traditionally taken from the male 'head of household' if there is one, so women can 'enter' a class through marriage. Women often have less skilled jobs than men so that a family might have a man in a professional occupation and his partner in an unskilled one. Thus Sima's father was a pharmacist and her mother a feather curler in the days when women wore huge feathers in their hats. Jo's two grannies each came from different class backgrounds. Among the middle-class families (Joan and Patricia, who are sisters - Charmian and Irene), there was a mixture of professional and commercial employment. A further complicating factor in our group was the change in economic circumstances caused by immigration. Thus Irene, with a professional background in Germany, worked as a domestic help when she first came to England as a refugee. So in spite of our willingness to label ourselves, we cannot be too categorical about the social class of our families.

In addition there has been a huge change in the definition of classes themselves during the century with the decline in manual work, the rise of new work opportunities for women, and the growth of service jobs. Nevertheless, there is no doubt that we had diverse class origins which have converged only in our generation.

The chapter on work shows how different are the three generations in terms of the paid work we did. Within our own generation our first jobs were of varied status but all typical 'women's' work; we have nearly all managed to make the transition to professional jobs and the education chapter will show how this came about. Education has been one of the most important elements in our convergence. Another factor that unites us is the extent of our working lives; given our generation one would expect long career breaks, or no paid work after marriage. In fact most of us worked almost all the time up to pensionable age whether we have had children or not. Some of us still have part-time jobs and between us we do a lot of voluntary work.

We shall trace in detail how this seemingly homogeneous group of U3A members, so geographically and socially diverse in our grandmothers' generation, have become increasingly convergent in our own. But this is only part of the story. We also remain distinct and diverse personalities, and this is reflected in the way we tell our stories.

Landmarks for Three Generations of Women

Our grandmothers were born between 1850 and 1880, and our mothers between 1880 and 1904. The last quarter of the 19th century and the first part of the 20th saw important social, economic and political changes affecting women, such as the Married Women's Property Acts, and the Guardianship of Infants Act. Women were admitted to London University, and after 1907 they could stand for local elections. Pioneering girls' schools and colleges were founded. Many women pressed for these changes, for example through the women's suffrage campaign and other aspects of the women's movement.

Ourselves

Birth dates

Irene	1917	(in Germany).
Sima	1918	End of First World War. Votes for women householders over 30. Women could stand for Parliament.
	1919	Nancy Astor first woman MP to take her seat.
Mary Joan	1922	Birth control clinics for 'married women in poor circumstances.' (Marie Stopes).
Patricia Charmian	1923	Matrimonial Causes Act. Equal grounds for divorce for women and men.
Renee	1924	
Estella	1926	General strike.
	1928	Equal Franchise Act. Women over 21 could vote.
Jo	1929	Economic depression. Wall Street crash. First woman cabinet minister (Margaret Bonfield).
Elizabeth Marj	1932	
	1937	Matrimonial Causes Act widened grounds for divorce.
	1939	Second World War. Evacuation, disruption of schooling. During the war the TUC pledged to equal pay; Beveridge reported on the 'welfare state'.
	1944	Education Act. 'Secondary education for all.'
	1945	End of war. Family allowances paid direct to women.

Equal Pay was not agreed for teachers and civil servants until 1955, and 'equal pay for equal work' not until 1970.

Chapter 3

Our Grandmothers, Our Mothers, Ourselves

(i) Irene: My Life and My Mother's Life

Elly: Irene's mother

Although Irene left her native Berlin as a young woman just before the 1939 war and never saw her father again, her mother, Elly, escaped to the USA and eventually settled in England. She lived from 1892-1989, and at the age of 92 she wrote her life story which Irene, her oldest daughter, now treasures. Irene says her mother was prone to dramatisation as befits an actress, but the main facts are not in doubt. The following account is based on this document, which has been summarised by Estella.

Elly, the youngest of two sisters, was born in Berlin. Her parents were well-off cultured people, affectionate and caring. She wrote: 'I'm sure I had the best mother. My father and us children - that was her entire world.' At the age of sixteen she went to a boarding school in Heidelberg to improve her English and French, attend history of art lectures at the university, and develop the social graces. She was a lively girl, always in and out of scrapes. Afterwards she went to drama school to train as an actress. In order to join a theatre company she had to get her parents' permission as she was only nineteen. At first her father protested that 'this was not a profession for a refined girl,' but when her mother suggested she could be chaperoned by an aunt, he relented. She became a Red Cross nurse at the outbreak of the First World War and married in 1916, following her husband to his training camp and nursing in the local hospital. Her first daughter, Irene, was born in 1917. In spite of the severe food shortages they made the best of things. On returning to Berlin at the end of the war, they acquired their own home, and enjoyed a busy social life and the arrival of their second daughter.

In the 1930s, their lives were deeply affected by Hitler's rise to power. Elly's husband was no longer allowed to carry on his profession as an antiquarian, and her daughter Irene was barred from journalism. Concerned about the future of her family, Elly decided to try to go to New York where she had relations. After an initial train journey in which she was subject to much harassment from German officials, she joined a ship in Antwerp. She had to spend three days on Ellis Island waiting for her aunt to claim her.

From the States she was advised to go to Cuba as it would be easier to get a visa there for her family to join her. She stayed two years, doing a variety of nursing jobs but never got a visa. She witnessed the arrival of the refugee ship St. Louis in 1939, and the heart-rending incidents associated with its enforced return to Europe where many of the passengers ended their lives in concentration camps. Irene's mother and several other people were taken on little boats alongside this big ship to see their beloved ones. They had to shout to each other because of the distance between them. After a few days like that they had to say 'Goodbye'.

In the meantime her husband had been put in a concentration camp; he was gassed in Auschwitz in 1944, but her daughters escaped to Britain just before the war. Elly continued to work hard as a nurse back in New York, and eventually saved enough to visit Irene and her family. She finally settled in London and remarried at the age of 64, to an 82 year old who had been a childhood friend. After he died in 1976 Elly had the opportunity to visit Berlin and she went back to the areas she had known as a child. The visit brought back so many happy and sad memories, and everything had changed so much she wished she hadn't gone.

Elly grew to love England; she enjoyed living near her daughter and granddaughter and kept in touch with her other daughter. When she looked back on her life at 92, she weighed up the pros and cons of the past and present. With all its advances in medicine, travel, TV, computers and so on, Elly still felt that the present was second-best compared to her life long ago, when family life mattered so much and respect of children for their parents was generally acknowledged. Throughout her autobiography she emerges as a vibrant, determined, fun-loving, out-of-the-ordinary woman. As she herself wrote, 'In spite of all the ups and downs, looking back on all that happened to me, I must say I have lived a full life.'

Irene's childhood

I was born in 1917 and my first name, Irene, was chosen because it means 'Peace.' I was born in Berlin in a private clinic, and my sister Marion was born in the same one three years later. At the time my father was in the army, as a Hussar, and he didn't see me until I was a few days old. I still have a photo of the two of us. He was stationed some distance away and my mother and I joined him a few weeks later. We stayed there for about a year, and the story goes that several of his friends changed my nappies.

After the war, my parents moved back to Berlin and took a flat near my father's business; he was a well-known publisher and antiquary. As a small child I was taken there often. I loved it, and used to watch the auctions, as I still like to do in London nowadays. Just before I was six, the age one starts school in Germany, we moved to a suburb outside Berlin, reached only by train as at that time hardly anybody drove a car. My parents had a house built there, and I can still remember being taken by ladder up to the roof, and, as was the custom then, putting a flower wreath on it. I went to a private school, which to my surprise still exists. I was taken to my first films, *Ben Hur,* and *Sleeping Beauty.* We had a lovely big garden, with a gazebo and lots of flowers and strawberries, and we had our first dog as a pet. We had lots of visitors, even relatives from America. We went swimming and skating on the nearby lake and of course wherever we went so did our nanny.

Three years ago we went to a wedding in Hamburg. My grand-daughter insisted on seeing where I lived as a small child, and so we went there as well. We even went inside the house. After more than sixty years it seemed even bigger, but it didn't touch me at all emotionally and I felt like a tourist. However, when I went to our former synagogue which had been burnt by the Nazis on the 9th November 1938 sharing the same fate as all the other synagogues, all of us were very upset. It is now a community centre for the few Jewish people still living there.

Coming back to my childhood, I stayed in this house until I was about eleven, and then, because of inflation, everybody had a rough time and we had to sell it and move back into a flat in Berlin. We went to a very nice area where all our nearest relatives lived; we saw everybody almost every day and always had Sunday lunch with the family. We were very close to our grandparents, especially my grandmother who had been a widow since she was 27. She was very orthodox, and on Jewish holidays and Fridays we often went to her house. We started new schools of course, and I went to one where I learned two languages. My favourite subjects were history, art, literature and languages. I had some Jewish and non-Jewish friends. By 1931 Hindenberg was still President and Hitler not yet Chancellor. We had Jewish instruction while the others had their religion class.

But then things began to change a bit. I went to my favourite teacher about an unpleasant remark which was made to me, but she took no notice. At that time my father's business was not doing well and my parents had to make some changes. My sister and I went to a Jewish boarding house quite far away near the Dutch border. Everything was much more primitive as it was a very small town. For instance, there was no hot running water and no central heating and everybody spoke dialect. I had never been away from home and hated everything and kept ringing my grandmother to take us

14

home; but then we made friends with the other children. For holidays we either went home or my parents came to see us. At the school I was the only Jewish girl in my class, but neither the teacher nor my fellow pupils treated me any differently. This small school was better than my other one, with a wider range of subjects. On my birthday I received several books from my father which I had to burn without reading them because they were by authors suddenly forbidden. The year was 1933 and lessons began to change. For instance, each day started with political questions like 'What is new in our internal politics today?' and 'What did Herr Hitler say?' But I was lucky enough to take my leaving exams there, and was even mentioned in the local newspaper as I had written the school play. However, my sister had to leave school at fourteen.

My sister and I went back to Berlin where my parents had taken a flat with my maternal grandfather after my grandmother died. I felt very sad, as I had only just taken a school holiday with her which we had both enjoyed very much. We were sorry to leave the small town as the family we had stayed with there had treated us like their own children.

My adult life. Disruption and family dispersal
My father had arranged a job for me with a well-known publisher to train as a reporter. I went to a business school to learn typing and shorthand, but of course I never got the job, as the publisher, being Jewish, had to close down. For a while I was able to work as a secretary until the various employers emigrated; then I worked as a house-daughter or looking after children as long as I could. My sister, being very artistic became a tailoring trainee. Soon we had to take boarders in our flat, as my father couldn't work any longer in his profession because it was culturally related. We weren't even allowed into a museum, theatre or restaurant, and only into one hotel, where I met my future husband Egon at a dance.

In 1937, my father tried to get the family out of Germany as we had relations in Holland and America, but he was unsuccessful. My mother who was working as a nurse, received a visitor's visa for America for herself, but she never succeeded in getting visas for any of the rest of the family. In 1939 a miracle happened and one after the other Egon, my sister, and I, were somehow able to leave for England, with ten shillings in our pockets, carrying nothing of value, having handed everything in before we left. My father and paternal grandmother took us to the station, and we never saw them again. My grandmother went to Rio de Janiero and my father later to Theresienstadt concentration camp. We heard from him for the last time on

30 September 1944, a reply to us telling him that I was expecting a baby. After the war we were informed by the Red Cross that he had been gassed ten days later at Auschwitz with one of the last groups when the camps were already being liberated. This was the worst news I ever had and stays forever in my mind.

But now back to June 1939. We all lived in Hampstead, and until war broke out I had a lovely job with an Italian family. Egon had put his name down to join the army in case war should break out, and my sister worked as a tailor trainee. We had lots of friends, all without money, just enough to live on. But we were thankful to be in England, and continued to try to get the remaining family out of Germany, without success. However we had several relations here and were never alone.

Egon and most of our friends were called up in 1940 and I started to do war work then. Our wedding was postponed several times; when he came back after the fall of France he had leave, so we were married in Hampstead Town Hall, and my aunt gave a very nice reception. Some months later I left London and from then on I followed Egon's company like many of the other wives. We had a week's honeymoon in Maidenhead, and it took us ten hours by train from Taunton because of air-raids. I saw a lot of England and Wales then, often in lodgings without indoor sanitation or running water. But we were lucky to be together. Everywhere we went I did war work; like pressing airman's gloves, inspecting mosquito nets, and working in a canning factory. In Stratford-on-Avon I nearly died of diptheria, but I was the only case luckily, and no one caught it from me. When my husband joined the Intelligence Corps I moved to Amersham and our daughter Barbara was born in 1944. In the meantime my sister had joined my mother in New York, and still lives there. She has been married three times. She can't come here any more as she is very ill so we visit her as often as possible.

After the war. A more established life

After the war we moved back to Hampstead into a very primitive flat because so much had been bombed. Our daughter went to school there and some years later we were allocated a larger flat with a big garden. My mother came to visit us in London, and then in 1954 she came to live here permanently. She had her own home again after 25 years, and we were very happy because it was a bit like old times.

After my daughter married in 1966, I took part-time jobs at Hamleys and Boots and joined art classes. In 1970 our first granddaughter was born and we bought a house in Kenton, the first house we had owned. We still have our old Hampstead friends and have made several new ones as well. I joined the League of Jewish Women and Wizo (a Jewish charity). I have done a lot of charity work, taking deprived children on holiday, working at a day centre, and collecting money. Seventeen years ago I joined a theatre class and I have been a member of the U3A for some years, attending art classes and women's history. We now have two grandchildren, aged 24 and 26; we see them often, go to the theatre and opera and ballet and I love reading. Although many of the family live in different continents, we keep in touch by visits, letters and e-mail.

My older granddaughter recently got married. She is a solicitor and her husband is a barrister. And where do they live? Five minutes away from the street where we used to live in Hampstead, but the price of their flat is enormous compared to what we paid. My younger granddaughter is a doctor, something she always wanted to do.

I have had quite a few serious illnesses in my time, and for the last two years have been suffering from osteoporosis. At first I couldn't walk or even sit and had to give up all my activities. I still have a lot of pain, but with medication I can again do most of the things I want to. We travel and visit our relations abroad. We have been married for nearly 60 years and enjoy life as much as possible.

[Sadly, Irene's husband Egon died on 21st February 2000. *Editor.*]

(ii) Sima: A Non-Academic

My maternal grandparents

My maternal grandparents arrived in this country in the 1880s with five children, a boy and four girls, one of whom was my mother Victoria. They were a middle-class Orthodox Jewish family from Poland (my grandfather had been a leather merchant), and they arrived in London with just what they could carry, as did most refugees. My mother was then aged five and she told me they were housed on the sixth floor of the Rothschild buildings in Stepney, where they had two rooms, and where the water and sanitation were in the courtyard. She remembered having to go to the soup kitchen in Stepney Green, which was some distance from her home, to get all the family's food. She went to school and learnt English very quickly. When my mother was ten, her mother became pregnant and had another son, but then became ill and died not long after. My mother (who was then aged eleven) and two of her sisters had to cope with the baby and all the housekeeping, as the oldest girl was sent to America where there were relatives, and their brother was apprenticed to diamond cutters in Antwerp.

When she was twelve my mother had to leave school because the family needed her to earn, although her teacher pleaded with her father for her to stay as she was a very bright girl. She was apprenticed as a feather curler at 2s.6d. a week (that is twelve and a half pence). Meanwhile, my grandfather had been peddling in scrap leather and had gradually built up a business. Some time later the family moved to a house in Dalston.

My paternal grandparents

My paternal grandfather was a well-educated man and a fierce Zionist. He had taken a pioneering boatload of Jewish refugees from Romania to Palestine and the Sultan of Turkey had granted him tracts of land in the Hula Swamp area to try to drain and cultivate it. The first settlement was started in the early 1880s and was called Zichron Jacob after Jacob Rothschild who supported them financially. My father's mother, Sima, who was a simple peasant woman, followed in the second boatload with her family of four children. My father, the fifth, was born in the new settlement where life must have been very tough. While they were there, my grandfather was said to have quarrelled with the bailiff who handled the settlement's funds, and he decided to come to England to seek new funding; but after he arrived he had a heart attack and stayed here. The family followed him and they took a house in Canonbury Square which became a centre of Zionist work in this country. When he died in 1917 my grandmother Sima came to live with my parents.

My parents

My mother met my father in 1910 when she was seventeen and he swept her off her feet. He was a man of strong beliefs: a Zionist, a Socialist, and later supported the Communists. He was an athlete and indeed ran for England in the 1908 Olympics. That was part of the glamour that won my mother over, and they married in 1910. Then he set about educating her; he made her read all the great classics and visit art galleries and museums, a regime that was also inflicted on us children. My sister was born in 1912 and my brother in 1914; I was born two years later during the last Zeppelin raid on London, above my father's chemist shop in North Finchley. Grandmother Sima had developed cancer and she actually died in one room as I was born in the next.

My mother was a wonderful influence on me. She had a lovely outgoing personality and was very even-tempered, even when she confronted my father's choleric temper. She kept house on a shoestring and was always short of money. She made all our clothes and was a wonderful cook. My father was a gambler; dogs and horses were his undoing. My mother looked after her mother-in-law, the house, her kids, and worked in the chemist's shop. My older brother and sister were well-bonded and I was an addendum, a nuisance. They were greatly encouraged in their schooling and proved to be very clever. I was a sweet little thing who could dance nicely and recite poems well but had no brains.

I went to a private kindergarten until I was seven when I was deemed strong enough for the rough and tumble of the local primary school. At seven, also, my mother took me to the Italia Conti Stage School, which gave me a scholarship and for two afternoons a week thereafter I missed school and danced. The Conti Kids were in many shows, including the famous *Where the Rainbow Ends* in 1930.

At eleven I passed the scholarship to the grammar school where both my brother and sister had been; my sister had already matriculated and won a place at London University. The education authority put a stop to my absences for dancing. At school I was made to understand that I had a reputation to keep up and I was constantly compared to my brother and sister. Halfway through my first year I went down with bronchial pneumonia and missed all the rest of the year. I decided to repeat the first year and, stopped from dancing, I went for drama instead and thereafter played a leading role in all school dramatics. If I could not shine academically I would shine in my own way, and I did.

In 1935 after school certificate, I was informed I would have to go out to work. My brother was a medical student, my sister had just graduated and I had to enter the civil service, which I hated. However, I enrolled to attend speech classes and by 1938 I had attained the Licentiate of the Royal Academy of Music (Elocution).

My whole family was intensely political and left wing. From 1936 onwards I was involved in collecting for the Spanish Civil War and I joined Unity Theatre and the Communist Party. With the rise of fascism and the Spanish Civil War, the voice of protest was heard and in 1935, Unity, a communist-identified theatre, was founded In London. In 1936 it acquired its own premises, a converted church hall, near Kings Cross. We had the support of many well-known people in the fields of drama and music, although no-one was paid for their work. In 1939 I applied for a scholarship to the Royal Academy of Dramatic Art and to my surprise I won the Leverhulme Scholarship - all fees paid but no living allowance. I left the civil service with no regrets and got an evening job to earn some pocket money.

Life at RADA, when I was already 21 and most of the other students were sixteen, was difficult and made more so as the war progressed. I spent all my evenings, and nights too, at Unity as part of the Outside Show group, visiting such places as factories and air-raid shelters. By May 1940, with France overrun, I realised I could not remain at RADA. I had a boyfriend there, the grandson of Sigmund Freud, and we would discuss what we would do if Hitler invaded. We were both Jews and politically-minded and felt we would have to join some underground movement which we were sure would be formed.

Then the blitz started and I got my call-up papers. I told the interview board that I did not want to leave the work I was doing at Unity Theatre, and they agreed that I would be directed to work in London. I was first sent to an office that had been set up to deal with air-raid casualties, but as I knew no shorthand or typing, that job ended after a week. I was then sent to a cigarette factory in north London where I was asked to work on accounting machines, but was hopeless at that. Then I was told that as I could read and speak well I was to go to a firm of solicitors in the City of London. I had to learn law costing and was given six months to read and study. All the law firms were fast losing staff to the call-up and the firm I was sent to was no exception. When I went to the law courts to defend my first bill of costs the registrar told the porters to 'remove that woman'. I explained why I was there and begged his help as this was my first case. After that he was most helpful.

In 1940 a neighbour asked my mother to help him out - he had a young nephew from Lithuania at public school but needed help for the holidays. Would my mother look after him? As usual, my mother said yes, and Leo came to stay with us. By 1940 his college had been bombed, and he had to find a job, as a firewatcher in the City of London. We fell in love and right through the blitz we cohabited in lodgings in the King's Cross area, until it was flattened and became a bomb crater. He lost all his belongings, including his family photographs, all he had left of his family still in Lithuania, which was then under the Nazis. We married in January 1942 and had two weddings: one for the family and the other for all our friends at Unity. We took a bedsitter in Maida Vale and I undertook to get rid of his foreign accent, which I successfully achieved. I had earned quite a bit by this time, teaching English to foreigners and specialising in getting rid of accents. Leo joined me in my work at Unity and I started the Unity Theatre School under the auspices of the London County Council. We ran classes three nights a week and trained people for our theatre to replace those called up.

My married life

By 1945 I was released from my law job and started to teach drama in various schools, and also continued teaching English to foreigners. Our daughter was born in 1947 and three years later our son arrived. We were still in a one-roomed flat and trying hard to get somewhere bigger and in 1950 a law contact came up with an old mansion flat on the fourth floor in a Maida Vale block.

The following years were very difficult. My mother suffered a dreadful stroke, my father developed cancer and died in 1953; my sister left for South Africa with her husband, and later went to Israel, and my brother, by then a Lieutenant- Colonel, developed multiple sclerosis. He decided to go to China where he felt he could still do a good job directing teaching. I was left with my mother on my hands.

The next few years were hell, trying to work when I could, travelling by bus with two small children between Maida Vale and my mother in Golders Green, loaded with food for the week, and trying to sort out a series of dreadful help/housekeepers. However, my husband and I got a car and both learnt to drive and in 1958 we got a house big enough for our family, my mother and a help. But life was still hell because my daughter developed migraine and my son an eye disease, both stress-related.

We had bought our first boat in 1955 and we sailed on a gravel pit lake near Slough. Both the children enjoyed the sport with us and later we got a bigger boat and an old caravan and sailed in the Blackwater Estuary. By 1975 we got our first cabin cruiser, and a few years later we bought a share in a catamaran sailing boat and shipped it out to Yugoslavia. We kept it in a marina in Istria and sailed there for many years, spending up to six to eight weeks a year. Alas, war clouds gathered in that beautiful country. We sold the boat just before the Croatian war broke out.

By 1962 my mother needed full-time nursing care and a year later she died. Free at last of my responsibility for her, I applied for a place at Trent Park Teacher Training College. I was allowed to do the course in two years in view of my previous experience, and after graduating at the age of 47 I started at my first school, a secondary modern 'sink' school in Tottenham.

The only good thing about this school was a drama teacher called

Marjorie Sigby. She was really gifted and it was said she could get blood out of a stone, which she did with some of the 'dumbest' kids. She certainly opened my eyes to what could be done with drama. My second job was at Woodberry Down Comprehensive School, which was a haven of good teaching and order. I specialised in drama and remedial teaching, using many of the new techniques I had learnt from Marjorie Sigby. From there it was a natural move to special education. Three years later I moved to a special school for 'educationally sub-normal and maladjusted' children in Camden. I enjoyed this work and made a few real breakthroughs which changed the lives of these young people. In 1971 I was given a year off from teaching to take a diploma in the education of handicapped children, at London University, and then returned to the school as deputy head. There I pioneered a work experience scheme after a battle with the local education authority about the insurance of pupils in a workplace. I specialised in teaching the fifteen to eighteen year-olds, often getting them into work experience and nursing them through their first year of work. I still have contact with some of these youngsters, now in their 30s with families of their own. This scheme was very successful and is now common practice.

My visit to China
In 1975 I went to China. My brother, who had spent sixteen years there, doing pioneering work in western medicine, had returned home for a few years and then gone back to get material for a book, but he had a heart attack while there. This was during the Cultural Revolution and travel to China was not easy. I applied to the Chinese Embassy in London for a visa and was given every possible help. I flew to China in the August and the Chinese Medical Association paid all my expenses once I was there. My brother had made good progress and we planned his return to London. I told my hosts I would like to see something of their country and a long tour was planned. I had my own interpreter who came with me wherever I went, and I saw a great deal of that vast country, travelling by air and train and car. I was one of the very few visitors from the west at that time. I came back to London greatly enriched by my experience. Alas, shortly after my return to England my brother suffered a second heart attack and died in Beijing.

Retirement
In 1984 I retired from full-time teaching and took up part-time work with teenagers withdrawn from schools, on a one-to-one basis. They were all school leavers who had not succeeded in settling down to adult life. I found

I could help to mould them and point them in directions they had not thought of. For example, a young girl with an overbearing mother who could not communicate with people. I found her work in a supermarket and got someone I knew there to protect and shepherd her until she settled in.

Two years later at the age of 68 I had had enough and retired for good. I joined the Workers' Education Association and took various courses there, and also the Labour Party and worked with them, particularly during elections. I took more time in the garden and in caring for my little dog, and we had good holidays: camping with a trailer tent all over Europe and, of course, sailing. We went to many concerts and theatres and In 1989 I joined U3A in London.

On the whole we've had a good life, made many good friends, and had very good experiences. We have just now, in the year 2000, had our 58th wedding anniversary. So perhaps being a non-academic was a good thing for me!

(iii) Contrary Mary: How My Garden has Grown

How do I know what I know?

After hearing about the work we were doing on this book, my niece became interested in the family genealogy and began to research into it. My sister has a few photographs and I have one of my mother when she was possibly in her thirties. Apart from that there are no diaries, letters, or documents, and my brother and sister know no more than I do about our foremothers. My father's two youngest sisters and my mother's half-sister used to visit us when I was a child and probably said things which I only half understood at the time. But we three children were very alienated and had given up asking questions.

Grandparents and parents

All my grandparents had died before I was born and I know almost nothing about them. My parents were very reluctant to talk about their past and became angry if questioned. So I only have scraps of information from other sources.

I believe that both my parents were first generation British, their parents having migrated from Eastern Europe. Both families were Jewish and both settled in East London. My maternal grandfather married at least twice, and both wives died fairly soon after giving birth to a daughter. My mother was the child of the first marriage. I have a memory of my mother saying she had a half-brother by a third marriage, but she did not know his name and had never met him. She and her half-sister were each in turn sent to be cared for by their mother's relatives, and neither ever saw their father again. My mother spent her childhood being passed from relative to relative; she was even sent out to New Zealand for a time.

My father was the only son, fourth in a family of six children, and seems to have been put under considerable pressure to succeed. However, my niece's researches have shown that my grandfather died when my father was in his early teens, which could explain why he became a pupil-teacher in order to stay at school after the age of fourteen. His two youngest sisters were placed in an orphanage. My father seems later to have cut himself off from his mother and older sisters, but he did keep in touch with his younger sisters.

My mother's education was, obviously, very much interrupted by constant moving, and she started work in her early teens, in a millinery workshop. She was small and nice-looking and probably quite lively. She certainly did not lack intelligence, though she was very submissive. But I doubt if my parents were ever really compatible, possibly because of my mother's poor education. My father was arrogant and self-important, and he made little secret of his low opinion of her. She had to account for every penny of housekeeping money she spent, and if she needed something for herself she had to ask for money separately, as she had no personal allowance.

I assume my parents were themselves badly parented. We always had a good material standard of living but there was no love or warmth in the family at all. We were dutiful to our mother but we each in turn lost touch with our father as soon as possible.

My memories of my life
What I remember of my own life is accurate but there are great gaps in my memory. When I was about eight or nine I developed a method of deliberately forgetting things which I didn't want to remember. It has stood me in good stead all my life and I still use it, but undoubtedly it has left me with a habit of not trying to remember, including some good things which my brother and sister remember and I do not.

I was born on 16 February 1922 in Aston, an inner-city area of Birmingham, in a short street of terraced houses owned by the General Electric Company, where my father worked as an accounts clerk. I was the first child and my father obviously wanted a son and had little time for me. My brother was born four years later, and my sister two years after him. I remember that I was not allowed to play in the street, so could not join the other children living nearby. The only toys I can remember were a spinning top which I enjoyed, and a doll in a pram which I rejected, much to my mother's chagrin as she had made all the doll's clothes and bedding. We children were never read to or told stories, and (as a result, I suppose) none of us seem to have learnt imaginative play. I can't remember a time when I was not afraid of my father. He never hit me, though he often threatened to, but he shouted at me a lot, and found fault with me all the time. Neither of my parents seem to have realised the necessity of making good relationships with their children. My brother once said, when we were both adults, that he could never stand the way our mother was always whingeing; I too was embarrassed by it, though not particularly sympathetic, I'm afraid, about her misery. Certainly her existence as a wife made me think that I would never get married because I would always want to be free to leave if I became unhappy. That was one reason why my husband and I lived together for so long before marrying, though he had his own good reasons.

When I was about four we moved house to Erdington, a suburb of north Birmingham, and I was sent to a very small infants school nearby. There I learnt to read and write and do sums and sing the multiplication tables. My brother was born that year but I was not allowed to go near the baby, and was shooed away if I tried to see him by a strange woman who came to live in our house for what seemed quite a long time (I suppose she was a nurse). I had not been told that a new baby was expected and I was rather scared that I would be sent away.

Our new house was much bigger than the old one, and was on a main road at the top of a hill and faced north. It was a cold house, and the only really warm place in winter was the kitchen, because of the coal-fired range, which was used for cooking and also heated the water. The other downstairs rooms had fires but the bedrooms were not heated unless someone was ill.

My father had had a car from our time in the first house, and now he had a bigger one. I began to suffer from car sickness in this car, and could hardly go twenty miles without having to get out. No-one else in the family had this problem and I was the object of much exasperation all round. We had a large garden with a lawn as big as a tennis court in front of the house, and an even larger space behind, most of which was used to grow vegetables. We were not allowed to play on the front lawn because we could be seen from the street. At the back of the house there was a small yard and a small lawn where we could play. There were no neighbouring children. One summer day when I was about eight I was left alone at home when the family went out in the car, because they knew I would be sick. I had a bicycle which I had never learnt to ride, for which I had endured the usual contempt of my father. That day, with no-one to watch me, I took the bicycle out onto the front lawn and taught myself to ride it. When the family returned I was riding confidently round and round on the grass (for which I was not reprimanded). It was a rare triumph.

At about this time I moved to a bigger school, headed by a woman graduate. I remember her with affection, the only school teacher I ever liked. I enjoyed my time there and learnt a lot. But I had become a commuter. It took 40 minutes to get there, including a tram ride, and as I went home to lunch, I had to make this journey on my own four times a day.

I also began to learn the piano. The teacher came to teach me once a week, and I had to practise every day. After a year my father became cross that I was not put in for exams, assuming I was not making proper progress. Throughout my childhood my confidence was very low because of my father's constant dissatisfaction with everything about me and the lack of any understanding from my mother. Later that year my sister was born. Once again I was not told in advance, and this time I did not try to see the baby and was never encouraged to.

We went away in summer for seaside holidays. In the early years my father came with us; later he did not. I was not allowed to play with strange children on the beach and had no idea how to play with my little brother and sister, so I spent most of my time reading. From the time I learnt to read, I read everything I could lay my hands on, including things which were not considered appropriate, which my father would take away from me and blame my mother.

My father was very much against religion and had decided we children should be brought up without it, so we remained in total ignorance of it until we each in turn started at secondary school. So when, in 1932, at the age of ten I went to Sutton Coldfield Girls Grammar School, I met with the subject called scripture for the first time. At the first lesson of my first term, the teacher started with Genesis and when she asked if anyone had any questions I asked: how did the man who wrote the Bible know what happened before there were any people? I was astonished when the teacher responded by calling me a wicked little girl, and said I would never go to heaven if I talked like that. I thought it was a reasonable question (I still do), added to which I knew nothing about heaven. I never asked another question in scripture and have remained religion-free all my life. With hindsight I realise that I was probably the only child she had ever taught who had no religious knowledge. Most of the others had been going to Sunday school for years.

I made friends at this school, the first of my life, and was one of a group of about six who stayed together throughout our schooldays. I very much enjoyed having friends, though we seldom met outside school. But I did not much like my new school. The teachers seemed distant and mostly critical, and my confidence remained poor. I was a plump and ungainly child and hopeless at games and gym. Music, books and friends were what I liked best, and in this period my brother and I gradually became good friends.

I also changed my music teacher to one who would (and did) put me in for exams. He taught me to love music and to enjoy practising, so that I became fairly proficient. His house was like an alternative school where there were classes to go to as well as my piano lesson, and other instruments were being taught. Here too, I made friends, two other girl pianists, and we met in our respective homes to make music. I also joined the Girl Guides but only stayed for a few months because my father forbade me to go on church parades, which meant I felt like an outsider. I did not at that time associate church with scripture.

I reached puberty at eleven. My mother was very upset and cross. She had told me nothing and I suppose she felt guilty, but fortunately I was a keen dictionary and encyclopaedia reader and had found out most of what I needed to know for myself. She never did tell me anything, and neither did anyone else.

At the end of my first term in the fourth year, my father announced, without warning or discussion, that I would leave school at Easter (when I would be fifteen). He offered me a choice of training either in domestic science or office work, and I agreed to the latter. All my friends expected to have at least two more years at school and it was very difficult to explain why I was leaving. I was sent to a small secretarial college for six months, where I coped well and got good skills, though I refused to learn bookkeeping, which annoyed my father. Afterwards I got a job as an office junior in central Birmingham.

This change was a psychological turning point for me, and a confirmation that my dislike and distrust of my father was an apt response to him, particularly as he had said one doesn't spend money on girls, though I didn't fully understand what he meant. I was very shocked and angry at the way my education was cut short and that I would leave school with no qualifications. However, I found that I was well-suited to office work and I always managed to do it well, but it took time for me to find a job I really liked, which I did when I was almost sixteen. I had begun to learn the violin that year, and I went to concerts and films regularly with friends, and sometimes to the theatre. I never had or wanted boyfriends.

Wartime

When the Second World War started I was working for a big electrical engineering company with a large branch in Birmingham. The firm, of course, immediately turned to war work and the staff were told that we would probably be classed as in reserved occupations, if we were called up. Despite that, the head of my section was called up almost immediately because he was in the Territorial Army. His senior secretary tried, and failed, to take over his work, and then left the company abruptly. I, the junior secretary, then aged seventeen, was asked to hold the fort for a few days until other arrangements could be made. In fact, a few days became several months, and then I was appointed to the post after some pressure on my part. I did not find any difficulty in doing the work, and the experience was a valuable one for me, as it built up my confidence and self-esteem.

Two years later, I suddenly realised that my age group would be called up quite soon, and then I would be reserved in my job for the duration of the war. I had been toying with the idea of joining one of the women's services and now the time had come to act - if I was going to join I would have to do so before my call-up date, when I would be reserved. I decided to join the Auxiliary Territorial Service (ATS, the women's army corps) and did so in April 1942, two weeks before my call-up date.

The branch manager was furious, because he found I could not be reserved as I was too young. My father was furious because I was throwing away a good job. I was very pleased and set off for my new life with optimism, which turned out to be fully justified. I was eventually trained as a high-grade cipher operator and was posted to exciting places, like the War Office in London, and the British military office in Washington D.C, America.

After the end of the war, as demobilisation from the ATS approached, I looked around for opportunities for ex-service personnel, and found that the Control Commission for Germany was recruiting all types of staff. This was the organisation which was set up after the war to rehabilitate the British

Zone of Germany and it offered two-year contracts with accommodation and other conditions of service not unlike the ATS. I applied and was accepted, and in Spring 1946 was posted to Hamburg, to work in the office of the Control Commission Police, which was staffed by police officers from Britain and ex-service people like myself. Hamburg was in a terrible state, levelled by bombing as far as the eye could see, with just a few buildings standing, most of which had been commandeered by the Control Commission. All the women staff were housed in one such building, and transport was provided to take us to and from our work each day. The Germans were living in cellars and bomb craters and any other shelter they could find. I was more shocked than I can say by it all.

My work was secretarial. For leisure time I found there was a college of the arts set up by the Commission, and there I joined an amateur drama group which was run by an Army lieutenant, and I played small parts. When our producer was posted, we found another one in the college, who was a serjeant in the Engineers, but had been trained at drama school before the war. I stayed with this group for the rest of my time in Hamburg. On leave I went to Brussels and later to the south of France. In Hamburg I met my first boy friends. At the end of my two-year contract, our drama producer, with whom I had become very close, was due to be demobilised, and in 1948 we went back to London together.

Return to England

Our first needs, of course, were a place to live and jobs. We were lucky to find a basement flat in Notting Hill very quickly, and I joined an agency to do temporary secretarial work. Eventually I found a permanent job in an insurance company in the City of London and I stayed there for several years. My partner got a few small parts in plays and films and worked as an extra, and between us we managed and were happy together. We were not married. I was against marriage after my family experience, and I had never wanted children. We did marry about eight years later, but I never changed my mind about not having children, and my husband readily accepted that. I was fortunate that I had no in-laws, as both his parents were already dead, and he was an only child. So no pressure was put on us, and I was totally out of touch with my own family in those early days.

In 1958 we moved from London to the Sussex coast, as my husband had got a job as a theatre designer/scene painter in that county, while I found a job with the National Health Service general practitioner administration. That was very interesting, but in 1960 I became seriously depressed. With hindsight I realise that I had been prone to bouts of depression ever since my early teens, but this was a particularly bad time. I lost the ability to speak and can remember nothing of what happened, I just found myself in hospital. I had six electro-convulsive therapy (ECT) treatments under general anaesthetic, which caused temporary amnesia and nausea, and were frightening. But the ECT treatment was surprisingly beneficial. Despite its bad press it seemed to have suited me, I lost the chronic depression I had suffered and after a considerable period on medication I found I was much more positive about myself and ready to think about a new career.

I was 44 in 1966 and it was time to make a move. I began to look in the local press but found every interesting job required at least five GCE O levels and I had none. This gave me the idea that O levels could hardly be difficult since so many people were expected to have them, so I had better get them, which I did, continuing with my job and teaching myself part-time. I then realised how much I had enjoyed studying, so I decided to take A levels as well, following which I applied to work for a degree in sociology at a polytechnic in London and was accepted.

The careers service

I graduated at age 50 and decided to train for careers advisory work. I was accepted for a year of postgraduate study at Reading University and got a qualification in careers work. In 1973 I joined West Sussex Careers Service in Crawley and we sold our house on the coast and got a flat there. I found careers advisory work much more interesting and satisfying than any work I had ever done before. My husband was now retired, but he came to life in our new surroundings and saw an opportunity to set up a youth theatre, which became very successful.

I joined a women's liberation group in Crawley, and later we set up a refuge for women who were victims of domestic violence, and also a women's centre. Since then I have been and still remain active in the women's movement, latterly in London.

Retirement

I retired from the careers service in 1987 and my husband died in 1990. I decided I wanted to move to London, and early in 1994 was lucky to get a tiny flat in a block run by a housing association for pensioners. My activities in the women's movement have changed and increased, and I also started a study group on women's issues in the University of the Third Age (U3A). I enjoy the many possibilities of life in London, and see friends and also my sister and her family from time to time, and my brother (now Australian), when he visits this country.

Looking back, I realise how difficult I found it to achieve a sense of maturity. For many years I could hardly believe how old I was, I felt too immature for my age; even though I was happily married, it seemed I was not ready. Apparently I subconsciously felt the need to complete my education, as I finally caught up with myself after I graduated. But I still do not feel elderly.

(iv) Joan: Myths and Memories

My maternal grandparents

My eldest sister has a photograph of my maternal grandmother, Granny Gill, in a basket-work bath chair pushed by my two maiden aunts. She looks shrivelled and is wearing a hat and a feather boa round her neck. She must have been widowed by then I think. She died in 1922 shortly after I was born - my mother showed me to her as she lay in bed and she thought I was too heavy to hold. My maternal grandfather's photo shows him white-haired, with a bushy beard. Curiously there seems to have been little knowledge of his working life handed down, apart from the fact that at one stage he was an accountant for the construction of the Manchester ship canal. He must have earned quite well to have built his own home, supported a large family, provided many of them with professional qualifications and left a small capital invested for my two maiden aunts to live on.

I asked my eldest aunt's husband what these grandparents were like, but all he could say was that he got on well with my grandfather but my grandmother was formidable in a way he found very hard to take. My grandfather's nonconformist faith was of central importance. I cherish the anecdote about him walking fifteen miles overnight to hear a famous preacher whom he enjoyed so much that he stayed on for the evening service and walked home again over the next night. He must have been typical of the values described by Tawney in his book *Religion and the Rise of Capitalism*. After long ages of feudal social structures it had at last become possible to envisage social mobility, particularly perhaps in the industrial north. They lived in Southport, a prosperous sea-side resort within commuter distance of Liverpool and Manchester and not so far from the Lancashire mill towns.

My paternal grandparents

My father's mother died of tuberculosis when he, her youngest child, was about eight. I have never been able to indentify a photo of her. An oil painting of my Grandfather Smith's portrait in oils hung on the staircase at home. He looked benign, with blue eyes and a fair complexion, and I felt him to be some sort of tutelary spirit. Alas, at some point, my mother took against it and got rid of the painting without asking anyone. He married his late wife's sister and had to go to the Channel Islands to do this as it was illegal in England at the time. His second wife died too after some years, possibly also from tuberculosis.

My father was sent to boarding school in Yorkshire where there was a whole clan of relatives; meanwhile my Grandfather Smith, his ailing wife, and my father's older sister, Ethel, travelled twice to the Canary Islands in search of health. It was Ethel who showed me a copy of a chapel magazine which eulogised my grandfather's family of origin for the signal contribution they made to music in the area and also described how my great grandfather had ridden on horseback over the Pennines to seek for his bride! My daughter now owns a handsome conductor's baton presented to my grandfather for his contribution to music in Bristol, where he had a musical instrument business before moving to Southport. After his second wife's death my grandfather married for the third time - the only granny I can remember, a slight, white-haired old lady who lived in lodgings with her retired schoolteacher sister. We paid regular duty visits, but they were unrewarding from a child's point of view.

The preponderance of anecdotes about men of this generation was probably more to do with the culture of the period than the personalities. Large families, no birth control and no machines to help with domestic chores meant that a housewife had little chance of an intellectual life or career.There there must have been a lot of frustrated ability hiding behind 'correct' behaviour, only occasionally lightened by extended family reunions with shared memories of youthful enjoyments.

My mother

Moving to the next generation, my mother, born in 1887, was the youngest of seven surviving children; there had been two or three stillbirths or neonatal deaths as well. Two of her sisters and three female cousins became trained teachers, two never married, one probably because she had tuberculosis of the spine as a child and thereafter had to sleep in a specially constructed hut in the garden; alone at first, but later shared as a treat, by

Patricia and me when we visited! Two brothers became respectively an accountant and an architect by apprenticeship rather than university training.

My mother herself missed a lot of school due to minor indispositions. I wonder if perhaps she was encouraged to stay at home as the family baby in her mother's widowhood, but don't have dates to corroborate this. She worked as a telegraphist at the post office until her marriage and never worked outside the home afterwards. She had a particularly close relationship with her eldest sister and lived in and worked from her and her husband's home in Sheffield for a time; this was a bond we were to benefit from later as we had many happy holidays there with my favourite relatives.

My father

My father had only one sister, Ethel, about eight years older than himself. She must have been an important continuity factor for him. She was a prim lady who only got married after my grandfather had died and there was a story among the cousins later, that when in old age she needed a medical examination, she was found to be a virgin. Her husband was quite a lot older than she was. My mother hated Ethel since the time when she was pregnant with my eldest sister and had to go and live with her after my father was called up in the First World War. Aunt Ethel lent my father money for his musical instrument business during the Depression and my mother always resented the fact that he paid her back with interest punctiliously, even though it meant more economies at home. My aunt eventually had to live in an old people's home and in spite of poor eyesight and ill-health, outlived my father, surviving into her nineties, no longer recognising any of us when we visited her.

My grandfather sent my father to London to learn piano-making and tuning, but called him back to sign the deeds of the house he had had built in Southport and which he lived in until his death. After my father returned from the war, he and my mother and their baby daughter lived there and that remained the family home until after he died. It had electric lighting, flush toilets inside and out, and a wash house and coal house in the garden; but money was always tight and little was ever spent on beautifying or up-dating it. Education and holidays took precedence.

Me

I was my parents' second child, born in 1922, after two miscarriages. My earliest memory was of our family staying with my mother's eldest sister's family in Sheffield when Patricia, fifteen months younger than me, was small enough to be bathed in a zinc laundry bowl in front of the kitchen fire, whereas I was bathed in the sink (at her eightieth birthday party my elder sister said her first memory was of being bathed by her mother and told that her daddy was coming home to stay soon. She must have been between two and three at the time - I wonder whether nudity and emotional communication go together?).

I appreciated being the middle daughter, not given a masculine nickname as my younger sister was and not the eldest who must have suffered from my mother's unhappiness while my father was in the army. I must have resented the abrupt transition from being the centre of my mother's attention when she became pregnant with Patricia, but I suspect that I was allowed to make more of an alliance with my father than the other two had opportunity for. My mother was experienced as a good provider of food and physical care, but was temperamentally invasive and controlling, with little ability to imagine what a child's feelings or experience might be; driven by duty rather than affection or fun. The emancipation of women and feminism came too late for her, and I suspect that her under-used intelligence soured her life. She was easily envious or disapproving. I remember one Christmas my mother's sad comment on hearing the Coventry Carol's words 'Jesus my dear heart, my darling.' 'Nobody ever said that to me,' she said - not surprising perhaps that she never felt able to say it to anyone else.

Patricia and I fought a lot. My mother was full of moral exhortation but my father played with us and was emotionally available in a way my mother never was, however much we realised that she meant well. I suppose I was the first child he was at home to see at birth, and maybe he had increased responsibilities for me when Patricia was tiny? We had live-in help at home, and Alice used to take Patricia and me to the park every afternoon. She was common-sensible and reliable in contrast to the maiden aunt who was supposed to be looking after me while Patricia was being born; this aunt was only alerted by my screams to the fact that I had reached out to the kitchen range and badly burnt my wrist. I don't remember this but still have the scar. In due course Alice got married herself and after a number of less satisfactory arrangements, Patricia and I started school and economies associated with the Depression spelt the end of live-in help.

I didn't start school until I was six, and remember mother stressing the importance of not lying, only to discover that the rivalry between fellow pupils was such that exaggerating the length of one's doll was expected in kindergarten culture.

At ten I moved to the church school that both my mother and elder sister had attended, but it closed down abruptly after only one term. My best friend in the playground told me that she was going to a small independent school near where she lived (in a 'good' part of town) so I went home and said I wanted to go there too. To my surprise Patricia and I were forthwith enrolled there. With hindsight I realise that this coincided with my mother receiving a small legacy from a childless uncle which she was glad to devote to obtaining educational advantage for her children. It turned out to be a happy place which nurtured my developing intelligence. I ended up being on my own in the sixth form, a very strange kind of adolescence. I passed my higher school certificate when I was just seventeen and in fact was only an immature sixteen year old when I was interviewed for university in 1939. When war broke out they reduced their intake and suggested that I reapply the following year. Had I got in then I would probably have become a teacher, and am very glad with hindsight that other possibilities eventually opened up.

Work

By this time I was tired of home constraints and isolation from a peer group so, with the idealistic intention of becoming a missionary, I allowed a family friend who was a health visitor (and much, much later became my step-mother, after my mother's death at 82!) to enrol me as a student nurse at the Children's Hospital in Liverpool. I got free board, lodgings and uniform and £15 pay annually, rising to £35 by the third year, in return for very long hours. The matron was an ogress and in my third year I caught diphtheria and spent eight weeks in a fever hospital without visitors; I was surprised to be promoted to acting staff nurse when I returned and eventually passed the state exam.

Again, I followed a friend in choosing where to do my general training, and in 1943 was accepted at the Radcliffe Infirmary at Oxford - a period of bliss, far enough from home not to have to visit more than once a year, a much more democratic atmosphere and easy contact with ex-service undergraduates to provide a social life at last!

Because at this time one was not allowed to change from a reserved occupation, I worked as a charge nurse after qualifying and did part one of the midwifery training; then I seized an opportunity to work in a hospital in Copenhagen under a professional exchange scheme (I had much resented the war and post-war embargo on foreign travel). I was allowed to take £15 of currency and would get half pay for four months or until I could speak the language. After three months I was put on night duty in charge of a ward, which involved having to answer the telephone, so I rehearsed my speech and went to claim full pay from the matron who was so tickled she gave it to me.

Being in a very different culture helped me to know what was me and what was environmental influence and I felt more in charge of myself when I returned to England after six months. By then I felt it was my sisters' turn to have a respite from coping with family crises. My elder sister moved to her employer's head office in London and Patricia followed her for her first job after ex-service teacher training. I enrolled at a fever hospital near my parents' home in Lancashire while I explored how to train as a social worker (I had always been fascinated by the almoner's reports on pink paper when I was nursing). The fever hospital was a dreadful place and served to confirm my resolution not to continue up the hierarchy of nursing.

Gradually, I found the courage to emancipate myself from my family and from the dependancy-creating institutions such as church and hospitals, and discovered not only that I could survive but that it was rewarding to venture into the unknown. Mercifully, I was accepted at Liverpool University to take a social science certificate. I withdrew my superannuation contributions and that, together with a small legacy from an aunt, enabled me to keep body and soul together for the first year when, abruptly, I realised it would not see me through the second. My parents were supportive - my mother bought me the typewriter I needed, but they were in no position themselves to finance me. The professor negotiated a grant of £100 from a shipping company and that saw me through. I was eligible for a government grant for the next stage to train as a psychiatric social worker at the London School of Economics. In the intervening three months, one of my tutors was able to arrange, through a French counterpart, for me to have live-in voluntary work experience with children's organisations in three different parts of France; this gave me a life-long confidence and pleasure in working through French.

After qualifying I worked in two different child guidance services, then when one of the tutors on my training course at LSE died of cancer, I was invited to apply for the vacancy. I got the post in competition with others who were better qualified academically, so embarked on yet another career with misgivings but feeling that I had won the post fairly.

For both personal and professional reasons, I underwent four years of psychoanalysis which freed me to make fuller adult relationships. I met and married my husband, a Reader, later Professor of Theoretical Physics at another college of London University and eventually, after a miscarriage and a stillbirth, gave up work to care for my two children.

Parenthood
I was 39 when my son was born and 42 when my daughter arrived and parenthood was a joyful discovery. I always felt that what I lacked in youthful energy was compensated for by my experience and a greater ability to pace myself. My children kept me young and I had had enough career satisfaction to put that on hold until they were both at school or playgroup. Fortunately, my husband's work schedule helped with childcare demands. I started back part-time in a neighbouring borough then a vacancy came up at a world-famous mental health training clinic only ten minutes walk from my home and the children's school, and I was able to start a very happy and developmental career for the last seventeen years of my employed life. I was involved with initiating new mid-career training programmes, research, writing and clinical work, was invited to teach abroad and had opportunities for consultancy training and practice. All this helped to hold me together through a disastrous period. My father died, and in the same year my fourteen-year-old son died after being knocked off his bike by a car that didn't stop. Two years later my husband withdrew from our marriage. I was 55, and was able to continue working until I was 65 and to build up some freelance consultancies which I could continue with after retirement.

Retirement
I wonder, if I had had a reasonable pension, whether I would have been as active in continuing work, and retrospectively am grateful that I really needed to go on earning. This is an age when we are increasingly aware that we may live for a very long time after retirement, and society can use our contributions as long as health permits. The burden on the youthful population of the increasing longevity of the older generation is often talked about, but by implication, there is also an increased opportunity for able-bodied oldies to continue being useful in society and to take greater responsibility for their own health.

Although there have been periods of depression in my life, there has also been an underlying optimism that has made me know intuitively that it is worth bearing adversity, that the tapestry of life is richer for acknowledging and incorporating the times of loss and anger among the times of happiness and achievement. In many ways, having health and work opportunities within quite modest means in retirement makes me feel unexpectedly privileged and grateful for my quality of life. I think this process must have started when I gave up the notion of blaming (mostly my mother), and decided to take responsibility for myself. For long periods I was just too busy to experience this to the full, and now that there is time to reflect I can relish it. I can accept that I too must have been an imperfect parent and perhaps that is what enables children to separate out from their families and in turn make their own mistakes.

Being part of this project has been important and pleasurable. I suspect most people review their lives as they get older; to do this in congenial company has added an enriching dimension.

(v) Patricia: My Life and Times

I suppose I must have been about four years old when the last complete eclipse of the sun, in 1927, was visible in Britain. Our parents took my sister and me to see the wonder up the nearby railway bridge; on the flat coastal Lancashire plain where we lived there were no hills to climb. We were awed when we were told that there would not be another such occasion until 1999, by which time, we were told, our parents would be dead. 'So who will take us next time?' we asked. The prospect of parental death was too foolishly incredible to warrant a response, I suppose. Now our U3A project encourages me to look back over three quarters of a century. Childhood seems impossibly far away and yet close enough to live on in the present.

My grandparents

As the youngest child of a youngest child, my knowledge of my grandmothers is scanty. My sister Joan has written about them elsewhere in this book and I have wondered how she came to hold on to such detailed information about our origins, while I apparently swam on, wrapped in my own life. Then light dawned; she had the stimulus of handing on the stories to her own children so must have taken more trouble to ask questions than I did. I am left with two pictures: a real-life memory of my father's stepmother, whom we visited on Sundays. Seated in her upright chair, like a white-haired porcelain figurine, clad entirely in black, she gave me the feeling that any loud noise or careless movement would shatter her into tiny pieces. My maternal grandmother, Granny Gill, died before I was born. She looks out at me with direct and disapproving gaze from an old photograph in which she sits in a basket wheel chair while our two maiden aunts stand sentinel behind her ready to push the chair when she commands. The basket chair gives no hint of disability; rather, it is her carriage and her throne; she grasps fiercely the wooden handle which is attached with a metal bar to the small single wheel at the front of the carriage. She is decidedly in control. She no longer had small children so maybe she needed her carriage and her control.

My cousin Sheila tells me of the fierce resentment felt by granny which she had confided to Sheila's mother. Grandfather Gill used the money belonging to his wife in order to build houses. He had the right to do this because an effective Married Women's Property Act did not become law until 1882, after they were married. This meant that granny had no money to buy presents for her grandchildren. Well, that is the family story; I can understand that the firm granny in the bath chair would not like to lose control of any of her possessions.

My parents

My father was a musical instrument dealer, owning the shop in Southport he inherited from his father. In the 1920s and 30s the economic slump forced such a business into the luxury class and trade was bad. We children always had clothes to wear, mainly made by the spinster aunts who appear in Granny Gill's photograph; we all had good nourishing meals. With hindsight, I wonder why 'nourishing' had to mean dull, though I did not complain at the time. Fresh fish arrived in a rakish cart, drawn by a trotting horse, while the fishman called: 'Codfish, hake and ray.' Milk arrived also in a cart. Jugs were put out on the back step and creamy milk with a hint of froth was poured from a metal measure by a smiling young man. He sometimes gave me exciting rides around the crescent in his swaying cart while he whipped the frisky horse as if we were riding a Roman chariot. My favourite meal was a thick cheese and onion sauce, served with mashed potatoes, and my least favourite was Lancashire hot-pot because it had barley in it.

We had a succession of live-in maids (one at a time!), but my mother was always tired and she rested on the couch every afternoon. She was a good cook but nothing was fancy or decorated. Even the Christmas cake stopped short at a marzipan covering and was never topped off with white icing. When I was older, she told me she would like to have been a domestic science teacher, but her health was not good enough to allow her to go to college. Two of her sisters became teachers and, years later, amazed us with tales of teaching classes of 70 children. Mother herself worked in the telephone exchange until she married. Nimble fingers and a clear speaking voice must have been among the qualities required, as all calls would have to be connected by plugging in the appropriate lines on a board in front of the operator. By the time I came along, I remember the phone on the wall in our hall, with its large dial and trumpet-like earpiece. One could make local calls without troubling the operator, but in my mother's working days there must have been few families with telephones.

My childhood

As children, we had a penny a week pocket money, which went a long way when sweets could be bought for a farthing. There came the time during the 1930s Depression when Saturday pennies were no more. I don't remember either Joan or me asking why this happened, but life was full of things we could not afford.

We had family holidays every summer, often staying in a small commercial hotel in Shap on the edge of the Lake District. I learned to love the hills and countryside as well as feeling at home in the village. We were there for the jubilee of George V in 1935 and I remember the unsophisticated bunting in the streets and the village fair in the evening. The main western rail route to Scotland ran close by and with my father we would go a few years later and wait to see the blue train, the Coronation Scot, race by, smoke filling the air and the steam whistle reverberating among the fells.

There were other young people who stayed regularly at the Kings Arms Hotel in Shap and we roamed the area together. As the youngest of three sisters, I was used to being left behind when interesting things were afoot, but paddling in streams to catch stickleback in a jam jar is still a fond memory. I must have been old enough to walk with the others to Mardale to see the village before it was drowned by Manchester Waterworks into the flooded valley of an enlarged Haweswater.

There was talk while we were at Shap in the summer of 1938, about forthcoming war and I remember my instinctive denial. I had seen the impotent rage of a Jewish girl in my form at school as she tore to shreds a newspaper report about Hitler, but politics were not discussed at home and I protected myself with a cover of optimism. When war came in 1939 I had to wake out of childhood. Evacuees came from Liverpool and I helped accommodate them in our church hall. So I saw and smelt real poverty for the first time. We had a mother and toddler billeted on us, and they sat with us on the Sunday morning when the Prime Minister, Neville Chamberlain, announced that war was declared. The serious horror of the occasion was obscured for me by the fascination of seeing our new lodger fling her white apron over her face and burst into loud sobs. I thought such emotional outbursts occurred only in books. Emotional display was not known in our family.

The second jolt I received was that I had to leave school and accept a job my father found for me in the temporary civil service. For the first time in my life I discovered boredom. For three and a half years I moved from one clerical job to another, failing dismally in each. I knew by then that I wanted to be a teacher but training courses were closed to me until after the war.

Wartime was a growing up period for me. In 1943, I joined the Women's Royal Naval Service and after training in London and Hampshire, was posted to Scarborough. Life in the WRNS was good; we missed the worst of the bombing, we had the freedom of living away from home, and the security of a controlled environment. The wearing of uniform was no problem. There were happy associations with uniform worn for school and Girl Guides. There was plenty of social life, without the complication of falling in love. I left that until later. I remember dances at the Royal Opera House, Covent Garden, converted during the war to a sort of superior Forces Club. There were walks along the cliffs with young airmen or soldiers and moonlight bathing adventures. Even practices for the drum and fife band were fun for us, however horrible the noises we produced. I also had the opportunity to take a postal study course in English Literature; the idea was put into my head by a friend that I might try for university as well as teacher training after the war.

Music was very important in wartime. Major orchestras left London, and we had a series of Sunday evening concerts at the Garrick Theatre in Southport, where we lived. In London, I found my way to the Promenade Concerts and met a whole new repertoire of classical music that excited and enriched me. I heard Myra Hess play in the National Gallery and Kathleen Ferrier sing in the *Messiah* at Westminster Abbey. In Leicester Square there was a kiosk that gave out theatre tickets to men and women in uniform; I remember the thrill of sitting in the second row of the stalls, though foolishly I cannot remember the name of the play we saw. In Hampshire, a batch of tickets was sent for a recital given by Moiseiwitsch at Portsmouth. Names were put in a hat and I could not believe my luck when one of the tickets was allotted to me.

War is a time of heightened awareness. Sometimes I felt guilty because I seemed to miss most of the drama and danger. It was a time when life was on hold; one could not get on with one's plans and dreams until the war was over.

A career in teaching

When I was demobbed in 1946, I was ready to take responsibility for my own life instead of being fed, clothed and instructed by the Royal Navy. I trained for teaching at Wymondham Emergency Training College, revelling in the chance for study, exploring the Norfolk countryside, and enjoying the chance of amateur acting. Teaching practice was hard but satisfying. I was accepted by the London County Council as a teacher and took up my first post in Holloway. I lived at first in a YWCA in Great Russell Street, sharing a room with my eldest sister who decided it was time for her, too, to leave the family nest. Joan was about to enter Liverpool University to study social science. We all began to get on with our lives.

In the early 50s I struggled to get to grips with teaching in a small secondary modern school under a very tough head who had herself grown up in the East End. London school children were an unknown race to me, but I soon came to be very fond of them. Every evening I was at Birkbeck College, at last taking up the education that had been stopped short by the war. I never regretted being a part-time undergraduate; both fellow students and staff were older and we all felt we could understand more at the age of 25 than we could have done at eighteen. Any spare time was spent in amateur dramatics, to my great delight.

From time to time as I have worked on this U3A project as one of the few members of the group who has remained single, I have wondered why I took that route. Certainly there was no explicit decision to do so; there were always interesting men around but it never occurred to me that I might want to spend the rest of my life with any of them. There was too much else to do.

In 1951 came the Festival of Britain. I must have visited it many times as relays of friends and relations came to London to share the fun. I have no recollection that there was the same fuss about that exhibition as there has been about the Millennium Dome. We seem to have become less able to celebrate and more carping with passing years. Perhaps we have become more sophisticated in our criticism of the use of money. Perhaps the media has become more pervasive and more opinionated.

I graduated in 1953, the year when Edmund Hillary stood on the summit of Everest and Queen Elizabeth II was crowned. It seems quaint now that these royal occasions, such as coronations and jubilees, should stand out like markers in a life story. We were not madly royalist and I was not strongly political. I had inherited from my nonconformist family background a middle of the road liberalism, and the royal family played a part in affirming one's national identity. The mood today, when every institution is questioned and most are found wanting, is one measure of how the world has changed in my life-time.

As a graduate teacher, I moved into grammar school teaching, which I found deliciously easy and without much challenge. By then I was living in a rented flat near Great Ormond Street, still with my eldest sister. I learned to drive and bought my first car for £210, thanks to a bequest from a maiden aunt. My salary had reached the dizzy heights of £500 a year. One could have three weeks in France with a Ford Popular, staying in one star, clean family hotels for a total cost of £40. I remember driving to Brittany on roads that were still pot-holed from the war.

In 1956, I was tired of London and took a job at the Grammar School for Girls in Southampton. Some friends and I marched in protest over the Suez crisis and again in support of the Campaign for Nuclear Disarmament. Our attitude to CND was ambivalent as we believed that if we actually joined that organisation, we should for ever be barred from visiting USA. Fortunately, that was vile rumour. No U.S. immigration official has ever demurred at my entering that country.

During the 50s I saw a computer for the first time, filling a brick building the size of a large bungalow in the grounds of Southampton University. As an ignorant non-scientist, I was not impressed. Much more interesting was the fact that the Equal Pay for Teachers Act was being phased in over seven years, and each April when the pay slips arrived we did a spontaneous dance in the staff room, celebrating the news that we were worth yet another seventh of a man.

The 60s brought the 'New Morality' which had much to offer women. We were no longer expected to be ruled by external authority; we took responsibility for our own decisions. I did not share the fears of those who thought schoolgirls faced ever-increasing perils. I found that young people were self-obsessed, of course, but also remarkably sensible. The ever-widening range of careers open to women gave opportunities waiting to be grasped; the young began to take charge of their own lives, rather than waiting to be told what to do by controlling parents or boy friends.

For me, the 60s brought wider experiences and more responsibilities. I went to teach in Hamburg, Germany, for a year as I had a German god-daughter and decided I had better learn German. I began to understand that I was not only English, I was European. I was in Berlin just before the Wall was built, at the height of the great tide of refugees moving from east to west. Visiting an East German family, I realised what it was to lack basic necessities. I took flowers to my hostess and sensed she would have preferred a supply of needles and thread. One day I drove from Hamburg to Bergen Belsen and stood where the concentration camp had been. My 'Pollyanna' optimism took a big dent and I absorbed something of the reality of evil. The emotional shock of that day has never left me.

In contrast, I was changed also by getting to know my amazing goddaughter. Close contact during the early years of a child's life, even when the child is not one's own, affects a relationship permanently; for us it gave total freedom to each but an ongoing connection.

Back in Britain, I found myself deputy head in a mixed school, then, three years later, head of a girls' grammar school about to become comprehensive. In education, the move from selection to comprehensive secondary education was the major event of the 60s. I moved to the Essex edge of London, experienced local government re-organisation and the birth of the London boroughs. On my first governing body there was a group of doughty women councillors aged between 55 and 75. They were mainly self-educated and totally committed to the local community. I learned to respect their courage, integrity and loyalty. A change came in the later 60s when local government attracted mainly those who saw it as a stepping stone to more glamorous national politics. Edith Pearson, Workers' Education Association member, self-educated, respected colleague in the Electoral Reform Society, was my chairman; an example of what could be achieved by women in a generation older than my own.

The change to comprehensive status was threatening to many in the local community who loved the security of knowing there were people behind them in life's bus queue. For me, who had experienced both grammar and secondary modern schools, noting the differing provision made to each in terms of finance and equipment as well as esteem, there was never any doubt. I knew too well the mistakes that the 11+ exam had made and I knew that selection at eleven was unjust. I enjoyed working with the neighbouring boys' school; their problems were similar. We both found that having a mixed staff and sharing some sixth form courses was very rewarding.

We were affected also by the wave of Caribbean and Asian immigration of the 60s. British insularity and colonialism bred unconscious racism. I knew the nervous insecurity of West Indian mothers, worried sick lest their offspring got into trouble; I loved the spontaneous response of Caribbean children and the earnestness of Asian families. Staff, at first, were all white, but gradually they got to know these new members of the school and not to fear them. Occasional incidents of unjust treatment by police or other institutions were tackled, and foolishly, we thought that education would solve all the problems.

In the early 70s I had a sabbatical term and spent half of it in the USA, visiting high schools and discovering that I really like the States – the positive energy, optimism and space to be found there. I recall being somewhat scandalised that Princess Anne's wedding on American TV was sponsored by someone's baked beans. There must still have been royalist instincts lurking in me! I was much awed by my first visit to the Grand Canyon and charmed by American hospitality.

In 1977 I moved to another headship and again took on the changing of a grammar school to a comprehensive school. I missed the multi-racial element of the previous school, but I sensed that this would probably be my final job before retirement so it was important to pull out all the stops. I was fortunate that my whole teaching career had taken place during a time when society believed that education was OK and teachers were OK (even if neither was perfect). As the 80s went on, life became tougher and I found I resented a regime of work and bed.

Retirement

Retirement from teaching in 1985 meant freedom, exploration and adventure. Work had been satisfying and enjoyable: strange how one forgets the bad bits. But I felt sure there must be more in life than work. I travelled to China, the Caribbean, India, Peru, Bhutan, and discovered the fun of photography. Being a teacher and a talker, it was not surprising that I tumbled into the hobby of giving illustrated talks on my travels or on nineteenth century novelists. It was so good to have more time for reading and revisiting authors I had not touched for years. Against my better judgement I was persuaded to take an honorary part-time job with a mission agency, which gave me the opportunity to argue out a contemporary philosophy of partnership, and the possibility of receiving as well as giving, instead of the religious colonialism I expected to find. I was sent on visits to Central America and Ghana, experiencing the richness of staying in people's homes instead of the ubiquitous intercontinental hotels that feature in most foreign holidays. Meeting people as well as seeing places was really good.

In 1995, macular degeneration set in; this is a hereditary disease of the eyes that I suppose had been waiting for me. It has been useful that I have a liking for problem-solving or finding different ways of doing things. I was registered partially-sighted, knowing that I would never go totally blind as the periphery of the retina, for some reason, remains inefficiently operational. Initially, one has to work through shock, anger and depression and then one gets on with living. There are so many more gadgets available to me than were available to my father. Talking books are superb; talking newspapers give me access to more leading articles than I would have bothered to read in the old days. Crossing roads can be scary, but beeping pedestrian lights are a passport to safety. Mercifully, close friends and relatives adjust helpfully and one learns to cope with the rest. There are the people who alternate between fulsome praise, 'You really are wonderful; the way you cope', and deep distrust, 'Are you sure you cannot see?' Seeing is not merely an optical event: it is a mix of memory, anticipation and imagination. Even those with perfect eyes see what they expect to see, or what they remember was there or what they imagine might be there. Being in a crowd of people, some of whom one knows, is uncomfortable; I have to wait to be greeted instead of taking the initiative. I have not yet worked out why that matters. A plus factor is how incredibly helpful people are, whether in reading out the 'use by' dates in the supermarket or helping with the morning mail. Like the traditional boy scout, they even help me across roads when I ask. More importantly, it has never happened unless I have asked.

I think my favourite Third Age hobby is having people to a meal. I am not a gourmet cook so there is nothing to prove, but as a single person who is rarely, if ever lonely, I love eating with people and I love conversation. What's more, I love it when people go home.

The task of looking back at my life has made me realise how unplanned and random it seems to have been. Most of the really good things (apart from teaching) are those I tumbled into rather than planned. The surprise has been part of the pleasure. I do not feel tempted at this stage to be aggressively in charge of the detail of any optional future plans; decisions will need to be made from time to time, but meanwhile the present is to be relished.

(vi) Charmian: Family Continuity

Sources

Unlike some others in our group, I have many sources of information (and doubtless misinformation) about my family history. On both my mother's and my father's sides ancestors have been traced back many generations, and they seem to have been assiduous in documenting their family histories. There is a monograph (privately published) on my father's family and a couple of heavy biographies of Victorian maternal forefathers. My brother has summarised all this material, noting the gaps and inconsistencies. In addition I have family letters dating from 1900 to 1943 and albums of photographs starting almost from the beginning of photography; portraits painted by artists in the family; diaries and drawings. Other sources of both myth and memory, are conversations with my siblings, particularly my older sister since I became involved in this group project.

All this gives an overwhelming sense of continuity in marked contrast to the disruption in the families of some of our group through migration or lack of communication. But I also have overseas connections as do many families calling themselves 'English'. My mother's father's family were Huguenot dissenters who arrived from France in the 18th century, and there was also a French branch to my father's family.

Grandparents

Dad's parents: industrial bourgeoisie

Both sides of my family were Unitarian middle class. My father's father was managing director of a family firm, a twine mill in Dorset near Bridport which was a centre for twine and net making. My father was brought up in this small industrial village in the manager's house which still stands in the middle of the factory buildings, the employees' cottages and the school. I can remember being shown round the factory by my paternal grandfather, and being most impressed by the rope walk which had to be extensive enough to twist a long rope. I have visited the site recently and found the remains of a typical Victorian industrial village fallen into disrepair, ripe for a heritage grant. My grandfather was a kind but somewhat pompous (according to my older sister), upright, honest gentleman; previous generations had been flax-spinners who had come down from Yorkshire in the early 19th century. His wife, my paternal grandmother left little impression on me. She was small, fussy, and supposedly not very strong, though she outlived him. Ineffectual I think, dominated by my grandfather.

Mum's parents: academic and professional

As a child I don't remember much contact with my father's family who were a bit stiff and formal. My mother's family was the defining cultural influence and my mother was the defining influence on my generation. My maternal great great-grandfather was William Ellis, an educational reformer who founded several schools, one of which is now a London comprehensive. His biographer writes that in the 1820s he used to walk regularly from his home in Croydon, nine miles to the City, to have discussions with James Mill and Jeremy Bentham before work. Obviously a man of the same vigorous and earnest mould as Joan's grandfather. My maternal great-grandfather, Henry Morley, was a professor at University College London, whose books until recently filled up much-needed space in my book shelves. Connections with University College have remained in the family; both his sons, and both my brothers went to the University College School and my son was born in the hospital. More continuity.

My grandmother Margaret (nick-named Peg), was the fourth of Henry Morley's five children. Her two sisters married Unitarian ministers, and one brother was a professional artist. She and my mother were emotionally close, and we used to visit her a lot as children. My younger sister and I were evacuated to her home in Bournemouth for the early months of the Second World War.

How do I remember her? As a benign ever-young old lady with a quizzical smile, emanating a great sense of warmth and security. There is a photograph of her sitting on a stone up a Welsh mountain at the age of 80. When I knew her she lived with and dominated my mother's two sisters, one single and the other widowed in the First World War. I also remember that she had mysterious 'turns' called 'dizzy spells' (migraines?) when she retired to bed; and that a certain puritan ethic prevailed in her household. We were rebuked if we asked what was for dinner as it was considered greedy to take an interest in food. My first and only lesson in lady-like behaviour (my mother didn't bother with such things) was when she reproved me for not cleaning the hairs from my hair brush with my comb: 'you can always tell a lady by her hair brush'. She was also not happy with the way I chatted to decorators working in her house when I was staying there. But we always had a good time with her, walking in the country, swimming in the sea, being read to. We often had family holidays on which she and my aunts joined us, renting a house in Cornwall or Wales.

When I knew my Granny Margaret she was separated from my grandfather, who during the First World War went off and built himself a big house on top of a hill outside Lyme Regis where he lived alone, pursuing his interests in geology and astronomy. Nobody ever commented on the reason for this. He was a difficult, unsociable man. He had a telescope and an observatory to look at the stars, and there is a story (I don't know the source) that local people thought at first that he was a German spy - though they must have overcome their suspicions as he was later elected mayor of the town. I think he retired early from his job with Marine Insurance, but he must have done well enough to afford to maintain two households. He remained in close contact with his family and my mother took us to visit him when we were little; she was his favourite daughter. I only remember him as a rather fierce, white bearded man who used to chase us round his garden waving a stick. This was his idea of fun, but I found it frightening.

From the 1880s until the end of the First World War my maternal grandparents were living in a big detached house in what was then the village of Potters Bar in Hertfordshire. They had servants (a cook, a parlour maid, a kitchen maid, and a gardener) to look after them and their five children. In spite of all this service my grandmother was always busy, according to her letters, though some of it must have been managing the household. She gardened and made her children's clothes, wrote endless letters, visited and received family and friends. The whole family went cycling and walking, and travelled up to London to concerts and the theatre. Their political allegiance was Liberal though of course my granny could not vote until 1918. She channelled her reforming energies instead into the British Women's Temperance Association, campaigning to get the villagers to 'Sign the Pledge', and chairing local meetings. I remember she wore a white ribbon in her buttonhole which was the symbol of the BWTA.

This busy Edwardian middle-class life was shattered after the outbreak of war in 1914. Granny Margaret and her husband separated and both her sons and a son-in-law were killed in the trenches in France (her own account of this period is in excerpts from her letters in our chapter on war). The family had already been dominated by women as she kept the family culture together through letters, visits and the routines of daily life. It became even more so in the inter-war period. My grandmother moved to a smaller house, though still big by modern standards, in Bournemouth, with her two daughters and her young grandson. Her letters show her determinedly facing these devastating losses, and turning her energies to the emotional and practical support of the next generations, including my mother Daisy and her growing family.

My mum: an Edwardian middle-class childhood

My mum, also Margaret, but called Daisy in the family, was born in 1889, the fourth of five as her mother had been. She was brought up with strong moral guidance, but very freely for the period in the family environment I have just described. They had a big garden and I have a vision of her (it's based on photograph) spending a lot of time up trees, eating cherries and reading. She never went to school but was certainly not uneducated. Daisy and her sisters attended lessons at home with a governess who became a life-long friend; as did her nanny, who returned to help later as each of my mother's children were born. She became accomplished in languages, humanities, music and art; quite ignorant of science; hopeless at sums. The family had cats, and dogs which needed walking. They led an active, informal and sociable life. I have a zestful account of a walking tour she did with her brother in 1904 in which they covered 20 miles a day in the Welsh mountains and the Welsh rain. The following extract from a letter written in 1912 by my grandmother seems to catch the essence of this idyllic family life.

'Skating has come, unspoilt by snow. We were all at it this morning. Daisy and a friend, and Bernard [her brother], were up by six; they prepared a feast of cocoa, bread and butter and jam and lighted lamps and cycled off to the pond before daybreak. There were two village dances in January, and we went to a Liberal meeting at the school. Roy cycled over for tea on Sunday. January has been a full month.'

Roy was my father, a trainee accountant in the City, from the Unitarian family in Bridport I have described; one of several young men who made regular visits to the hospitable house and courted the daughters. It was a case of: 'Daisy, Daisy, give me your answer do!' Alas there was no time for the 'bicycle made for two'. He married my mother in 1915, served in the Royal Navy during the war and was the only one of the young men in the family to survive.

My childhood: a strong self-sufficient family culture

My parents set up home in Whetstone, Middlesex, and then Edgware, which had become convenient for commuting to the City when the Underground reached it in 1925. They had five children between 1916 and 1924. It seems to me looking back, that our family life was as far as possible a replica between the wars, of my mother's in the early years of the century, though the servants had dwindled to one and were later replaced by au pair girls. When we were small there was always someone to help look after the family, though it was much more difficult to get suitable people and my mother seemed to spend as much time looking after them as they did looking after us. Our large, ugly house was always open to family, friends and people in need. My memories of childhood are inextricably bound up with memories of that house which I have described fully in my contribution to the chapter on our homes. We played family games, had strenuous walking holidays, climbed trees, and learnt to swim and row a boat on the nearby lake. Boys and girls were treated equally, and I spent much of my childhood wearing boys' shorts. The family culture was strong and self-sufficient; relaxed, argumentative, stoical. We were told 'don't make a fuss' but we sometimes did; urged 'when in doubt, have a go!' which we certainly did. But I know we helped very little in the house, and grew up lacking in domestic and social skills.

Moral values were strong but not oppressive. My mother gave my younger sister and me 'Sunday lessons' from a Unitarian book called *How to be Good*. Unitarianism is strong on behaviour but lacks ritual and mystery; the 'miracles' in the Bible were explained rationally to us. My mother followed her mother as a strict teetotaller, and my younger sister and I were taught about the damage alcohol does to the liver when we were eight or nine years old. When she was in her 80s, I enticed my mother into a country pub for lunch, and she was amazed to find it was not the den of iniquity she expected.

My mother was the matriarch of a lively household, as her mother had been before her. She didn't have economic power, but she determined the culture. She was always busy - darning, making our clothes, gardening, reading to us, walking our two large dogs, taking in lonely people. Strong-willed and generous, she emanated a kind of radiance, and I knew that as long as she was around everything would be all right. Politically naive, she thought that if everyone was kind to one another all the problems of the world (which she felt deeply about), would go away. My mother influenced me strongly, but there are problems about being the daughter of such a mother. I always wanted to follow her example, but I have had to learn that I don't have the necessary selfless and outgoing personality.

My father was more politically aware than my mother but too shy to participate in public life. He was often uncomfortable with my mother's plans and lack of conventionality. I remember for example, his dismay when she befriended 'Old-Alice-who-lived-under-the-hedge', who was 'a tramp' as we called homeless people then. She brought Alice to our house for tea, as well as helping her to find accommodation as she grew even older and her partner, Old Joe, died. However, my dad's devotion to my mum allowed the whole family enterprise to continue.

Myself in the family: a free life experimenting with different roles

I was born in 1923, the fourth in a family of five, like my mother and maternal grandmother. My oldest sibling was born in 1916 and my younger sister is as close in age to me as are Joan and Patricia whose life stories precede mine. She and I did everything together and were known scornfully by the older three as 'the babies.' We shared friends, and a bedroom where we used to talk and make houses from the bedclothes after we had been put to bed at what seems now the absurdly early hour of six or seven o'clock. My mother (known to everyone as 'Millibar') used to come up and scold us if we made too much noise, though I can't remember ever being punished for anything as a child. My sister and I were also rivals as we shared the same interests and she sometimes did better than me at school. A part of me resented being 'lumped' with her; I was expected to act as a protector. I aspired to the prowess of my brother, four years my senior and in another world.

On the whole though the two of us got on very well and led a free life, often up to mischief in the surrounding trees, the lake, and the golf course where we used to trespass to steal golf balls. We had a gang of girl friends, and modelled ourselves on the antics of Arthur Ransome's parent-free *Swallows and Amazons*. As a pre-adolescent child I was naughty at school and courted popularity (I think I've always been over-dependent on the opinion of others, though it's gone off a bit with age!). At home I didn't misbehave as I was consumed with guilt at any sign of my mother's disapproval. Anyway there were few rules, so it was not easy to break them.

In those days, the label for a child like me was a 'tomboy,' a girl who behaved like a boy. I was proud of this label but as I grew up I experimented with different roles; I would try being bossy, being dreamy and poetic, deceitful (but guilty about it), a changeling. In my teens the dreamy bit took over and I became unassertive and took to writing poetry and novels which my friends had to listen to (did I say unassertive?). I was a late developer, physically and intellectually, and didn't work at school except at what I enjoyed - English, art, gymnastics and sport. I didn't go to school until I was seven, being taught at home by a governess until then. We were lucky to have the North London Collegiate School, Miss Buss's pioneering girls' school, within cycling distance and most of my schooling was there; a very privileged education.

I took my School Certificate in 1941 and although I passed, I didn't do well enough in the range of subjects needed to matriculate whereas my younger sister did. I felt humiliated. I spent one year in the sixth form, and it was only then that I began to be academically interested. However if I had stayed to qualify for university I would have been called up because of my age, so I decided to leave after a year and go to college to become a physical education teacher. I had a crush on my games mistress and felt all that admiration was just the thing for me, swanning about in shorts and being physically active too. Being called up and ordered about was definitely to be avoided.

I was a student for three years, and as my college was evacuated to Cornwall, I left home for the first time at the age of eighteen. It was extremely strenuous, there were a lot of exams to pass as well as all the physical activity, and if you didn't pass them you were called up.

This experience was a turning point in my life. First, I discovered that there were secondary schools of different status. Many of the students were from girls' boarding schools, while others were from state grammar schools. According to the principal of the college, the girls from boarding schools played games with style, and those from state schools played games to win. A nice comment on the social class system. For some reason mysterious to me at the time, my own school was ranked by her more highly than either.

Secondly, I took a subsidiary course in social science and began to become more socially conscious. I gained intellectual confidence as I did very well in exams (though not so well on the games field), and was advised by the principal to go on to take a degree. Physical education was not a degree subject in those days and she was keen to raise the status of the teaching profession.

My career and family life: groping through a fog of immaturity

I have always been some kind of teacher and have always worked full time outside the home except for maternity leaves. When I left college the war was finishing. I shall never forget the terrible film footage from the Belsen concentration camp in 1945. I took my first job that year and taught in girls' grammar schools for eight years, during which time I matriculated by correspondence course. I had aspirations to do medicine until I discovered I would have to do physics to qualify for entrance. I went to one evening class and decided that was not for me. Instead I turned my attention to education and to sociology.

I was still very immature emotionally. All my experience had been in girls' and women's institutions, and in spite of having brothers I didn't communicate easily with men. Going to dances held at the college for members of the nearby army camp didn't help. I remember the agony of sitting waiting to be asked to dance; too tall, gawky, and shy, in a dress made by my mother. Later I bought a red dress, had my hair 'permed' and was more successful, but I never got beyond one or two 'dates'. We had to introduce anyone we went out with to the principal, and be home by 10.30; I was too bored to want to stay out longer.

But I had a happy time teaching and was successful at it, though I always felt my success to be precarious, depending on the pupils wanting to do what I wanted them to do. I could never convince myself of what should and should not be allowed, which I like to put down to my rule- free upbringing, though it's probably part of my tendancy to see too many sides of every question.

I became more conscious of my own privilege through doing voluntary social work and a job in a school in a poor area of Southwark. Communicating across class divisions was not easy for me as I had no experience of it and was very diffident.

In 1953, at the age of 30, I took a further qualification in education and the following year was accepted at the London School of Economics to read sociology. I owe this second turning point in my life to my sociology tutor on the education diploma who enthused me with the subject and encouraged me to apply. She was also a role model for my subsequent life, combining family and career. I lived at home until I graduated, earned money by supply teaching and qualified for a grant in my second year, but I never contributed to my home finances nor would I have been allowed to. I was always free to live at home when I needed to as was every one in the family. LSE was a turning point for me in two ways. First, it gave a theoretical framework to my ill-informed but developing awareness of social inequality (hooray for Marx!), and confirmed to me that I could do academic work. Secondly, in an institution with students from different backgrounds and both sexes, I met my future husband.

We became good friends. He was a fellow mature student brought up in the Jewish East End; we discovered when we were embarked on this project that his family home had been very close to that of Estella, whose life story follows. Both families were in tailoring and he and Estella had even been to the same school for a while. He had educated himself the hard way after leaving school at fourteen and becoming an apprentice in the printing industry. The broadening of my horizons continued. However, he was married with two little children, and it was not until some time after his first marriage broke down that we married; in 1960, three years after graduation.

Arriving at last? But does one ever arrive?
I think it was only then that I felt I had arrived where I wanted to be. Before, I seem to have been learning about life very slowly, groping towards a future I was hardly aware of, enjoying myself but... anyway, after a couple of years teaching social science back at my P.E. college (not a happy experience) and a year's unsatisfactory, isolating post-graduate studentship, I fell into a job at the University of London Institute of Education. I was in the right place at the right time with the right combination of qualifications. Sociology was all the rage in teacher education in the 1960s. Alas no more. In 1962 I bore a son, an unmitigated joy, hoped for but not expected as I married at 37. Three years later we adopted a baby daughter of mixed ethnic origins, another joyous experience. With holidays and weekly visits from my stepchildren, our family was complete.

This was my fourth turning point. I had never particularly wanted children or marriage; but the experience of both has made me more happy than anything else, and I have been lucky enough to be able to continue with teaching, with the help of good au pair girls. In bringing up the family we tended to reproduce the free atmosphere of my own childhood following the only model I knew.

After I had been twelve years at the Institute of Education my husband got a job at Plymouth Polytechnic and we moved to Devon. The move was ideal for our children as they enjoyed a rural life during their adolescence; much more relaxed than inner London. Our daughter complained of the lack of ethnic mix in her Devon school, but pony riding was some compensation. I taught in a college of higher education in Plymouth, where my interest in social class began to extend to matters of gender and ethnicity.

In 1984 my husband took a job in higher education in Hong Kong, as our children had nearly finished their schooling. I spent a couple of years commuting back and forth until our daughter was established in her degree course and then moved to Hong Kong too, coming home for two or three months each year. By this time I had retired from my teaching job, aged 62. I took a course in Teaching English as a Foreign Language and enjoyed teaching Chinese adults for the British Council, a good way to meet local people. I was also involved in the Hong Kong Council of Women, a rather 'Establishment' feminist pressure group.

Hong Kong was the last place I had expected to live, but it was a fascinating experience. It gave us opportunities to travel all over the Far East, and I even got to enjoy the insulating cocoon of the twelve-hour plane ride home. Chinese culture is translated in a unique way in Hong Kong; we made Chinese friends and friends from many other countries, but I didn't much appreciate the weather or the expatriate way of life. It gave our children the chance to travel in China, and indirectly it has enlarged the ethnic mix of our family as our son has married a Chinese woman. I consider it a further turning point in my life and that of the family in the way it developed our international perspective.

Retirement? It implies withdrawal; we don't feel retired
We returned to London in 1988, and have lived in Camden ever since, though my husband has often been back to Hong Kong on consultancies. This has meant I have had periods on my own in London, developed my own interests, and appreciated the times of independence. I think it is essential to maintain this even if you are as happily married as I am to a man who accepts and encourages my autonomy. Mind you, I did the wifely thing and followed him around, getting jobs where his work was located. I don't see how it can work out unless one of you gives way. As I'm not particularly ambitious I didn't initiate job change. For me the combination of work and family, though stressful at times, seemed the best of all worlds.

After 'retirement' I continued to teach English to adults occasionally; attended adult education classes including the U3A, travelled a lot, and 'spent time with the family' which now includes five grandchildren, one half Afro-Carribean and one half Chinese. I consider a mini-turning point in my life to have been joining the U3A Women's History group. Through the way the group has developed, taking a three-generational historical approach, I have discovered a whole new field of academic and personal enquiry. This has led to my following a course in life history studies which has enabled me to see the wider possibilities in what we are doing. I have also met a whole set of interesting women. I have reason to be thankful to the group.

How can I view this life? It is obvious that I have been privileged in my family background. Only gradually, through a mixture of academic work and experience, did I become aware of the struggles and conflicts of the world. But I am hopeless on committees and in public argument, unlike those members of our group who campaign actively against injustice.

I am privileged not only socially, but because of my family culture and the personality of my mother. I have been lucky too in my happy marriage, my health and my career. But it may be (must be?) that I see my childhood through a mist of nostalgia. Our sheltered lives did not prepare us well for adulthood. I was slow to grow up, not used to handling conflict, and very unworldly. And of course we were not happy all the time. There were sometimes tensions in the family because we were an obstinate lot. As I was rarely involved myself I may have minimised these. But I'm sure that basically my siblings would agree with my interpretation of our family life.

(vii) Renee: It is a Changing World

My grandmothers

My maternal grandmother, Brana, came from Poland, as far as I can find out, probably around 1860-70, as all her children, two boys and three girls, were born in London. Her next youngest child, a boy, was born with Down's Syndrome, and lived until he was 28 years old.

The family lived in the East End, and were in the gentlemen's tailoring business, with their own workshop at the bottom of the yard behind their house. According to my eldest sister they did quite well and lived very comfortably. My grandmother died three or four years before I was born.

My paternal grandmother Rose, whom my eldest sister was named after, came from Romania to London around 1894, when my father was two or three years old. She travelled with four small children, two boys and two girls. Her youngest daughter was born in London. Rose died at the age of 36, some months after the birth of her daughter. According to my sister, who was told by my father, the midwife did not ensure that the afterbirth was removed, and it caused a great deal of unnecessary suffering and consequent death.

My grandfather remarried, but the stepmother was never really accepted by the children. I remember her quite well. She had a stall in the market and we would go and see her sometimes. After my grandfather's death she became a cook in a restaurant.

My mother

My mother was born in 1897 and was named Gertrude. She was the youngest daughter in a family of six children. People thought she was extremely beautiful and she was probably spoilt on that account. She learnt to play the piano and loved reading, although she had very poor eyesight. After she left school she was not put to work in the workshop, which would have been usual in those days, but became a cashier in a Lyons teashop. She never learnt to sew. She married at the age of twenty and had nine children, three boys and six girls. She had a very hard life.

Looking back I realise that there was no need for her to have had such a terrible life. My father was a master tailor with his own workshop employing five or six people. The work was seasonal so the business had its ups and downs. The main problem was that my father spent most of his money on his own pleasure, that is gambling, and his family was not his main priority. Amazingly enough, in spite of this, my mother loved him and he always came first.

In 1940 my mother was for a time evacuated to somewhere near Blackpool, taking with her my youngest sister who must have been around three years old. For my mother it was as though she only had one child and I know she loved it.

My mother died at the age of 54, from stomach cancer.

Myself

I was born in 1924, the fourth child in a family of nine children. From when I was born until 1933, we lived in two rooms on the upper floor of a small house in Stepney. Eight children were born there, only one in a hospital. There was no running water or toilet facilities, but at the back of the flat was something we called the 'orf-room', where there must have been a tap, and also a pail instead of a toilet, which consequently had to be emptied very often. My mother cooked in the front room, on a gas ring placed on a chair. As a result, my mother's legs were burnt more than once. According to my sister, she later had a proper gas stove.

In 1933, when the eighth child was born we were given a council flat nearby, where we had three bedrooms, and an indoor toilet, but with a bathtub in the kitchen. Two years later we moved to a three-storey house near Aldgate. It was in a very bad, damp condition, but it also had three bedrooms. We kept the ground floor front room for best. The toilet was in the yard and there was a tap just outside the kitchen door. In 1937 my mother bore her last child. We lived in this house until the outbreak of war in 1939. It was bombed during the war and the street has since completely disappeared.

I remember very little of my early life. We were very poor, but so were all my contemporaries, so I didn't feel that I had a deprived childhood. I started school at three, which was quite common in those days, and probably learnt to read at a very early age, because I can remember going to the library very often and losing myself in books. After school we would go to a play centre, and I also joined the Brownies. My brothers and sister quarrelled amongst themselves quite a lot but I never took part.

One incident that stands out. In the council flat where we lived, there was a boiler for washing clothes. One day when I was nine years old, it burst as I was passing and my leg was badly scalded. It had been repaired the previous day but my mother refused to claim any damages as she didn't want the man to lose his job. I spent nine weeks in hospital and a further six weeks in a convalescent home in Hampstead.

At ten I won a London County Council scholarship, which included a grant of £27 a year for uniforms. I went to a grammar school in Spitalfield. My aunts were against my taking up the scholarship, as they said we couldn't afford to let me go, but my mother was so proud of me as the first in the entire family to go to a grammar school. I stayed on until I was seventeen.

I have a tendency to accept things at their face value, and mostly don't wish to probe too deeply. It must have been during my school years that I created a shell around myself in order to block out unpleasant incidents and humiliations. The headmistress of the school seemed mostly to be taken up with pupils whose parents reached her standards, and I was obviously not one of them. I wasn't a particularly good student, and as my mother had so much to contend with, I didn't get any encouragement to work hard. When my school reports were given to me to pass on to my parents, I used to sign them myself, forging my mother's signature, without their ever seeing them. One regular comment was: 'Renee has the ability but talks too much.'

In 1939 the war broke out and my school was evacuated to Ely. We were able to walk to Liverpool Street Station the day before, that is 2nd September. We had no idea where we would end up. Myself, two of my younger sisters, plus two younger brothers, were put on the train. I was fifteen at the time, and was upset that I was supposed to have the responsibility for keeping an eye on them all. I felt that I had more than enough with myself, which may sound very selfish, but I was really too young for this, and wasn't a great help to any of them.

My two sisters and I were billeted on two ladies in their 70s, who owned a large house and had two servants. The eldest one, Miss Hilda, had originally wanted German boys as apparently she spoke some German, but had to settle for us. The two ladies kept to their part of the house and we lived with the servants. It was only later, on a visit to Ely, that I entered their morning room. To be honest, in their own way, they were kind to us, and Miss Hilda, who ran a fast car, sometimes took us to Cambridge or

Newmarket for treats. She took care, however, to sit at a separate table in the cafe whilst we were having our tea. My brothers were billeted separately, just round the corner from us, but we didn't have a great deal of contact. I didn't stay in that billet for too long, but moved around to various homes. At one place, where they took in other lodgers, they had a daughter of my own age, and we became friends.

I took my school certificate and matriculated whilst evacuated. We were the first to sit the exams after the outbreak of war. I only got fairly average results, as I wasn't into swotting, but as we were away from home, we weren't really expected to do so well. After that the entire class moved up to the sixth form to take a commercial course, where I did very well. I had no thoughts of going to university, and in any case most of the universities were closed for the duration. I understand that one girl went on to university and presume that she took her degree.

My first job after I left school was while I was still away I stayed on in my last billet and paid a weekly amount. I think I was paid 30 shillings a week, so I probably gave up half for my board and lodging. The job was with an estate agent managing farms. There was very little work and I found it boring, especially when I was asked to do some bookkeeping. They must have had quite a problem sorting out some of my mistakes!

A short time after I returned to London, I moved in with an older sister actually not more than fourteen months older than myself. She had married at eighteen and had a small child. Her husband was away in the army, so it was convenient for both of us for me to live with her. I had no problem in obtaining a position with a firm of chartered accountants. My work mainly consisted of correspondence and typing accounts, but it was a job. Due to the shortage of accounts clerks as so many had been called up, my boss asked if I would be interested in training to become an accountant. However, I thought that would be even more boring and turned down the offer. I stayed there for less than a year, and then took a secretarial job with a well-known corset manufacturer with very elegant offices in Regent Street. Again business was very limited. My boss was a very sophisticated refugee from Czechoslovakia, and one of the things we did was to write a short history of that country. Again, I didn't stay there too long.

For some reason or other my year was not called up, but I felt I should be doing something for the war effort and joined the Air Ministry and sat in various typing pools for the rest of the war. However, it gave me the advantage of further training and I took the RSA first class certificate in typing and shorthand. I changed departments several times, once because I was subjected to anti-semitism, especially from one woman who objected to me even before I started there, as my name was so obviously Jewish. Another time was when Bush House received a hit from a V2 and the London School of Economics building where I worked was closed off because of the damage. All these changes gave me a great deal of experience, which was a help when looking for a better job after the war.

We had to stay on at the Ministry after the war, but I made the excuse that I was going abroad, and was able to leave. The only reference I got was that I had worked there from one date to another.

For a young girl, London was a very exciting place to be, apart from the bombing, V1s and V2s. There were lots of young men around from so many different countries, and we went out dancing two or three times a week. I had no supervision at home so was able to come and go as I pleased. However, I had my own rules and was quite a prim and proper young girl. During the time of the V1s my friend and I had quite a lot of contact with Norwegians, so much so that we went to evening classes to learn Norwegian as we thought the language was much more exotic than French or German. At that time quite a few girls had married Norwegians, and classes had been set up in order to prepare them for moving to Norway after the war. This came in very useful when at the end of 1950 I met a Norwegian journalist, who was at Oxford on a British Council scholarship, and who later became my husband.

My last job before going to live in Norway, was with a firm of manufacturers of sound equipment, and I stayed with them for eight years. I had a good deal of responsibility, as the secretary to the managing director, and liked the job very much. Funnily enough, when I left I was given a substantial sum of money, as my boss said that he had not realised how much work I had taken on, and that he had underpaid me.

I stayed with my sister until 1949. By that time her husband was back and the flat was cramped. They found me a room of my own in Willesden Green. I was very pleased to go, to be on my own and look after myself. It meant that I could have friends home when I wanted, something I had never been able to do before.

A new life in Norway

I moved to Norway in 1952. My future mother-in-law didn't exactly welcome me with open arms. She shared the common belief that everything in Norway was better than anywhere else, and as she already had a Swedish son-in-law, she didn't take kindly to an English daughter-in-law. Actually we didn't marry until 1955, and in those days it wasn't the done thing to move in together before marriage. I spent the first years living in a bed-sitting room, and my living conditions always came with the proviso that the host family should be helped with their English. My then fiance was still living at home. We were on the waiting list for a flat as very little building work was going on in Oslo just after the war. The whole of the north of the country had been razed to the ground by the retreating Germans and had to be rebuilt first, so we had to wait our turn. We finally obtained a two-bedroomed flat but had to show our marriage certificate before we were allowed to move in. We lived there for ten years, after which we moved to a small three-bedroomed house. Most of the building at that time was carried out by semi-co-operative organisations. You paid part of the cost yourselves, and the rest was in rent, but you never became the real owner. Then in 1968 we were offered a plot of land just outside Oslo, through the local council, and we put up our own detached house. It was large and roomy, with lots of cupboards and storage space, and surrounded by trees. We had to do an enormous amount of work to get the garden into shape, the climate not helping very much.

In Norway one of my first jobs was with a large pharmaceutical company importing antibiotics, mostly from the States. They also had another company importing cosmetics and perfumes from France. All communications had to be in English as Norwegians don't usually know very much French. My English was essential. I stayed with them for about eight years and eventually became the secretary to the managing director. I left because my husband had obtained a three-month scholarship to study in England, and of course I wanted to accompany him.

During my time with the pharmaceutical company our first child was born, and I continued working. We were still living in our first flat, but we hired a young girl to come and live with us, and she looked after our daughter. In 1961 our second daughter was born, but by then I was no longer working.

Just before we moved to the new house, I decided that it was time to get back to working outside the home. I had always done a fair amount of work at home, typing manuscripts and translating or correcting English for various organisations, but I needed to get out of the house. My first job was with the state hospital, on a temporary basis, working for a doctor who had a short-term contract in the sociology field. After that I joined the trade union bank and was with them for 22 years. During that time I went from being a secretary to being trained as a loan consultant, and was responsible for all loans in connection with the erection of houses and other large buildings. I was for a time elected as a shop steward, which meant that I took part in wage negotiations, making decisions on staff placements, the bank's policies and in general helping to solve any problems that arose amongst the staff.

In Norway children began school when they were seven, but only went for three hours a day to start with. Full-time nursery school places were very hard to come by, being mainly for children with special needs, divorced parents, etc. I didn't have a problem with the first child, but for the second one we had to come to an arrangement with a lady living in the same street She was extremely religious, but after the first year our daughter decided that she no longer wished to continue with her. Both the girls then had their own door keys and came and went as they pleased. Fortunately we had no problems. The schools they went to were near our home, within walking distance, and it was a very safe environment. We realise to-day how lucky they were to have grown up in such surroundings.

Owing to my husband's various moves, from being a journalist on a daily newspaper to working as organising secretary with the Labour Party, some time with the Norwegian Development Agency and as a junior minister in the Prime Minister's office, we came into contact with many prominent people, both in Norway and abroad. I was very fortunate that we were able to travel extensively. In 1980 my husband left the Prime Minister's office and we spent almost four years in Israel,where we still have very many good friends. I was able to keep my job with the bank open, but wasn't allowed to work in Israel as my husband was with the embassy. Whilst I was in Israel I attended archaeology courses at the Tel Aviv University and also studied Hebrew.

I was able to accompany my husband abroad on many occasions, and in 1974, on a trip to Israel organised by the Israeli Foreign Office, we had a private interview with Golda Meir at her home. The reason for visiting her was to tell her about a fund that had been set up in Norway, called 'Let Israel Live' to help after the Yom Kippur War. At that time Norway was very supportive of Israel and part of the conversation was about the fact that many members of parliament objected to Yasser Arafat speaking in the United Nations General Assembly for the first time. Even though she was no longer prime minister, she took the problems very much to heart and this showed in her face. We had heard about her kitchen cabinet, so we were not surprised when she offered us coffee and went into the kitchen to make it herself. We were told that the meeting should only last about twenty minutes, but it actually went on for about one-and-a-half hours.

Whilst my husband was at the Prime Minister's office, we were always invited to state banquets given for visiting prime ministers and other heads of state. In this way we met some very interesting people. A couple of events stand out: one was that we were asked by the Foreign Minister to chaperone the Prime Minister of Poland and his wife during their state visit to Norway; Included in that assignment was lunch at the King's palace. I don't remember much about the lunch. What stuck in my mind was that the communist prime minister's wife was the only one to wear a hat. Another event was King Olav's 75th birthday. At the state banquet, attended by all of Scandinavian royalty, and also Prince Charles, the Norwegian crown prince (now King Harald) stood right behind me to deliver his speech in honour of his father, and I appeared on television, and was seen all over the country. My mother-in-law was quite peeved about this: 'How was it that I appeared on television and not her son?' At all these banquets you did not sit with your husband but were always placed in order of rank, so that I could end up with a very high-ranking personality and my husband with that person's wife, and they would be sitting at another table.

In connection with the Nobel peace prizes we also met, amongst others, Menachem Begin and Mother Teresa.

Return to England

My husband had always promised that as soon as he was able to retire we would move back to England. This did not mean that I didn't enjoy Norway, but our two daughters were already living in London and we had grandchildren. Also I felt that I had seen enough snow to last me a lifetime, and the older you get the worse it becomes in the winter. We sold our house at a ridiculously low price, there being a depression on, and at first moved into a rented flat, later buying our present accommodation, which suits us very well. We are centrally placed to keep in touch with the family and see them once or twice a week. Our grandchildren are our greatest joy. My husband has been able to maintain his connections with his organisation, and we have on many occasions been asked to represent them at various conferences around the world.

Since returning to London I have worked as an assistant in classes for people with literacy problems, taken painting and drawing courses, and last but not least, taken part in the women's history class at U3A. This has given me a great deal of pleasure and added to my knowledge of both myself and the other participants, who have become my friends.

We have retained our house in the mountains in the western part of

Norway and visit at least once a year. The area is very beautiful, but we are rather isolated, especially as we are unable to drive up to the house, it being too steep.

To sum up I would say that in spite of all the early trials and tribulations, I have had a very good and interesting life, met many famous people and travelled a great deal. I am very fortunate in that my marriage is a good one, and my husband is both kind and supportive. Even though, as I have said above, I am fond of Norway and have many wonderful memories of both the country and its people, I am very happy to have returned to London. Once a Londoner, always a Londoner.

(viii) Estella: My Grandmas, My Mother, Myself

My grandmas

Both my grandmas and their families emigrated to England from Eastern Europe in order to escape the pogroms that were being inflicted upon the Jews. My maternal grandma reached this country in about 1897/8 and my paternal grandma in 1900/1. There is no official substantiation of these events, only 'family' knowledge. The task of writing my own history has shown me that two sets of so-called 'facts' have emerged; those that are irrefutable and those that can only be surmised. Sometimes it is difficult to differentiate between the two.

Some years ago, having attended a genealogy group at U3A, I felt inspired to do some research into my family background, beginning with Betsy, my maternal grandma, born in 1861, a date that was verified by recorded details of her death. Records of her birth, her marriage and the births of her first two daughters might be somewhere in Eastern Europe; indeed they may never have been officially recorded. However, Betsy married and lived near Vilna (at that time in Russia). Legend has it that she and her family were involved in market-gardening, coming into Vilna to sell their produce. It has also been said that she acted as midwife within her own community. My mother adored Betsy, often saying that she was a 'witch' or wise woman. Betsy's husband was unable to accompany her to England as he had been conscripted into the Russian army. A long time ago my aunt showed me a photograph of my maternal grandfather dressed in Russian military uniform. Unfortunately all my aunt's photos seem to have vanished.

Betsy arrived in England with her two young daughters and pregnant with my mother; she must have travelled to England sometime between summer 1897 and early 1898, because my mother's birth in England in March 1898 is confirmed by her birth certificate.

Betsy found work as a cap-maker, doing this for a number of years. Local schools accepted children from the age of three, which enabled her to devote more time to her job. Even so she felt obliged to withdraw her young daughters at various times to help with the cap making, so increasing her earning potential. but not furthering their education. At that time and in that area of East London, poverty was endemic. Like Sima's mother, my mother talked about getting food from the soup kitchen at a cost of one penny.

Betsy died in 1935 when I was nine years old, and I have quite clear memories of her as a plump little woman with snow-white hair. Often I would sit with her as she sipped her glass of lemon-tea through a sugar-cube clenched between her teeth. Sometimes she would pour some sweet milky tea from her cup into the saucer for me to sip, and sometimes she would allow me to dip fingers of dry bread into her bowl of cocoa. In her parlour she had a dark, horsehair-filled sofa. Whenever I sat on it, it would stick to and prickle the backs of my bare legs. In a household of five adults and seven youngsters, she was much loved and revered by us all.

Rebecca, my paternal grandma, was born in 1879. She, her young husband, and her extended family of father and sisters, came to England at the beginning of the twentieth century, from Romania. My father was born in 1902 in London, followed at two-yearly intervals by his three sisters. The young family moved from town to town, probably as my grandfather tried to find work. Seven years later, when they were living in Swansea, my grandfather died of a lung disease, brought on by his work in the steel industry. He was 34 years old. Rebecca was 30 when her husband died and her four children were all under eight. She and her children returned to London where she found work in the tailoring trade. Working in the East End sweatshops and perhaps receiving help from the Jewish Board of Guardians she tried to support herself and her young family. She struggled on for a couple of years but eventually put her children into the West Norwood Jewish Orphanage. Then she was able to concentrate on working full-time, advancing her prospects, knowing that her children were well cared for and educated in a harsh but stable institution. As they reached the school leaving age of fourteen, each child returned home to her and began to work themselves.

When I was a child she was still living in London and I was taken to visit her once a week. She was very small and thin, a bit sharp in figure and manner. Her house always seemed to be dark - the curtains were often drawn to protect furniture and carpets from sunlight. My cousins, my brother and I, all loved her garden, playing on a home-made swing tied to a tree, and balancing on the brick wall that ran along one side. Rebecca also baked cookies and other goodies for us.

At the outbreak of the Second World War Rebecca and her two unmarried daughters moved to Manchester. My brother and I were evacuated, and I only saw her again when the war ended. She seemed even tinier and was bent with age, but somehow her manner had softened. On one occasion we talked about dancing, and she showed me how she had danced as a young girl in Romania. Rebecca and her daughter-in-law, my mother, never really got on; each was critical of the other, and perhaps some of this attitude rubbed off on me when I was young. I have my father's apprenticeship certificate which shows he had served a full apprenticeship to become a qualified tailor, cutter and designer. Rebecca thought that his marriage to a mere felling-hand in the workshop was beneath him. Rebecca died in 1958 in Manchester.

My mother

Gertie, my mother, Betsy's youngest child, was born at the end of the 19th century, into extreme poverty. Her birth certificate gives her name as Kate, possibly because the registrar could only interpret my grandma's oral yiddish version, Gittel, in that way. 'Gittel' became anglicised to Gertie, though grandma always used the yiddish name. Gertie, her two sisters and her mother Betsy, lived in Backchurch Lane, just off the Commercial Road in East London.

My mother told me the name of her first school in East London. My interest in genealogy took me to the Greater London Records Office where I found the actual school admissions register. I saw my mother's name and address in the year 1900 admission lists; Betsy had given a false date of birth for her youngest daughter. This deception must have been discovered, because the following year's admissions included my mother's name and correct details. I imagine that Betsy was desperate for paid work, and having all her three daughters at school (the eldest was ten) might have enabled her to get a full-time job more easily.

Gertie herself left school at the age of thirteen to go to work in a tailoring sweatshop as a felling-hand. Apparently she always worked in the tailoring trade and met my father, a jobbing tailor, while she was working in a workshop supervised by Rebecca, his mother. Unbeknown to both their parents, in 1923 he and my mother married in a registry office. Each continued to live in their respective homes for another year, when all was revealed. They then went through a 'proper' religious ceremony. They went to live in two rooms in Betsy's multi-occupied house.

My mother was always concerned about 'bettering herself'. She used to boast that she dressed very smartly, saying that when she took the tram to work, she looked more like an office-girl than someone who worked in a sweatshop. On setting up home with my father, she dropped paid work and took on the conventional role of housewife, and eventually, mother. My father would hand over his wage-packet to her every Friday night, and they would work out how much money was needed for the following week, with him taking his share for personal expenses. This was a weekly ritual which I well remember (it often caused arguments). Somehow, out of these irregular wages, my mother managed to make savings. For a short while, to satisfy her aspirations, she employed a 'skivvy' to come once a week, and I can remember her talking about 'my hubby' to friends - 'hubby' being a typical term used by some 1930s suburban housewives. How she dreamed of becoming one of these housewives in a neat suburban semi with its manicured garden, just like the pictures used by estate agents to advertise the 1930s houses! In 1938 my parents bought a small, Edwardian semi in Tottenham, but it was not at all like those neat mock-Tudor semis so alluringly advertised.

As far as living in Greater London was concerned, the suburban dream never really came to fruition. However, my father, who was not called up for service until the end of the war, had earned enough money by then for my mother to make substantial savings. They used some of these to venture into the property market. Using their small house as collateral they bought a house on the Essex coast to let to holiday makers and eventually to retire to. They were desperately disappointed when this financial venture failed and they had to sell it again.

Completely devoted to her family and her home, my mother died in 1970. Immediately following her death my father retired. He is still alive at the age of 98 and I visit him every week.

Myself

Born at the beginning of the General Strike in 1926 I was the first living child of my parents. A year earlier their first child had died after living only 36 hours. The household I was born into consisted of my grandma Betsy, my aunt and uncle and their son, and my other aunt's four sons. Later my parents had two sons, making me Betsy's only granddaughter. We lived in Bethnal Green in a poor but respectable area. My mother fed my body, my father and school my mind. On the whole I was adequately clothed, though I do remember a couple of times when my shoes were worn out to the extent that the nails in them were exposed and made my feet bleed, or there were holes in the soles through which I could pull my socks!

I remember clearly how the three women, my grandma, my aunt, and my mother, ruled the roost, and by their ingenuity satisfied their families' needs of food and clothing, using to good effect every penny given them by the six wage earning men.The men were kind and supportive and revered my grandmother. Sometimes they would all gather together in her parlour to discuss politics, boxing, horse racing and cricket; or they would play cards or sing the current popular songs; all of this of course while the women were somewhere else clearing up, putting the kids to bed or doing some other chore. As a child I wished I was a boy as men's lives seemed so much more interesting.

My life revolved around home, school and street games. We children used the local East End streets as our playground, especially the narrow traffic-free ones. The streets were by no means quiet. Vans and carts made their deliveries to the many small shops. There was the milkman, the coalman, the rag-and-bone man. Other street vendors were the cat's meat man, and the 'India-toffee' man who carried his spiky sugary confection in a biscuit tin slung round his neck, from which he would take fingers-full of toffee to put into paper cones and sell for one halfpenny. There was also the toffee-apple man, the hot potato/chestnuts man, the ice-cream seller, and, usually on Sundays, the shrimp/winkles man and the muffin man. Add to these the newsboys and the local characters like Prince Monolulu, who sold betting tips; the old man who played his great horned gramophone on a home-made cart, and the woman who roamed the streets with her dog in a baby's pram. The calling out, the ringing of bells, and the music from the barrel organs, all contributed to the concert of sounds, tastes and smells which made such a lasting impression on me in early childhood.

Occasionally we had a family outing, even a week or two's holiday. I can remember when I was about ten I went on a school journey for a week to Devon. Full board and lodging cost 27s.6d, i.e. £1.38p a week. On my return I was met by a cousin who put me on a train with the guard. I stayed in the guard's van until I arrived at Westgate-on-Sea where I was met by my family. What an adventure!

Up until the outbreak of war in 1939 my schooling was nothing but joy for me. In that year came evacuation, which involved a five-year chunk of my life (which I have described in the chapter on war). At the age of seventeen or eighteen and in my last year at school, I did not really want to apply for university entrance as I felt that I had had enough of education. However, teachers advised me to carry on with my Higher School Certificate studies (equivalent to present-day A-levels), and to go through the motions of university applications.

Not knowing what else to do, I just drifted into university. Possibly the changeover from cosseted schoolgirl evacuee living in a small country town to the comparatively adult life of a university student, living at home in war-torn London, commuting daily on a long journey to the bomb-damaged college in Bloomsbury, presented something of a culture shock to me. Although I had friends at college, I wasn't happy. I felt a bit lost and disappointed with some aspects of my degree course and still didn't know what I would do when I graduated. Lectures became a burden and academic progress began to take a back seat to my social life. Exam results were so poor that the faculty dean told me that I had to leave. That year, 1945, the war had ended, and universities were under a certain obligation to offer places to those people whose call-up into the services had deprived them of further education. I was not offered a second chance, and this rejection had a profound effect on me; I felt a complete and utter failure. That autumn I became ill with pleurisy and was admitted to hospital, followed by convalescence on the south coast, a period of fragile health lasting three to four months.

Then in April 1946, just before my twentieth birthday, I obtained a clerical job in the Foreign Office (German Section). This turned out to be so boring and mind-numbing that after the first three weeks I asked for a transfer, a request that caused a few ripples in the sluggish puddle in which I was trapped. It took seven months for this request to be acted upon, and then I was transferred to a department where I could use my knowledge of German. When this rather 'way-out' department was absorbed into the Foreign Office proper, I transferred to an accounts section, where I eventually met my husband, who was also in the Foreign Office.

We had different cultural and religious backgrounds - I was Jewish and he was not - and although my parents were not very religious, they objected to our marriage. Life became miserable for all of us, especially for my parents. My father, brought up to abide by certain traditions, felt deeply shamed by the knowledge that his daughter wanted to marry 'out'. He spent painful hours trying to convince us of the problems we might have to face as a couple in a 'mixed marriage'; the anti-semitism, the question of the religion of any children we might have, the adverse effects of our cultural differences, and so on. We, so sure of one another and the strength of our love, and completely self-centred of course, withstood all his pleading. To my mother he confessed that he felt like cutting his throat; she must have been sick with worry. Trivial though it may seem, the fact that I was their only daughter meant that she would be deprived of all the fuss, excitement and showing-off associated with a Jewish wedding. My parents had even thought of spiriting me away to Israel.

Eventually, having promised to wait a full year before making a final decision, and amidst all the trauma, we married in a registry office in December 1949. I was 23 and my husband just 29. My husband's family welcomed me with open arms. As time went on, my parents too came to love my husband like another son.

After more than three years of saving up, we bought our first home, a small semi in a West London suburb. There we brought up our two daughters, who were born in 1953 and 1955. Apart from the usual family ups and downs, there was a painful break for us all in 1958 when I was taken into hospital suffering from tuberculosis. The bad attack of pleurisy when I had just left college at the age of nineteen, had scarred my right lung, and the scarred tissue had played host to a gathering of TB bacilli. As I had had a bad reaction to one of the drugs I was taking, it was decided that I should enter Harefield Hospital to have that part of my lung surgically removed. Before the operation could take place, the bacilli had to be killed off, and afterwards there had to be a time for convalescence. I was in hospital for ten months, a huge separation for all of us. Arrangements had to be made for the children. The neighbours were wonderful, but it was a very worrying time, especially for my husband.

In 1965, aged 39 and fully recovered, I decided to work on a part-time basis. I started as a 'Saturday girl' at a local department store. My husband was at home on Saturdays to look after the girls, and to them as well as me, Saturdays became like special treat days. There were other part-time jobs, all of which fitted into keeping school hours; no-one could accuse me of neglecting my family! A significant step came when I entered a college of education in 1967, and I began a teaching career two years later. During this period I employed a 'cleaning lady'. What a relief! I loathed housework and still do; even more so now that I don't have a 'cleaning lady'.

We spent 22 years in that little semi, but in 1975 when both girls were away at college, we went 'upmarket' to our present detached house. We enjoy family visits from our children and grandchildren. Those first 22 years seemed so long, and in contrast the last 23 years seem to have flown by. My husband retired in 1981, and I three years later.

When I first started at U3A in 1984, I was rather apprehensive about joining groups of people ranging in age from mid-50s to 80+. Colleagues at school had ranged from mid-50s down to early 20s, and our relationships with one another did not appear to be affected by age differences. How would I relate to people who were mostly older than myself? Would I experience the stimulation from new ideas, be infected by the enthusiasm of others, care about and discuss other people's opinions, have fun and enjoy the presence of mental and emotional vitality? Yes is the answer to all this. Being a member of U3A in London has given me the chance to dip my finger into so many pies and to sample so many different tastes, from architecture to genealogy, from painting to history, from jazz appreciation to graphology, and of course, women's history and this project; all with groups of like-minded people.

(ix) Jo: My Life as an Escapologist – and What I was Escaping From

My two grannies

My two grannies came from very different worlds, yet each knew great insecurity. My father's mother, Granny Eva, suffered insecurity from losing her parents as a child, her husband as a young wife and three of her five children. My mother's mother, Granny Bertha, knew all her life the insecurity of grinding poverty.

Granny Eva (who was born some time in the late 1870s) lost both parents in a train crash and was made a ward in chancery. As this indicates, there was money in the family, which was part of the prosperous commercial middle class of South Yorkshire. She married a businessman and they had five children, including my father who was the second born. One day when the youngest child was still a baby she and her husband had quarrelled and she refused to make it up before he went out to business (the family never referred to 'work'). During that day he had a heart attack and was brought home dead.

She then moved to an East London suburb and opened a high class dress

72

shop. Why she chose to move such a distance I don't know, nor where the money came from, her original inheritance or her husband's life insurance perhaps. Her oldest son, Lionel, died in the influenza outbreak at the end of the First World War, her third child, my Aunt Dorothy, died of cancer during the 1930s, and my father died of coronary thrombosis at the age of 50. (My father had become estranged from his family when he married my mother, see below). She herself lived well into her 80s in a fifth floor converted flat in a house in Mayfair without a lift. She never quite lost a faint Yorkshire accent, nor the values of her class. I can still remember her saying: 'Best is cheapest in the long run'.

Granny Bertha grew up somehow in the insecurity of being virtually a strect waif. I know nothing about her family, nor the reasons for their poverty, nor their neglect of her. She somehow acquired a skilled trade as a tailoress. In those days, one hundred years ago, people had to pay a premium for such training as well as serve an unpaid apprenticeship. I have no idea how she managed this, nor the extent of her new skill. As a young woman she set up house with a married man. He was a skilled metal worker and had a wife in an institution of some kind. He was a political radical, although I don't know how active, and would talk of hanging dukes from lamp posts. When she moved in with my grandfather, Granny Bertha had his two sons from his marriage sent out to Canada under indentures.

In order to have her first child in hospital Granny Bertha had to borrow a neighbour's wedding certificate or the lying-in hospital near Waterloo would not have admitted her. This made problems for that first child, my aunt Gertrude, when she came to claim her pension at 60. That of course was not her mother's fault. Granny Bertha was though, more to blame in two ways for further reducing my aunt's life chances. When Aunt Gertrude won a scholarship in the years before the First World War Granny Bertha would not allow her to accept it, in spite of personal visits from the school, in case it would educate her beyond her class. In spite of this aunt Gertrude managed eventually to get a prestigious job that she enjoyed. However when my grandfather died in the 1940s, Granny Bertha declared herself an invalid (it was never clear what the problem was), and Aunt Gertrude gave up her job to become a carer; her caring lasted for over twenty years.

My mother
My mother grew up in a close family, but her mother, my Granny Bertha, was as I've shown, needy and domineering, and mother found her life stifling. She was an adventurous woman, and tried various means of escape.

She tried to be a nun for a while (the family was Roman Catholic), and then a nurse. Granny Bertha resented this and so my mother became semi-estranged from her family. One day when she was in her early twenties and was out with a man who became obnoxious, she was rescued by my father. Three weeks later in August 1928 they were married, and discovered on their wedding day that they shared the same birthday, although four years apart in age. On the day itself there was some confusion over the arrangements, mother waiting inside the Registry Office and father outside. My mother had her mother with her who enjoyed giving dire warnings of how little she knew of my father and how he was already letting her down.

They started their married life against the wishes of both their families and this was to cause them considerable hardship. My father had lied about his age to get into the army in 1918, was commissioned and sent on an expedition to Archangel that was supposed to meet and support the White Army in the Russian Revolution. The Whites never reached the rendezvous and the expedition made a chaotic return in dreadful conditions. When my father left the army his medical condition had changed from A1 to C3, but he hadn't been wounded and so didn't qualify for a pension. By 1919 his mother (Granny Eva's) dress shop had become a small clothing factory and my father was employed there as a dress designer. When he met my mother he had been engaged to a nice young lady from the tennis club. Granny Eva was furious about the marriage: it was so quick and improvident, and my mother came from a working-class Roman Catholic family. So my father lost his job in the family firm.

From then until the Second World War he never had a proper job, although he did his best and took many unskilled temporary jobs. Because he was a dress designer and had been a director of the family company owning the factory and therefore management, he didn't qualify for the limited national insurance of that pre-Welfare State time. Within five years my parents had four children, of whom I was the first; they had to seek what assistance they could get from the parish. In those days this was very harsh and parish officials made them sell some of their beds and bedding so that all four of us slept in one bed under coats in winter. They were unable to afford decent or secure housing and we moved from one unsuitable set of rooms to another, landlords being shy of four unruly children. My mother was not at all strong and all this was a dreadful strain on her health, as well as on my parent's marriage. They did the best they could within their limitations but family life was far from happy, and they were clearly trapped in their circumstances.

During the Second World War they both managed to get employment and that eased their finances. But the demands of their jobs meant there was little time or energy to spare for the home or children. I was expected to do a lot of the housework and to keep my younger siblings out of trouble, responsibilities which I hated. My mother was unable to sustain her job and that meant we had to start the moving series again (she had been managing a shop that had a flat over it). During these moves the family became split. Mother took a residential job as a school matron and took my little brother with her. My two sisters were temporarily sent to a convent orphanage, I was now fifteen and left home and came to London to live.

At the end of the war the family all came back to London. At sixteen, as a London resident, I was charged with finding a family home. A two-roomed condemned basement in a slum was all I could find at the time. For some reason, my father wasn't able to come home until a few weeks after the others and during that time the family had no income other than my £1+ wages as a shop assistant. My mother would come and meet me at lunch time on Friday to collect my wages to buy the week's rations.

The new housing conditions did nothing to help my parents' health, nor their marriage. Housing was given as the reason for their temporary separation as my mother took a residential job as a housekeeper. Both died early, my father in 1950, just after his 50th birthday, and my mother in 1954 of lung cancer when she was 50. I am convinced that the hardships and worries of their lives killed them.

Looking back on such hard, wasted lives is painful. I admire the courage and integrity they showed in their attempts to keep something like a family life. It pains me that my father never queried the conditions that led to such hardship for himself and for so many others. He retained throughout the middle-class values of his background and saw our circumstances as the result of his personal failure.

Myself

I was born in June 1929, four months before the Wall Street crash. I have no memory of either of my sisters being born, Barbara in 1930, and Madeleine in 1932, but do have a vague memory of the arrival of my brother Tony in July 1934. The family story is that I was dreadful to Barbara. Neither of us can now remember, but it's all too likely. I was a difficult, strong-willed child, resisting parental wishes and going on hunger strike.

I still remember the strength of the longing to read, coming from my delight in *Winnie the Pooh*. I was always greedy for more than my daily ration of having it read to me and so persuaded my mother to move her finger along the line while she read it, thus learning to read at the age of three. Another early memory is Barbara and I playing at mummies and daddies by throwing a dolls' tea set across the room at each other. I was four and she was three, and we neither of us remember our parents actually behaving in that way. At the age of five I bullied my mother into admitting the non-existence of Father Christmas, but agreed to keep it a secret as it was nice for the children to believe in him.

When I was six I had a series of childhood illnesses and some very painful surgery. This was the occasion of a reconciliation between my father and his mother, and I was sent to stay with Granny Eva in her flat on the seafront at Brighton. I had a wonderful time there as the only child and playing on my invalidity as granny tried to tempt me to eat. I still remember my faint voice announcing: 'I think I could *just* manage some bananas and cream.' Granny wanted to adopt me and send me to a local private school but somehow it didn't happen. I wonder now how my life might have been. With an adequate childhood education I might not have been driven to become an adult student and would probably not have gone to university.

Another memory from the age of nine is being part of a rehearsal for evacuation from the local rail station with my label tied to my coat and with my suitcase. I felt really cheated that Chamberlain came back from Munich with 'peace in our time'.

By the age of eleven I was noticing how convenient for adults were all the things we children were supposed to do for God, and so I decided that like Father Christmas he didn't exist. From that time on, my mother's ill health and harassed life were apparent even to a child and I remember looking at her and determining that I was *never* going to allow myself to get into that situation. About that time I made my only ever life plan; I would get a job in a fashion store earning £3 per week, of which £1 would be rent, £1 food and the rest pocket money.

When I was fourteen I left school (this was my first escape, Granny Eva's had been only a temporary break). Since the age of five, when I'd started, I'd been a new girl thirteen times. Why we were changed around so often I don't know since sometimes it would be a school we'd left only a term ago. I think part of the motivation was to play the holiday dates of different schools so that we'd be at home for the shortest possible time. We were difficult, unruly children, and the confused conditions of wartime might have helped disguise what was going on.

My first job was at the direction of the local Labour Office, at an aircraft repair factory. I was thrilled to be away from school and doing war work, hand writing out clock cards and announcing when there were air raids. The next year there was a constant procession of tanks and armoured lorries on the road to the South coast, and so we were all prepared for the announcement of D Day, shortly after my fifteenth birthday

At the end of that year I left home and came to live in a hostel in Gordon Square, with a job at Marshall and Snellgrove, where Debenhams now stands in Oxford Street. I felt that I was now truly embarked on my real life. The budget, though, was markedly less generous than that of my childhood imagining. I was paid £1.2s.6d. (£1.15) per week, my hostel cost 17s. 6d. for bed, breakfast and evening meal, leaving five shillings (25p) for fares, tooth paste, soap, lunches, etc. It wasn't enough. I used to walk to and from work and take bread from the breakfast table for lunch. At the end of my first day at Marshall and Snellgrove, I left to go home and realised I didn't know the way, not a nice moment. I supplemented my money by selling sweet and clothing coupons. Also I occasionally visited my aunt in Kensington and her husband used to take me to the bus stop and give me five shillings for my fare home. The fare was actually twopence so this virtually doubled my income for that week.

I felt I was really adult and sophisticated, but in fact was dreadfully ignorant and childish, especially compared to teenagers nowadays. I remember hearing that the Labour victory in the 1945 General Election was 'a revolution', only to be disappointed when the tumbrils didn't roll along Oxford Street to Marble Arch. I left the hostel to share a room with Rita whom I had met there. The basis of our sharing was that she was a Fleet St. teleprinter operative on night shift which meant that we took it in turns to sleep in the bed, just sharing it at week ends. The room was in a mouse-infested slum off the Harrow Road. Soon afterwards I had to find a home so that the rest of my family could come back to London. This was just round the corner from my room with Rita, which I then had to leave. That period of escape was over for the time being. This was the time I mentioned earlier when my mother came to collect my wages on Friday lunch time. About then my only pair of shoes became unwearable. The holes in the soles were so big the newspaper stuffing would fall out. With no sense of guilt, but feeling very frightened, I stole a pair from Marks & Spencer near Marble Arch, leaving my old ones in the rack in place of the ones I took!

All this sounds very dire and Dickensian, but it didn't feel like that at all. I was, in fact, thrilled with life in war-time and immediate post war London. Being so poor was just part of the adventure of living - I felt like a character in a novel. I remember one day in Spring 1945 feeling so happy I had to restrain myself from skipping along Oxford Street. I was grown up now and grown ups don't skip along the street. Soon after this I left Marshall & Snellgrove and took a better paying job in the millinery department at C&A Marble Arch, where the customers were very different from the up market clientele of the old job and the staff less servile then the ones at Marshall and Snellgrove had been.

After about a year at C&A, I noticed when walking along Brook Street, a very smart hat shop as part of Claridges Hotel. I liked the look of it so went in and asked for a job, which I was given, although at a much lower wage than at C&A. I was there when the 'new look' was introduced. A friend's mother copied it for us and we were among the first in London to wear it. I loved the excitement and high fashion of the hat shop, which was an education for me, although after three years I became bored. The smart set that shopped there for their Ascot and Royal Garden Party hats seemed shallow and silly and I was tired of having so little money. It was time for a change.

My next job was as an accounts clerk at the Old Vic Theatre. In fact I knew nothing about accounting but pretended that I'd helped with the book-keeping at the hat shop. Naturally the system there had been different so I needed to be shown the Old Vic system. That job, too, was an education, attending all the plays, seeing some of the rehearsals and hearing the discussions among the cast in the canteen. The atmosphere was totally democratic with everybody, including the director, on a weekly wage, and all basically friendly in spite of some surface bitchiness. By the time I left after seven years I had a store of new knowledge and the position of deputy chief accountant. I had decided to leave as the very small permanent staff made for a claustrophobic atmosphere and as the chief accountant was only a few years older than me there was little chance of further promotion. It was during those years that I met and married my husband. I used to go to a club that had dances on Sundays and that was where we met. We were immediately strongly attracted to each other. He was Italian, in London on a one year contract buying cloth. After we had been seeing each other for four months he was due to return to Italy. We were neither of us prepared to be separated and in order for him to be able to stay here we would need to be married. So, although neither of us was marriage minded, we decided that the circumstances left no alternative and we were married on the 14th February 1953. We had no money so looked for rented accommodation where we met quite a lot of racism.

The job I moved to in about 1958 after the Old Vic was as cashier and 'responsible clerk' at the Design Centre. The Design Centre was a government funded semi-official body run on civil service lines. It soon became apparent that with my lack of education or qualification I would never be promoted from a boring routine. My husband had become a language teacher at an adult education institute so had long summer vacations. I resigned my job and worked instead on temporary assignments for an agency, leaving us both free to travel to Italy in the summers.

By the early 1960s our marriage was in difficulties and I was tired of doing a series of boring jobs. I had fallen into a 'poor me, life hasn't given me a chance' mode which was horribly negative. The escape was provided by my seeing an advertisement for a residential college where one could have a grant-aided (those were the days!) chance to make up for missed childhood education. This would stop my 'poor me' feelings and give us both space from our marriage without all the drama of a trial separation. The grant was discretionary and the local authority took some persuading but finally agreed.

I enjoyed my year of study, although it was very frightening to call my own bluff, as it were. Suppose I wasn't worth educating after all! But I did well and was encouraged to apply for university, which hadn't been part of my original intention at all. I got my degree in modern history and politics when I was 39 and went on to do an MA, and then a year's teacher training. My school job I simply couldn't cope with, I'd forgotten how much I'd hated school as a child and how pleased I'd been to escape when I was fourteen. I was fortunate enough to get a lectureship in government at the Open University, working on inter-disciplinary courses and international relations. I stayed there until taking early retirement when I was 57. I continued tutoring for the OU until I was seventy, when I gave up because they don't employ people over 70. I found parts of the academic atmosphere stressful, feeling a dual handicap of gender and class background. But I have a tremendous respect and admiration for OU students, to whom, of course, my own educational experience is highly relevant.

Retirement
As with many retired people, I can't imagine how I ever found time to work! I enjoy literature at the University of the Third Age, and am engaged in a number of voluntary activities: I am part-editor of the news letter of the Older Feminist Network, and active in the causes it supports. These include the 'Justice for Women' campaign concerned with women imprisoned as a

The Child and the Adult

Jo aged 11

Jo at a demonstration in the 1980s

Roman Catholic Irish community who had their own church and school. The Irish were considered by the Welsh to be intruders and looked down upon; these attitudes continued well into my own childhood as I lived there with her during the 40s.

Apart from her paid work, Mary had considerable midwifery skills, was sent for at times of illness to give advice and help, and, together with other senior women, always needed to prepare the dead for burial. Her daughters left school in order to work and contribute to the housework when twelve or thirteen years old.

In common with the other women in this community, lack of money dominated Mary's life, but they had many domestic skills, grew their own vegetables and were adept at making ends meet. The women were very close, often getting together in the evenings to talk and reminisce about their lives; social and family history was handed down through the years in this way. At times of crisis or illness they rallied round offering support and sharing what they could spare. Mary and her family were greatly respected in the village.

Eventually my mother, Brigid, married and came to London with my father in search of work. Her sister Kate stayed on in Aberkenfig, married and had fifteen children. Mary, my grandmother, died there in 1960 aged 98.

Brigid – my mother

Brigid was born in 1896 and lived with her widowed mother, an older sister and younger brother, in the Welsh village which was their home. As part of the Irish Catholic community she attended the local Catholic school where both she and her older sister were considered bright, and there she learned to read and write. Because of the lack of money at home both girls had to leave school at twelve or thirteen to contribute to the household. Both started in domestic work, but my mother later on worked as a live-in barmaid in the local village tavern. This establishment opened at 5.0 am to offer food and drink to workers returning from the night shift in the local mine and steelworks. The landlady was a feisty, indomitable widow who kept a roaring fire going all day and hot food was prepared and served throughout. Brigid loved this job and became a great friend of the landlady, leaving reluctantly after several years when my grandmother insisted she was needed back at home to help with the lodgers.

As a young girl, my mother loved going to dances and often told stories of how she and her girlfriends would walk for miles to get to a dance and then walk back home afterwards in the early hours. Another great love of hers was the cinema and although often chronically short of money, she and her sister would scrape together the few pence needed to go on a Friday night (this habit was disapproved of by my grandmother who thought it was a shocking waste of money). She went to the cinema throughout her life and always took me with her as a little girl. My mother had a wonderful sense of humour which never left her, she was a great talker with a clear, melodious speaking voice who loved to recount memories of her family history and events that had happened in her local community.

An avid reader all her life, she never lost her enjoyment and engrossment in books. Light romances were never her 'thing' as she preferred classical writers. She also studied the newspapers closely and did so all her life.

In 1914 when the First World War started, my mother was eighteen; she never spoke much about this period of her life but it had a long lasting effect on her family and her future. My father, sixteen at the time, volunteered for the army and lied about his age in order, I think, to escape from a harsh, unaffectionate home. He went to France very early on in the war and spent the next four years in the trenches. Somehow he survived despite the terrible casualties, and returned to Aberkenfig where he frequently displayed unstable, erratic behaviour as he was traumatized by the experience. He and my mother married in 1919 but his war experiences affected him adversely throughout his life and, as a result, influenced our family life considerably.

Brigid was a remarkable woman in my view who had to adapt to considerable change and hardship after her marriage. She and my father left their village in 1932 to travel to London with three small children and few possessions to seek work, but they both missed the family network and the support and cameraderie of their community. My mother's lifestyle changed dramatically as a result and in London she was never able to replace the essential closeness and support she had previously known in her life.

As an old lady she still spoke vividly and warmly of her early life in Wales and to her that was her real identity. Both she and my father found London alien and rejecting, their only friends were also from South Wales. They formed a small, close group. Their early years in London were particularly hard and stressful with little money, insecure housing, and finally the death of their daughter Mary aged nine, which left them bereft for years afterwards. Despite this, Brigid's humour and intelligence sustained her, she was still a great reader and a loyal socialist, sharing these beliefs with my father. A wonderful cook, a good thrifty housekeeper, she lived simply and without pretension. For the last ten years of her life she was disabled and housebound, but continued to laugh, to read, to enjoy company, showing a great spirit to the end. Since her death in 1988, I miss her greatly. I owe her a lot as my interest in family history and my own understanding of myself have been formed and influenced by her sense of family identity.

Elizabeth

I was born in 1932 in London, the youngest of a family of four; my sisters were aged twelve and six, my brother was nine. We lived in a council house on the edge of an estate between Southall and Hanwell. My father had fought to get us housed after they moved here from South Wales; they had been in London only twelve months and were struggling. I have few early childhood memories but recall a sad atmosphere as my six-year-old sister had been ill for some time and died aged nine when I was three years old. The household was dominated by this trauma and, in my opinion, my parents never fully recovered from it. However, as the youngest I was spoilt and was very close to my mother whose temperament I shared. My family were Catholic and I had been christened at birth, but following my sister's death my parents lost touch with the church. I began school in London when five years old and attended the local Church of England primary school.

In 1939, aged seven, I was sent to live with my grandmother in South Wales for the duration of the war and this was a formative experience. I had her entire attention; we got on very well, living alone together in her tiny house with the rest of the extended family nearby. I was sent to the local Catholic school and attended church regularly. The school was excellent and I obtained a place at the local grammar school where I went for about a year. The war ended and I rejoined my family in 1945; for a time I tried to keep up with my religion, but not for long as I had no local contacts in the church and it had become irrelevant to the rest of the family. I cannot remember that this change caused me any difficulty and I do not consider myself a believer. Back in London I attended Southall Grammar School until 1949 and obtained school certificate with matriculation exemption. I was asked by the school to stay on, but my parents were in conflict about this; my father was the breadwinner and thought the time had come for me to go to work and contribute financially.

In 1950, I got a job with the London County Council as a clerical officer working in the vehicle licensing department and later on in town planning. I had a great time socially and made many friends during this period (1950 to 1965). I left home in 1953 when aged 21; by this time life at home was fraught, mainly due to the difficult relationship I had with my sister. There was a big age gap between us and she had reluctantly returned to live at home after being away during the war years. We had to share a bedroom where she constantly monitored my social activities in a disapproving way. I had little money to buy clothes and was always 'sneaking' out of the house dressed in something of hers and fearful of being discovered, which often happened. This was an exciting time of life for me, but a depressing one for her as she had chosen to return to live with the family when she should have made the break from it. Both she and my brother never married and remained at home all their lives.

After leaving home I rented a 'bedsit' in Maida Vale with a mad landlady and felt 'liberated'. I joined Unity Theatre shortly afterwards and met many amusing and, I thought, 'daring' bohemian people. I took small parts in several productions and 'hung out' there most evenings and weekends for a couple of years.

In 1958 I began a relationship which had a great influence on me; it lasted for eight years, and through it I met many lively, artistic people whose expectations and experiences were vastly different from my background. I learned about art, writing, furniture, antiques, drinking, and general 'joie de vivre' (although many of us were broke a lot of the time). They were good days but ended in 1965 when the relationship broke up though we remained good friends until his death in 1992. I embarked on a more sober and in many ways productive way of life by being accepted at Hillcroft College (a residential college for mature women) at the age of 33.

Hillcroft was a milestone and a challenging experience. It was a full time residential course for one year (similar to an access course now). On leaving, I was advised to try to get into university by winning a state scholarship award. I worked hard at writing an essay for this but wasn't successful, which was a setback. However, I rallied and got a job with the Family Welfare Association working in their Citizen's Advice Bureaux throughout the London area. I enjoyed this job tremendously and learnt a great deal. In those days we dealt with anyone who called in with every kind of problem, both practical and emotional. I was with the Family Welfare Association for five years when, having heard about the probation service, I applied to the Home Office and was accepted as a student in 1970. After one year's training full time I qualified in 1971, and from then until 1991 I was at the office in Haringey, a multi-cultural working class area, where after four years, I became a senior and was team leader until I left. Again, I loved this job, it suited me and I trained many new officers who were straight from social work courses.

These twenty years were a positive era in my life, as in 1971 when I was 40, I met my husband (he is five years younger); the saying 'life begins at 40' was certainly true for me. We have had a very good marriage, and weathered many difficult times together. He is introvert and I am extrovert, and it works very well. We have no children, and occasionally wonder what difference it would have made, but we are not preoccupied by this. Instead we have a number of difficult relatives who make frequent demands on us for support, and a number of caring, loyal friends who don't.

I left work in 1991 in a curious way. I discovered very suddenly that I had breast cancer. I left my office one evening to go to the GP and never returned and, within two weeks, I had surgery and had to come to terms with the fact that my life had changed. I could have returned to my job but decided not to do so. Coping with cancer and the aftermath has been another challenge and one that is always with you. When in hospital I met many courageous women and found that we frequently communicated with great honesty and a total lack of pretence.

Looking back on my life it is inevitably a progression with some success and some failure. On the whole it has been fulfilling, enjoyable and eventful, and I consider myself fortunate to have lived a fairly liberated lifestyle both emotionally and socially. I made choices in my personal life about which I have no regrets. Professionally I was seen to be successful. I made a choice to go into a potentially difficult job which I found well suited to me at a time when people from many diverse backgrounds were being recruited. I consider timing to be an important factor in life; to make the right decision at the right time, even though painful, is vital for progressing and achieving. In my case I found my judgement and intuitive feelings were sound enough for me to have made mainly the right decisions at various turning points in my life.

The transition from work to retirement and the resulting adjustment to ageing has been another major turning point. After many years of full time work as a professional woman with a busy career, the impact of retirement proved to be unsettling and demoralising for a short time. Now, nine years later, I cannot imagine how I ever coped with previous demands as there seems so much to do and enjoy, with greater space and time for oneself, one's family and friends.

Finally, joining U3A and finding the women's history group has given a terrific boost to retirement as the opportunity to share ideas and exchange knowledge with another remarkable group of women continues to be immensely stimulating and exciting.

(xi) Marj: My Story

Antecedents

My mother's family travelled from Glasgow to England in the early years of the 20th century, when she was still a babe in arms. They settled in a village called Stillington in Yorkshire, but the work was in Middlesbrough and they eventually went to live there. Thirteen children were born but only four (including my mother) survived to adulthood. One, John William, was killed in the 1914 war, and another two brothers (Alec and Tom) married and settled in the same town as my family. I remember my grandmother telling me about some of the ones who died: little Katie (Gran was also Katie) died from pneumonia at the age of four, and Francie, a little boy met the same fate as many of the children living in the yard or compound which my grandparents shared with other families. As there was no running water it had to be carried in large tubs or pails from some baths close by (it might be boiling hot or very cold) and was often left lying about the yard. Perhaps the children were curious about it or perhaps they tripped and fell into the tubs; at any rate, like little Francie, they were either scalded or drowned, or maybe died of shock. It must have been an anxious time for parents then.

I don't know where my paternal grandfather came from but he also moved to Middlesbrough and worked in the steel mills which was where both grandfathers (Alex and James) met. James had lost his wife and wasn't able to look after his son (my father) who was therefore taken in by my maternal grandparents; that meant my parents were brought up as brother and sister from the age of twelve. Later when they married they returned the favour, taking in my grandmother when she was widowed. She lived for a time in 'The Flats' which had gas lighting and an oil lamp (I liked the smell when I visited), and later came to us and shared a bedroom with me and my two sisters.

My parents married in 1928 when they were both 24 years old. They had basically a good marriage although I remember a lot of bickering when I was young. I remember also that my father called mother 'Kidda' which is what he must have called her when they lived as brother and sister. I liked this but she objected strongly every time (I suppose it's understandable), until one day she made a stand and said 'My name's Agnes and I want you to use it.' From that day on he did.

Childhood

I was born into a working-class family on a council estate in Middlesbrough, Yorkshire in 1932. I had five siblings and there were only a few years between each birth. Doreen was born first and was followed by Howard, then myself followed by Clifford, Katherine, and then Leo.

We had a nice house with three bedrooms and a bathroom upstairs, and downstairs a living-room and large kitchen. There was a front and back garden and a yard at the back in which there was a stick house for chopping and storing wood, a coal house and a wash house. Hot water was obtained by lighting the fire in the living room which heated the boiler in the bathroom. There was also a copper in the washhouse in which water could be boiled and clothes washed. I remember a few occasions when my mother popped us small ones into the copper – it was fun and probably saved her having to light the fire to boil the water for our weekly bath. My mother had a tub and a mangle and later what I would call her first washing machine, a mechanical one with a handle on top which was turned in order to agitate the clothes. She then graduated to an electric machine with a mangle on top. My mother was a resourceful woman; for example, she didn't have a refrigerator so when she needed a cool place for certain foods she would place a large bowl in the wash house and drip cold water into it from a hosepipe and the food would keep cool in the bowl.

There were difficult times: my father had a debilitating illness due to working in the steel mills. His Union fought for him to get some compensation and it was decided that he needed convalescence which the union would pay for. There was (and I think still is) a hospital in the Manor House area in London which has some connection with the union. He was sent there for some months and my mother visited him and took things to him. I suppose Grandma took care of us then. However, on the whole we weren't badly off. My father had a steady job in the steel mills (he was there for thirty years), and my mother was a 'good manager'. It seems a setting for a happy childhood but for some reason I wasn't happy. I didn't seem to communicate with any of the family and spent most of my time reading – my great escape! My mother said I could read almost as soon as I could talk.

She would tell me often about the two wonderful children she had had before me and how everyone commented on how well-behaved and smart they were. I surmised that she was thinking: '…and then the rot set in!' She also told me how her quick thinking had saved me from being lame. When I started to walk my ankles were so weak that my feet bent under me and I couldn't walk properly. My mother took me to hospital where they broke my ankles and re-set them. I don't remember the time in hospital but do remember wearing callipers on my legs for some time afterwards, and I also remember asking my mother why the nurses called me 'Peggy'. She gave me a rubbishy answer which just confused me (perhaps she didn't know) but some years later I realised that they must have thought my name was Margaret, for which Peggy is a nickname. I also learned later that I must have had rickets, due to malnutrition. It puzzled me how that could happen to me and not the others, and how could she not see it and prevent it – there was probably a good reason.

This was the time of the Great Depression. I didn't cause it, but I may have contributed to it as far as my mother was concerned, and the Depression may have contributed indirectly to my illness. We lived in the kind of neighbourhood that people tend to feel nostalgic about - neighbours very friendly, popping in and out of each others' houses without invitations. They were very interested in each other's lifestyles, but when I grew old enough to understand the things some of them would say about the others it didn't seem quite so friendly. However, they were compassionate and would always be supportive in times of trouble and would collect for wreaths, etc., whenever there was a bereavement in the street.

Education

I attended St. Francis', the Catholic school about fifteen minutes' walk from my home, where I was taught a lot about the Catholic religion and how to sing the Mass and the Benediction in Latin. I also learned some Scottish songs which I still remember. If I missed any lessons it wasn't because I was looking out of the window, it was because I had a book under my desk and my nose buried in it. This was particularly noticeable in needlework class when the teacher would inevitably become aware that my needle was poised in mid-air and I was peering at the book hidden under the material I was supposed to be sewing.

Just before I left this school in 1944, I had to sit for the scholarship (the next year the name was changed to the 11+). That day I had a horrific cold, had come to the end of my hankies, and was really afraid of the headteacher (a nun) who kept telling me to stop sniffing, so that I concentrated on not sniffing rather than on the exam. I wasn't surprised to learn I hadn't got a place in the convent. I was surprised at my mother's reaction to the news that I would be following my older siblings to a Catholic school some distance away which had the reputation of being a 'rough' school. She hadn't shown much interest in my education and suddenly she was rebelling – she told the school authorities I had weak ankles. I thought this must be a lie as by then I'd repressed the hospital experience. She said I couldn't travel far and unless they found me a place at a better school (such as St.Philomena's which was nearer and was also considered more genteel) she would send me to a nearby non-Catholic school. The blackmail worked and I found myself at St. Philomena's which bore that name until something sleazy was discovered about this saint; it is now called The Sacred Heart School. Both the infant-junior and the senior schools I attended had nuns as headteachers and some as class teachers.

Wartime

I was seven when the Second World War began. When I heard the announcement I felt excited at the change that must happen in a rather humdrum life. It was exciting not knowing whether we would go to school. Sometimes instead of lessons we would sit in the air-raid shelter in the schoolyard telling jokes and stories, and the bangs and whizzes were like a gigantic bonfire night. In the middle of the excitement I would remind myself of the bad things happening to other families but not to us as my father had bad eyesight, and was not called up, but was in the Home Guard. I do remember my mother's cousin coming to stay straight from the Blitz and how he cried at having to go back. Fortunately he returned unhurt. We were fairly safe living on the edge of Middlesbrough and only saw shrapnel, but there were houses and some schools bombed in the town. My parents felt we didn't need to be evacuated which disappointed me, especially as the next door kids went to Canada! In spite of the rationing and other hardships I had a 'good war'.

Leaving Home

Whilst I was living at home I was unable to make any real friends and stayed in most of the time, to the annoyance of my mother. A lot of my reading was about London and I longed to go there to meet all the authors and poets who according to the books, were to be found on every street corner and in most of the good restaurants. As a child my unhappiness had made me want to run away from home but I suppose I was not desperate enough to do it. As an adult I still wanted to leave home and this time I knew where I wanted to go but was still not desperate, and was scared of going off on my own.

When I was 23 a young woman moved into the house next door and because she had no friends she chose me as a companion. We went dancing at the local Institute, then on holiday to London. She asked me to go with her to live in London and of course I agreed. I felt an immediate freedom there, as though I had dropped some chains, and after my companion returned to Yorkshire I got a room of my own in the house of a friendly landlady. She introduced me to psychology by way of a weekly psychology magazine of which she gave me the back numbers. These set my mind working – particularly when I read that a young child can be traumatised by a separation from her parents. Especially if this time is spent in hospital, in pain, it can have a grave effect on the personality of the child. I recalled my mother's remarks about my weak ankles and the reason why they might be weak. I remembered that I'd been in hospital when I was young – could this be the reason for my being so shy, awkward and fearful?

I haven't really found the answer to that yet, but by searching for it I have managed to find a way through the misery, or most of it. Coming to London gave me a new lease of life and I began to experience some of the things which others of my age had by then become used to, such as making a first real friend and later, with another friend, staying overnight in her family and not feeling strange and awkward. All this happened very gradually but it began when I made the journey from Yorkshire to London.

Work

I left school at fourteen in about 1946, and started to look for a job. It was really scary that everyone thought I was adult enough to get a job when I felt just like a child. I went into a factory because that seemed the safest place; I felt I would be too exposed anywhere else. My shyness would be too visible in a shop and I couldn't envisage working in an office. It was interesting in the factory, we made every kind of brush and also tiny Xmas trees to use as ornaments. After about three years I thought I had enough confidence to go into shop work and in fact obtained a job in a large department store which is now one of the Debenham chain.

I was wrong about the confidence, I still wasn't ready to face people. I was too scared to look them in the face, let alone the eye. I stayed in the job for a year and was then encouraged to leave. I found a smaller shop selling cooked meat and was much happier there, but in winter the cold conditions made me ill and I was encouraged to leave, this time by our doctor. I started working at another department store though not so large nor so prestigious as the first one. Things went better for me except that I discovered that my habit of brooding on current and past unhappiness could cause me to make mistakes at times.

In 1955 when I moved to London I went back to factory work, packing chocolate at Lyons chocolate factory. Wisely the boss gave us carte blanche as far as eating on the premises was concerned, but dug in his heels at anyone taking the product home. I had a good time as they had a large sports ground and often put on events for the staff. I remember having my photograph taken with Norman Wisdom and, I think, Bob Monkhouse, both of whom I was quite keen on at that time.

I wasn't very interested in education whilst I was at school but some years later I got the bug of learning and took evening classes in English language and literature and French and, later in London, psychology, philosophy and sociology – always trying (and failing) to make up for what I had lost. It was not until I was about 40, in 1973, that I got the opportunity to re-enter full-time education.

I had gone back to factory work in order to please and to be with the companion who had instigated the move to London. When she later returned to Yorkshire I sat down and reconsidered my career. I didn't want to return to working in a shop. I now had a better idea of what working in an office would entail as I had taken training in shorthand-typing. I therefore took what I thought was another step forward, but like my last big step (into shopwork) it proved to be a false one, I wasn't ready for it. I found I was unable to concentrate well enough to do the work properly, and was encouraged to leave job after job. I was at my lowest ebb, sitting in my room one evening listening to the radio, when I heard the City Literary Institute advertising for people who felt they needed to return to education. I applied the next day, left the job I was in, and started the course two weeks later.

It was an exhilarating year, as also was the interview for the degree course which was my next step, and I still remember the surprise on the face of the principal at the extent of my reading. However, the depth of my reading was a different matter and because of this the degree course was much harder than I had anticipated. I just scraped through and then found myself back on the job market with no idea of what to do next. I enrolled for teacher training and loved being in the college but it was a different matter when I was faced, after a few short months, by a class of children – most of them hostile. I hurriedly left and went back to secretarial work, discovering to my delight that things had improved considerably in this area. I had by then discovered co-counselling (a form of counselling in which people learn to counsel one another), and had learned that talking about things rather than brooding about them can really change one's outlook. I was much more confident in the office and much better at the work; I was even encouraged to stay rather than to leave. When I discovered that I was also good at counselling I began training and eventually took clients in the evenings. Later I trained as a psychotherapist with some financial help from the organisation for whom I worked, a job I really enjoyed. I stayed there until 1982 when I was 50 and then left to start up a practice as a psychotherapist. This didn't work out. Perhaps one needs capital; one certainly needs the courage to put oneself forward. The centre I trained at sent me clients now and then but as we were discouraged from taking either people we knew or friends of clients, I was unable to build up a practice and eventually settled for working with the few clients I had, and also working in a voluntary capacity.

On Being Single and Childless

People ask why I didn't marry or have children and seem to expect me to answer in one sentence. Maybe one word would do: 'circumstances', or I could explain that I used to be afraid of people and that included males. By the time I had largely recovered from this I had passed the age when I was likely to marry. I did have at least two affairs, but in each case we both knew that there was no future in it. We just enjoyed each other's company for a while and the nice thing is that they are both good friends of mine now. Although I got no pressure from my family I seemed to feel it from society and if I sometimes daydreamed about finding someone suitable to marry; part of the reason was that I might then look better in the eyes of society. It's easier nowadays when on the whole there is less concentration on women being married. I find it surprising when some people, after hearing I'm not married, ask: 'Any children?' I suppose I associate children with marriage. I admire single parents but don't have enough courage for that. Maternal feelings don't seem to bother me; maybe I displaced them on to animals. I enjoy children and love to spend time with them but there are no pangs when they go off home.

Retirement

'Je ne regrette rien', well almost 'rien'. I used to bemoan the fact that I hadn't become a successful psychotherapist. Now I concentrate on being successful at the things I am involved in, and enjoy being busy and being fit and healthy. Sure, I'd like more time and more money, but they're not the important things. I'm at a voluntary society, doing administrative work, some mornings and on the helpline one evening. I visit someone in a special hospital once a month, and a sick woman most weeks, and I'm a member of a feminist group, which means I'm involved politically in a non-party way.

One of my sadnesses has been that there hasn't been a lot of contact or closeness with my family, as they all live in Yorkshire. Within the last ten years my younger sister Kath and I began to meet and get to know each other again. We even spent a weekend together and planned to go on holiday. Sadly she died of cancer before we had that opportunity. I'm glad that we had at least begun to get reacquainted.

In the summer of 1999 I went to stay with my eldest sister who used to be so wrapped up in her family that we rarely met. Now that the family are getting married and/or moving away she has more time to spare than she used to have. We're beginning to get to know each other and I hope and trust that this will continue and get even better.

Although I've never been able to afford (or even wanted), to go on expensive holidays I have been able to travel to India through knowing two sisters who invited me to their home in Goa, and also to Sri Lanka through a Sri Lankan friend who has a villa there. The second holiday was shortly after I had retired so I was just able to afford it, and I accepted that that would be the last big holiday for me. However, another friend contacted me and said she could get cheap tickets and had a friend in the USA. She was so keen for me to go that she paid most of the expenses. I imagine that must be my last big holiday, but the exciting thing about my retirement is that I never really know what's around the corner.

Charmian's mother aged 15 in 1905

Three Mothers

Sima's mother aged 15 in 1908

The Old and the Young

*Elizabeth's mother
as a baby 1896*

Irene aged 3

*Joan & Patricia's grandmother and aunts –
Late Edwardian period*

PART TWO: SOME THEMES FROM OUR LIVES

Chapter 4

What is a Family?

Estella and Charmian

When we began talking about our families, each of us thought we knew what a family was. As discussions continued, however, it became clear that even amongst our small group there were variations in our notions of 'family'. We knew that there must be hundreds of books, giving as many definitions of the word 'family' (even a simple concise dictionary shows ten definitions), provoking much scholarly discussion according to each author's premise. For our particular purposes, we decided not to worry too much about this, while being aware that we might each have a different group in mind when we talked about our families.

Starting with our own parents and siblings, we found our discussions ranged widely; backwards to a past involving our grandparents and even a few great-grandparents, forwards to our present-day lives, and for some of us, our children and grandchildren. Not only were we able to draw on our personal memories, we could also avail ourselves of the memories of past generations, recollections that between us encompassed almost 150 years, and included many relationships beyond our immediate families.

For some these wider families loomed large. They were ever-present for Estella, whose household when she was a child in the East End included twelve family members. Even when they didn't live in the same house they might not be far away; Joan comments that her father had a 'whole clan of relatives in Yorkshire' where he was sent to school. It has been difficult for some of us to stop digressing into long stories about cousins and aunts who are very real to us if somewhat confusing to others. At times they have been crucial sources of support financially or emotionally; so our recognition of their significance in our lives varies according to circumstances. Elizabeth, aged seven, was sent for safety at the beginning of the war to live with her grandmother in Wales. She has good memories of that time: 'I had all her attention', she says: 'and the rest of the extended family was nearby.' Jo, whose childhood as the oldest in a family of four was fraught with problems, had a brief escape after an illness to her grandmother in Brighton (she sees her life in terms of one escape after another). She had a wonderful time: 'I think I could *just* manage some bananas and cream!' she remembers saying plaintively. She wonders how different her life would have been if she had stayed there, as her grandmother would have liked. Joan remarks how she was brought up 'without much fun or room for fantasy; occasional visits from or to relatives offered temporary glimpses of something different.'

So the wider family could provide insights into different ways of living. Sometimes they gave ready advice for good or ill; Renee's aunts were against her taking up her place at grammar school, but her mother was proud of her and insisted. Although some of us make much more mention of them than others, there is plenty of evidence that the views of relatives were to be taken into account particularly in our early childhood, even if they did not live close by. However, there are always branches of a family that become 'lost,' and we can only speculate about Estella's paternal great-grandfather, who married for the second time, much to the disapproval of the children of his first marriage. He produced a second family, but the children of the two marriages never really got on, and parted company very quickly. 'Somewhere in or around Manchester there are people with whom I share the same great-grandfather. We are complete strangers,' says Estella.

These examples are all taken from our childhoods before or during the Second World War. The idea that the extended family is increasingly irrelevant as members live further apart has become a part of everyday thinking. It is true that telephones, e-mails and letters have often replaced daily visits, but that does not necessarily mean people care about each other less. With increasing divorce, more single parents or both parents working, grandparents are often the first to be called on in times of need. But because they live longer, and are in better health they are often very busy with their own lives. Although delighted to see their grandchildren, they may also be pleased to see them go home so that they can get on with things while there is still time.

For some in our group the next generation of the family is flourishing. Irene, Renee, Estella and Charmian with fifteen grandchildren between them, see those that live near enough often, between all their other activities. Irene's granddaughter is a great support to her. Estella and Sima both have daughters living in the United States and we notice how they drop everything else when they and their families visit this country. But we are not typical of our generation as half our group has no children. For them any continuity between the generations will be less direct.

What do we really know about our families?

Documentation can confirm the facts of family history, such as birth, death and family size. But it is the emotional response to what happens, to events both trivial and traumatic, conveyed by anecdote and legend, that brings warmth and substance to stories of family lives. Some of us have written about the sources of knowledge we have or which we lack. Maintaining continuity between generations depends a great deal on women passing on life stories by writing or talking. Elizabeth says: 'My interest in our family history and my own understanding of myself have been greatly influenced by my mother's sense of family continuity and identity. Information comes entirely through accounts of family events passed down orally. Diaries were non-existent in our family; letters were rarely sent.' In contrast, Charmian's mother and grandmother wrote many letters, recording their family life since the turn of this century. Joan and Patricia have a fund of anecdotes. These are all families with a strong sense of continuity. In contrast, Mary knows almost nothing about her grandparents: 'My parents were always reluctant to talk about their past and became angry when questioned. So I only have scraps of information.'

Continuity is more difficult to maintain and sources more difficult to come by, when family members have had to start again in a different country, as half our group have done. They know little about their families before they arrived in Britain; but in these circumstances recovering the past through stories, documents, or treasured objects, can become imperative. Estella has carried out genealogical research and uncovered records of births, deaths and school attendance from the time her family arrived in England early this century. Irene, whose life was the most disrupted of all, has the personal story of her mother written at the age of 90 and lovingly bound by her children, recalling her childhood in Germany and her escape to America.

Although the amount we record about our mothers and grandmothers reflects these differences in the facts and stories available, we found examining these previous generations simple compared with sorting out our own childhood worlds. We have commented on the trickiness of memory earlier in the book, particularly for unravelling our relationships with our mothers. Emotion may bring our stories to life but it also makes it hard to see clearly. Mary writes: 'There are great gaps in my memory. When I was about eight or nine I developed a habit of deliberately forgetting things I didn't want to remember. It has stood me in good stead all my life and I still use it.' There are memories we block out, and others we remember but don't want to discuss.

100

Why, in the midst of all these complexities do we have such vivid memories of trivial incidents from our childhood? In Joan's family all three sisters seem to remember being bathed in zinc baths or the kitchen sink as small children. She wonders whether nudity and emotional communication go together!

An area of our lives we have not expanded on concerns our partners and children. None of us lives with a female partner or with a woman friend. Those of us who have, or have had, male partners wish to protect them; they didn't ask to be involved in a project which is becoming public. Nor did our children, though it would be fascinating to extend this study to the next generations if we live long enough and they agree.

Some younger women hearing our stories have been surprised by the lack of reference to sexuality. We have talked about singleness, sexuality, and friendship, but not publicly. We are of a generation which still considers these things private. Sex was never mentioned by our mothers except in a prohibitive way, and they did not prepare us for puberty.

But some of us have written frankly as well as spoken about painful memories. Marj, writing about being a single woman in a society which expects everyone to be in heterosexual couples, admits: 'Sure I get lonely at times but one can get lonely in a crowd or in a relationship, especially if it's the wrong one.' Joan describes the pain she suffered at the death of her fourteen-year-old son following a bicycle accident. The after-effects of this tragic occurrence took a heavy toll on family relationships. She also reflects on the delights of having children relatively late in life, which she found a transforming experience, putting into practice what she had only known professionally. 'Life was never the same again.' Charmian agrees!

Changes in attitudes to sex outside marriage during the century are of course illustrated by observations in our life stories. Jo's Granny Bertha set up house with a married man; she had to borrow a friend's marriage certificate in order to have her first child in the Lying-in Hospital at Waterloo (the building still bears the name), otherwise she would not have been admitted. Both Estella and Irene had problems with landladies suspicious of men coming to the house, during or after the Second World War. Estella remembers a prospective landlady asking to see her marriage certificate: 'I'm not having any of that carry-on here.' However, in the 1950s and '60s several of us lived with men we were not married to, which was not generally accepted in those days.

What kind of family cultures do we come from?

The divergent class and religious backgrounds of our grandmothers and mothers are reflected in the cultures of the families in which we have been brought up: Catholicism, Christian nonconformity, Judaism and secularism are represented. Almost half of our group are of Jewish descent, and some of their grandparents were forced to abandon their homes in Eastern Europe to make their way to England in the late 19th or early 20th century. A few of these immigrants experienced a change in their fortunes, from 'riches to rags'. For others, the poverty they faced in England was probably not much different from that which they had left behind. But for most of them there must have been a sense of relief at escaping from life-threatening circumstances in a physically hostile environment. Sima's maternal grandparents were middle-class orthodox Jews. 'They came to London in the 1880s from Poland, with just what they could carry. There were seven of them, all housed on the sixth floor of the Rothschild Buildings in Stepney. All water and sanitation was in the courtyard and they had two rooms.' Despite the drastic decline in their economic circumstances, all the family was alive and together and they could look forward to a future, whatever hardships may have been in store for them.

People emigrate for a number of reasons, the most obvious being to escape dire poverty or persecution. They seek a better life elsewhere. Elizabeth tells how her grandparents moved from Ireland to South Wales in the late 19th century, where they became part of a Catholic community in a village divided into Catholic and Protestant factions. Marj's moved from Glasgow to Yorkshire probably in pursuit of work.

In our own generation, family cultures are created from the fusion of different influences as several of us have married across cultural boundaries. Joan, brought up a Methodist, married a Jewish man. She writes: 'My husband and I had both emancipated ourselves from our different religious upbringings and were freer to choose the family life we wanted.' Renee, Estella, Charmian and Jo also married men from different religious or cultural backgrounds. Charmian and her Jewish husband have a family of different origins, including adoption and stepchildren, with whom they try to maintain the continuity and inclusiveness which was characteristic of her foremothers' families.

Such marriages have an effect on the parents-in-law. Estella had to endure dire warnings from her parents and friends as to future problems, but her family life has not suffered. Charmian's mother Daisy, and her mother-in-law Rachel, were both open, warm, yet socially naive women. When they met they liked each other. On one occasion they were admiring the educational achievements of their daughter and son: 'It was not like that when we were young,' says Daisy, 'we never went to school' (an image in her mind of a cosy group of girls and their governess in the family schoolroom). 'No,' agrees Rachel, 'nor did we' (a vision in her mind of playing truant or staying at home to help in the tailoring workshop). They never did discover the cultural gulf revealed by this simple conversation.

Poverty and wealth affect cultures but do not entirely determine them. People don't necessarily feel poor even if objectively they are, nor did those of us who were better off think of ourselves as being able to spend freely. Marj writes of the poverty experienced by her grandmother's family, living in a building without running water and sharing a large yard. Her grandmother, undaunted, bought a sack of potatoes and a sack of onions, cleared the front room of her house and started selling. Renee is able to write: 'We were very poor, but so were all my contemporaries, so I didn't feel that I had a deprived childhood.' Estella felt exactly the same way. Jo, whose father came from a middle-class background but had lost his job, writes about her parents: 'They led a life of extreme poverty and insecurity, unemployed most of the time. They were quite unable to cope with the conditions resulting from being dependent on the parish. We the children, felt the unhappiness of the home. There was no normal family life, surviving took all our parents' energy.'

Patricia and Joan, as well as Charmian, came from middle-class families who shared the somewhat austere attitude to self-indulgence associated with religious nonconformity. Their contrasting accounts show how important the personality of the dominant parent can be in determining the family culture. Patricia tells us: 'Our mother was very class-conscious, wanted to control, and knew what she wanted her house and family to be.' Joan confirms: 'Our mother was full of moral exhortation, but my father was emotionally available in a way my mother never was. Materially and physically I was well looked after in an unchanging environment without much fun or room for fantasy. Moral probity was important.'

The picture of family life described by Charmian, in contrast, makes her childhood sound like an endless round of family fun. Her mother, like her grandmother before her, was the matriarch of the household and determined its culture. In a full and happy life, she remembers Sunday evenings when the whole family, five children, both parents and possibly a friend or relation who happened to be staying, all sat round the big centre table playing games.

Another family with a strong culture passed between the generations, but this time through the father, was Sima's. Her paternal grandfather had been a 'fierce Zionist' and he was the dominant influence over his wife and children. Her father was also a Zionist, a socialist, and later supported the Communists. He also ran for England in the 1908 Olympics. Sima comments: 'That was part of the glamour that won my mother over; they married in 1910 and he set about educating her. He made her read all the classics.' These educational and political interests were passed on to Sima and her siblings: 'My whole family was intensely political and left wing. From 1936 onwards I was involved in collecting for Spain, and I joined the Communist Party.'

In some families, apparently following the ideal of the two parent 'traditional family', circumstance and personality combined to prevent the passing on of a strong supportive culture. Both Jo and Mary experienced this.

Jo writes sadly: 'When a family isn't "working" all the positive features of family life become negatives. Closeness becomes stifling and imprisoning, warmth and affection become irritation, support becomes a burden. Family life can become negative without there necessarily being any spite or malice. My parents loved us, they would have liked to care for us, but were simply unable to cope with the conditions of their life which were very hard. Other members of our group have experienced a childhood of poverty in happy families. Poverty isn't necessarily a reason for family life to fail. What seems to be essential is that parents be strong enough and able to handle the harsh physical conditions that are inevitable when money is insufficient and housing inadequate. My mother was not strong physically, she was desperately worried about my father who was having what today would probably be recognised as a nervous breakdown, because of his inability to find and keep work. His conservative middle-class values led him to perceive our situation as personal failure; he didn't have the political awareness to see what was happening to us as a system failure. My childhood dreams were all of leaving home and escaping what I experienced as stifling disharmony.'

In a largely uncommunicative family environment, Mary was made aware of one fact: that her maternal grandfather had been married three times. At the deaths of his first two wives, their children were 'farmed out' to relatives, though never on a permanent basis. To those children, who included Mary's mother, the idea of a 'close family' would have been irrelevant. Of the third marriage, Mary knows that it 'produced a son, but I know nothing about him - not even his name.' Mary's dominant and uncommunicative father completely suppressed whatever will or self-esteem her mother may have had. 'My father was able and autocratic and bullied my mother. They split up after the war and he sold the house. Having been very badly parented themselves, my parents were hopeless with children. My sister and I left home as soon as possible and lost touch with my father as soon as we could.' Mary decided that when she married she didn't want children. What a contrast with the secure and supportive childhoods of Estella and Charmian!

Mary describes herself as 'contrary', Jo was determined to escape. Their accounts of their subsequent lives show what can be achieved by spirited girls released from oppressive families. The sense of being 'different' from their siblings is also apparent in the stories of several others in the group. Renee writes: 'My brothers and sisters quarrelled a lot amongst themselves. But I never took part.' She was the first to go to grammar school. Marj always felt the odd one out: 'My mother would tell me about the two wonderful children she had before me; how well behaved and smart they were. I got the feeling she was thinking, "and then the rot set in!"' 'Sima suffered from feeling the non-academic one after two bright siblings: 'I was the addendum, the nuisance.' They think this sense of difference helped them achieve what they did.

A range of diverse family situations has emerged from this examination of even our small number of life histories covering over a hundred years. Our families had origins in England, Ireland, Scotland, Wales, Eastern Europe and Germany. Their economic status has varied from intense poverty to comfortable middle class, and has included both improving and deteriorating fortunes. Economic struggle has existed within both middle and working-class families. Not all our families have been able to maintain the traditional pattern of two parents supporting their children which is the stuff of rhetoric about family stability. We have known divorce, separation, and widowhood, sometimes resulting in the need to bring up young children alone and with meagre resources.

There are several examples in our grandparents' generation of informal solutions to the problems presented by family breakup. For instance, Mary's mother was passed around a succession of relatives; Jo's grandmother disposed of the responsibility of her grandfather's two existing sons by sending them out to Canada under indentures. When she became the only support of her three young children, Estella's grandmother placed them in an orphanage while she sought work. They had to stay there until they were of working age, so the institution became their substitute family. Such unregulated distribution of 'inconvenient' children would be much more difficult today.

Changes in women's lives this century

The biggest change has been the expansion of choice. Better health and longer lives allow more opportunities. With one or two exceptions we come from long-lived families, more than two-thirds of our parents having lived to their mid 70s, 80s or beyond. Elizabeth's mother-in-law is still alive, and so is Estella's father, both in their 90s. However, four of our grandmothers were widowed when their children were young. Elizabeth's grandmother Mary, widowed and pregnant at the turn of the century, applied for a parish grant and was offered 2s.6d. (twelve and a half pence), and told 'she was a strong young woman and could work', and so she did. Joan and Patricia's paternal grandfather was widowed twice and married three times. There is a lot written these days about family problems caused by the increase in single parents, and step-parenthood; but this is not new, only the cause has changed.

We have certainly enjoyed better health than our foremothers. Infant mortality remained high during the first half of this century, and several members of the group report infant deaths and stillbirths among their foremothers. Infectious diseases such as measles and chicken pox ran through whole families when we were children. Mary remembers being put to sleep with a sibling who had one of these, in the hope she would catch it and 'get it over with.'

There must have been many childhood deaths caused by accidents in the home. Marj records a particularly horrific example of a child in her family being scalded to death in a tub of boiling water left lying in the yard as there was no running water in the flat. He was not the only one to meet such a fate. She comments: 'Perhaps the children were curious about it or perhaps they tripped and fell into the tubs; at any rate, like little Francie, they were either scalded or drowned, or maybe died of shock. It must have been an anxious time for parents then.'

There was also a great deal of undefined ill health among women, particularly poor women. A survey carried out in the early 1930s found only a third of working class women reported feeling 'fit and well' most of the time. They considered they were lucky to keep going. This is hardly surprising given the amount of hard labour involved in raising a family in overcrowded conditions with only a cold water tap and outside lavatory. Most of our parents who experienced such conditions moved to better housing in this period.

Apart from childbirth, tuberculosis was one of the main causes of early death, and is mentioned in more than one of our family histories. Elizabeth's grandfather died of it. Joan says: 'One of my mother's sisters had tuberculosis of the spine and had to sleep in a specially constructed hut in the garden.' In our own generation, Estella went through a period of serious ill health with TB when her children were young. Between the wars, poor diet was linked to rickets in babies. Marj spent a long time in hospital with 'weak ankles' she thinks were caused by rickets.

Our family histories reflect the problems of ill health, unwanted pregnancies, and early deaths faced by families before the Second World War, which our children and grandchildren rarely suffer. The hazards they face are very different.

One of the most important changes in the shape of the family has been women's ability to control their own fertility. This is very clear in our group, families of six, nine, and seven being recorded. Marj's Catholic mother was one of thirteen, of whom only four survived. In our own generation, of those who have had children there are none who have had more than two, though Charmian also has two stepchildren who were brought up by their mother.

It would be wrong to overgeneralise the extent of choice open to women today; even in prosperous Britain some are still trapped by cruel circumstances. But women have better health and live longer than their foremothers, they own property, and make decisions about employment. They can choose to marry or live with a partner or alone, and decide when and whether to have children and how many to have. They can plan for a lengthy retirement. Some of our foremothers led happy, fulfilled lives, many were resourceful in coping with large families and difficult conditions. But they were all locked into their expected role as wives and mothers. We on the other hand, have been able to make a wide variety of decisions about our family lives.

For the generation of our children and grandchildren the changes faced are even more far-reaching than those which have affected us. They involve the separation of the biological and the social to the extent that a single-sex couple may bring up children, or an infertile couple have them through surrogacy. A woman on her own can make a deliberate decision to become a single mother. The expansion of choice brings its own problems as more and more women in their thirties postpone parenthood for a rewarding career.

So what is a family? Can we choose them too?

Patricia, while revealing the pain of losses through deaths within her family writes: 'There were gains too, as other relationships developed. Friendships were always important and the mutual support of groups where I had a sense of belonging.' Elizabeth, whose brother and sister never married, writes: 'My major contact is a cousin living in London. We are very close, were brought up together and have shared the same memories of listening to our grandmother and my mother.' Jo only has occasional contact with her extended family: 'I have a small circle of long-standing friends who are important to me. They are my family.'

Buried beneath all the trivialities and simplifications of our family stories lie a complex set of truths - historical, structural, cultural and emotional truths. It is easy to fall into the trap of making dogmatic distinctions between 'good' and 'bad', 'happy' and 'unhappy' families. No wonder so much has been written on the subject. If there is one thing our life stories show it is the impossibility of making sweeping pronouncements about 'the decline of the traditional family', or 'the erosion of family values'. We define the family in different ways; we find it oppressive or nurturing; if we haven't got one we wish we had, or invent it for ourselves. The family seems infinitely adaptable, and will surely survive in one form or another.

A Family between the Wars

Renee's mother with Renee in her arms and her three older siblings 1925

Chapter 5

There's no Place like Home

Elizabeth and Charmian

> *'In my beginning is my end. In succession*
> *Houses rise and fall, crumble, are extended,*
> *Are removed, destroyed, or in their place*
> *Is an open field or a factory, or a by-pass.'*

> *T. S. Eliot, East Coker*

Housing for our grandmothers and mothers

We are recording our foremothers' housing in the period up to the Second World War, during which there was an enormous expansion of house building, and a revolution in housing policy. Between 1850 and 1914 England was transformed into a nation in which most people lived in towns, and some of these towns were very large indeed. It was not until the interwar period that council housing became a major alternative to rented accommodation, and only a few people could afford to own their own homes. At the beginning of the century the only alternatives to private housing were employer-built estates such as Saltaire in Bradford and Bourneville near Birmingham; or charities such as Shaftesbury, the Peabody Trust or Sydney Waterlow's Improved Industrial Dwellings Company, all established in the second half of the 19th century.

Sima's maternal grandparents, who came to England in 1895, were found a flat with their family in Rothschild Buildings in Stepney, charitable housing for Jewish immigrants. Estella remembers living opposite Waterlow Buildings in her Bethnal Green house, which was part of a long row, some of which were shops with living accommodation above, and some residential properties, let out as flats. She says: 'The Buildings were very large, red-brick, with black iron railings, and further along the road were Columbia Buildings, dark and forbidding, with gloomy, draughty corridors lit during the winter with flickering gas-lamps. They were built around neglected and empty courts, where the poor could live, paying low rents, breathing the "fresh" air that whistled through the narrow passages, up the stone stairs, and round the inner spaces. There was a social "pecking order" in our road. The shopkeepers were considered the local aristocracy, the inhabitants of the houses were next in line, the people in the buildings opposite were graded as "common", and those in Columbia Buildings were really the lowest of the low.'

Most of our mothers and grandmothers lived, however, in private rented housing as was typical of the early part of the century even among the middle class. Elizabeth, Marj, and Renee's families were able to take advantage of the expansion of council housing between the wars. Cheaper house prices and lower interest rates had begun to put house ownership within reach of a wider section of the population. The more middle class families in our group were owner-occupiers before the Second World War. By 1939 Elizabeth's paternal grandmother in Wales had achieved this too, probably by a lot of scrimping and saving.

Our foremothers were on the move both socially and geographically in the inter-war period. Elizabeth's parents left the Welsh countryside for London in search of work. In their moves from a relatively small area of the East End, fanning out to more desirable north London suburbs, Sima's and Estella's parents were following a general pattern of Jewish families seeking a better environment as they established themselves.

Such moves were made possible by speculative building. New suburban housing was built along the expanding transport routes, the arterial roads, the railways, and the underground system. For example, as the London Underground extended its lines further and further out in North London they advertised for buyers for the houses being built around the new stations. In the early 1900s Golders Green was portrayed as a rural idyll of pseudo-Tudor houses with big gardens. In 1924 the Underground had reached Edgware, which had been a small village on the London - Holyhead Road. It became a fashionable suburb advertised rather over-romantically as: 'an alternative recipe which...will convert pleasant , undulating fields into happy homes...a shelter which comprises all the latest labour-saving and sanitary conveniences. Edgware is designed to give us that much more.' When Charmian's parents moved to Edgware in 1925, the undulating fields were still there. By 1939 their three storey Edwardian 'semi' had become surrounded by pseudo-Tudor houses. The fields had disappeared under drives, parks and closes.

Our houses and homes

At first this topic seems a mere chronicling of house types, facilities, and moves, which throw light on the changing conditions in which our mothers and grandmothers spent their lives. Labour-saving devices gradually improved the lot of housewives during the century at the same time as servants, for those lucky enough to be able to afford them, became increasingly difficult to find. But a study of housing is much more than this. We distinguish in English between a house and a home; when we described the furnishing and ornaments in our childhood homes we found we were involved not just in a physical description, but a cultural one.

Where you live, what kind of house you live in, and your security of tenure, have important status implications. Moving house is a big social step as well as a geographical one. Moving is often a critical event for a family, symbolising a new start; but even where this is so, there is often a tinge of regret at the loss of the familiar, and a need to preserve continuity. Families who moved to better housing in outer suburbs between the First and Second World Wars, while rejoicing in their improved environment, became nostalgic about the hugger-mugger 'community' they left behind in the inner city. In an earlier generation nearly half our families left behind a home in a different country, and the need to preserve continuity with the past must have been even greater for them.

Most of us in the group have improved our housing as we grew older. But better does not usually mean larger. None of us have children living at home any more so we are either alone or with a partner. Our housing conditions have converged, not only geographically but because we have been able to choose how we live in a way impossible for many of our parents. Everyone seems happy in their present homes which shows how they have become extensions of our personalities. We are mostly in a settled stage of life. We still have the urge to learn and discover but there is not much sign of the continued urge to acquire things. How far do our present homes represent the summit of our housing dreams and how far do they reflect our stage of life? Are we are happy in our homes because we are, broadly speaking, happy in our lives?

'Home' is defined in the dictionary as 'a family's place of residence; a domicile; a house; a social unit formed by a family living together; a congenial and pleasant environment.' Popular songs like *There's no Place like Home*, *I want to go Home*, *My Little Grey Home in the West*, *Home on the Range*, offer a more romantic and sentimental definition, and express the powerful emotional, nostalgic and often patriotic use of the word. Even Spielberg's alien in the film *E.T* longed to return home.

For the group, remembering and recording details of the housing conditions of our grandmothers, and later on, ourselves, 'home' is where we started from as children and where our roots are. We have revived many memories of our childhood and family cultures, and as a group of women from differing social and religious backgrounds there are perhaps a surprising number of similarities in our early experiences.

Descriptions of houses, flats, rooms and furnishings are intertwined with memories of affection, warmth, shared fun, or alternatively of darkness, cold, gloomy interiors and a rigid unloving atmosphere. Recalling in detail our early homes we have shared with the group some of our personal identity and found a shared identity through the similarity of basic living conditions.

For instance, outside water taps and toilets were commonplace; whether property was rented or owned, shared bedrooms or beds were taken for granted, especially when wider family members were visiting or living in. Overcrowding was a major factor, lack of privacy was significant, front rooms were kept for 'best' if they existed at all, and many of us have depressing memories of them. Estella says of her paternal grandmother's front parlour: 'The curtains were always drawn to keep out the sun, the carpet always seemed to have a layer of tea-leaves spread over it.' She felt it to be a forbidden area, dismal and dank smelling. Floors were often covered in lino, only the living room was generally heated. Of course, these factors were influenced by differing financial and social circumstances but in spite of the differences we all seem to remember how cold our homes were in winter.

These conditions made an enormous amount of work, washing the family clothes, cooking, ironing, cleaning, carrying coal, laying the fire every day. Joan remembers the washing hanging on ceiling rails or 'maidens' in front of the fire when it was wet; and the annual spring cleaning when the carpets were hung over the washing lines in the garden and beaten vigorously with clover shaped bamboo beaters. Charmian's mother's routine was washing on Mondays, ironing on Tuesdays, but started on Monday evening if it had been a good drying day. There were different days for 'turning out' the different rooms in the house. These memories are from the larger homes with gardens and some domestic help, which was not the situation for most of the group. Their mothers and grandmothers must have been literally slaves in the home as well as often working to earn money. Although labour saving devices gradually lessened the work, it is our generation which is the main beneficiary of the domestic revolution.

We are all living in the London area because for us 'retiring to a rural cottage with roses round the door' is not stimulating enough. Most of us are able to own our homes either privately or through a housing association. We have books, pictures, carpets and reasonable space for our needs. The size of our living space has changed to suit our changing circumstances but our living conditions are much less diverse than those of our mothers and grandmothers.

The personal accounts of our past and present homes tell us a lot about our family background, class, social standards and values.

Irene

Irene remembers her homes in Berlin where she lived until 1938; flats and not houses were usual. Her grandmother's flat had a big stove for heating and Irene enjoyed baking apples on it. Her parents' flat was large enough to accommodate a big family with room for a maid. Breakfast and supper would be served on the balcony. There was a lift for the tenants and a tradesmen's entrance. She remembers good antique furniture, a piano, lots of silver and crystal and a gramophone. The floors were parquet and had to be cleaned with wire wool and polish and the rugs beaten on the balcony or yard. Her parents' bedroom was full of white furniture and rugs, both elegant and beautiful and they complete a picture of gracious living and prosperity. Sadly, towards the end, due to repressive Nazi laws forbidding her father to work, the family had to let bedrooms to make money and they slept in the sitting rooms.

Irene and her husband came to England in 1938. They settled in a flat in Hampstead for 25 years and then moved to their present home, a three bedroomed house in Kenton, to be near her daughter who told her: 'You are not a good grandmother-to-be if you are not prepared to baby-sit!' They have lived there for nearly 30 years and must have done a lot of baby sitting. It is light and cheerful, a mixture of modern and antique; lots of modern and old paintings. They have often eaten on their patio and enjoy entertaining in their garden. Irene appears to have recreated the same ambience here for herself that she left behind in Germany. It is the first time she has lived in a house rather than a flat, and the first house she has owned.

Sima

Sima's maternal grandmother rented two rooms on the sixth floor of the Rothschild Buildings, Stepney, a charitable foundation where her mother was born. Facilities were minimal, the water and toilet were in the courtyard.

After her parents' marriage they had one room in her father's family home, a large leasehold property in Canonbury Square, where all his family lived together with numerous visiting Zionists. Canonbury was, and is, a fashionable area, and the house became a centre for Zionists. Sima thinks it likely that leading Zionists had paid for the house. Later on, her family rented a flat above a shop in North London. From here they moved to rent large premises in Finchley, again above a chemist's shop which her father ran. This was multi-occupied, on four floors with other families plus a lodger. Sima describes some of these other occupants. There was a family they called 'Creepy' because they never heard any of them moving about. A lodger, Florrie, who 'did' for them, was light-fingered and Sima's mother used to go through her pockets recovering anything she found. There was plenty of space, they kept chickens in the back yard, and later on a goat. Sima recalls lots of good mahogany furniture and many pictures, a telephone, radio and a gramophone. In 1932 the family moved to a large rented semi in Golders Green where her mother stayed on until 1958.

After her marriage, Sima and her husband owned a large house for 25 years and moved to a smaller maisonette in Muswell Hill fifteen years ago. Their current home is in a quiet cul-de-sac, with spacious rooms, gardens, and a wonderful view over London.

Mary

Mary has no knowledge of her grandparents' housing or that of her parents before they relocated to Birmingham. There, they started in a small rented terraced house backing onto the works, an inner city area with factories around. Mary was born there. Four years later, her father bought a piece of land and built a house with a garage in a middle-class suburb of Birmingham. The house was large, a best room, dining room and kitchen, four bedrooms and bathroom. All the heating was coal fired, all upstairs rooms unheated. Lino prevailed as floor covering but there was some carpeting. She remembers heavy, dark furniture, a radio and telephone. Later on, the best front room had a baby grand piano. In the kitchen was a mangle, and a scullery extension with sink, copper, work table and gas cooker. Beyond it again the coal hole, back loo and a door into the garden. There was a large front garden with a fine tree in it, but it was never used, because 'you could be seen from the road.' A gardener came once a week to tend the gardens - very grand!

Subsequently, Mary lived with her husband in Crawley, but after his death she decided to move back to London where her new activities were based. But her plan to sell her flat in Crawley hit the big drop in house prices so she investigated housing trusts and was eventually offered a purpose-built pensioner's flat in Wimbledon where she now lives.

Mary installed masses of shelving for her books; she says, 'I may be short of floor space but there is plenty of wall.' She has a large room, a tiny kitchen and bathroom, and everything is sufficient for her needs. Public transport is excellent and she has no problems with travelling around. People ask her how she could think of retiring to London, but she says: 'I wouldn't live anywhere else, there is so much to do and see. I am an urban bird, and for me London is best.'

Joan and Patricia

Both sides of the family lived in a genteel seaside resort in Lancashire. The maternal grandparents lived in one of a pair of semi-detached houses which grandfather, whom Patricia describes as 'surrounded by an air of Victorian self improvement' saved up to build, as debt was unthinkable in their family culture. The family occupied one of these four bedroomed houses. They had eight children, with an extra room built in the garden for an aunt who had TB when young. Later on, the ground floor became the home of Joan and Patricia's two maiden aunts and they have photos of them in long dresses and Edwardian hats. The house had a bathroom and indoor and outside toilets, and was lit by gas lamps. Joan remembers that when they stayed there the contents of their potties would be deposited round the roots of the apple tree in the garden 'to improve the crop.'

Their paternal grandparents lived initially on two floors above the musical instrument shop owned by grandfather. He then built and moved into a semi-detached four bedroomed house in 1913. After his death, Joan and Patricia's parents lived there from about 1919. The house was freehold. There were winter curtains, summer curtains and net curtains; it was a house where Patricia says 'respectability mattered.'

In this new house Joan and Patricia shared a bedroom and a bed, though with a bolster between them, called for some unknown reason, 'the pulpit'; their older sister had a room to herself. There was a maid or live-in help who had a small bedroom. Joan describes the house as light and spacious. The front room was for use on Sunday afternoons or when visitors called. Most of the family living went on in the dining room which had easy chairs and a sofa; the radio was in there. All the baking, clothes-drying and ironing went on in the kitchen where the 'help' ate her meals and passed her leisure time.

There was no refrigerator but food was stored in a cold pantry; their mother made her own bread, potted meat and brawn, plus pounds of home-made jam. Joan describes a 'black bombazine-dressed lady calling with a big bread basket lined with muslin and filled with cooked and peeled shrimps'. The fish cart called on Fridays. She also comments that, in those days, it was not considered proper to exchange more than civilities with neighbours, so no patterns of mutual help were ever developed. Both Joan and Patricia recall their past home in great detail and with obvious affection; their descriptions vividly describe a bygone era.

Later the sisters moved to London and shared a flat in Bloomsbury which boasted the only bathroom in the street. Patricia changed teaching jobs and this meant moving homes. In 1972 she bought a three-bedroom flat near Epping Forest, not too far from the lights of London. She has no urge to move again.

Joan moved on to share the top floor of a Georgian house in a nearby square until her marriage, later moving to a one, then a two, then a three-bedroom flat with a garden in Hampstead where her children were brought up. As for many in the group, the best was yet to be. After her retirement, she by chance heard of a vacant first floor flat in an Islington square and was eventually able to enjoy gracious proportions, balcony gardening and excellent local transport and shopping. Her flat makes a splendid central location for some of our meetings.

Charmian

Charmian has photographs of the large detached Victorian pile where her mother was brought up; it seems to have been mock Tudor and had lawns and vegetable gardens. There are pictures of tea parties on the lawn and of her grandmother lying serenely in a hammock. After the First World War her grandmother and her two daughters and grandson moved to Bournemouth and lived in a smaller detached house. But there was a summer house, a tennis lawn, a garage. Charmian remembers a sunny atmosphere, roses, a grand piano and Victorian furniture.

The house her maternal grandfather built for himself after he left the family was absurdly large for one man, on top of a hill outside Lyme Regis. There were wonderful views of Lyme Bay and it was sold as a guest house in 1927 for £2100.

Charmian's mum and dad bought a house in Whetstone after the First World War, which was probably subsidised by their parents. It had five bedrooms but was described by her mother in a letter as 'small and modern'. It was sold in 1925 and the family moved to Edgware which had acquired a tube station.and soon became a London suburb. Charmian describes the house, named Heatherdene, as 'the heart of the universe, somewhere you could always come back to and feel safe.' She recalls it being cold due to little heating, open windows and the door to the garden flung wide, as her mother felt stifled without all this air. 'To sleep with the windows shut would have been bordering on immorality.'

There were six bedrooms for the family and a mother's help. Charmian shared a bedroom with her sister, and her brothers also shared a room. The hub of the house was the living-room, called the nursery, where the life of the family was played out. There was a coal fire, a big table, old armchairs, bookshelves, a piano, a toy cupboard, a gramophone and often clothes-horses grouped round the fire. Here, her father worked at his accounts, amid the hubbub of the rest of the family. Everyone gathered to do homework, play games, argue, tease, draw, paint, make models, together with visiting friends and, of course, the dogs.

The walls were covered with pictures cut from magazines and stuck on by family members; they reached as high as the family could reach and were mostly of animals and beautiful scenery. This arrangement was an idiosyncratic family tradition. Pictures were everywhere in the house, some painted by artists in the family, and there were also masses of photographs. The garden was large and used by all the family.

This family home evokes a memorable and loving atmosphere.

Subsequently, Charmian has lived in rented rooms or flats, a council flat for a short time and luxury high-rise flats in Hong Kong. She has owned small mews houses in Camden and her largest house was a Victorian family house in a small market town in Devon. After leaving Hong Kong she and her husband bought their present mews house where they can cycle to the West End and where, as Londoners, they feel at home; they also have a cottage in Cornwall with a sea view. They feel lucky to be able to move between these two contrasting environments.

Renee

Renee lived until 1933 with her parents in two rooms on the upper floor of a very small house in Stepney. Eight children were born there, and conditions were very overcrowded and difficult with no running water or toilet facilities. At the back of the flat there was something called for some reason the 'orf room,' with a tap, and a pail which served as a toilet and had to be emptied continually. Cooking arrangements were inadequate and dangerous. There was gaslight and an open coal fire.

After 1933, when the eighth child was born, the family moved to a council flat in the same area; here they had three bedrooms and at last a separate toilet. Two years later, after the ninth child was born, they moved to a three- storey house near Aldgate, in a very bad damp condition. The front room was kept for best. There was still only an outside toilet and tap, and the family lived in this house until the outbreak of war in 1939.

Renee's life style changed considerably during and after the war. In 1952 she went to Norway with her Norwegian fiance, where she lived in bedsitting rooms. Traditions of housing were very different there; plenty of land and plenty of trees. After their marriage they moved into a new two bedroomed flat (part owned, part rented), and after ten years moved to a small house financed in the same way; the house was built completely of wood and was all on one floor. Later, they bought a plot of land and had a four-bedroomed house built, two bathrooms and three toilets, laundry room and lots of space. It had a large garden with trees.

On returning to London during the past few years, Renee and her husband moved to a smaller place and now have a flat on two floors which they own. It has a garden with lots of sun and they don't at all regret giving up their big house in Norway and all the things they used to own. They still return to the family home in Norway for summer visits.

Estella

Estella says: 'Like me, my homes have come up in the world.' She describes living with her parents and baby brother in one bedroom of her maternal grandmother's house, a rented three-storey opposite Waterlow Buildings in Bethnal Green. The house was shared by the extended family (twelve in all), was large, crammed with good solid furniture, a china cabinet with Royal Derby china, and her parents' pride and joy, a cabinet style gramophone constantly used by the enthusiastic singing and dancing family members. Different groups of family had their own bedrooms which appeared to double as a 'salon' for entertaining. They had privacy but the children of the household used to run up and down the whole house, regardless. There were lots of ornaments and pictures and a wonderfully described ambience full of life and warmth.

In 1938 Estella's parents moved to an Edwardian semi in South Tottenham, which was freehold and mortgaged.

After her marriage, Estella's first aim was to save enough money to buy a house, and they achieved this by living for a time in cheap furnished rooms. They bought a typical 20s semi in a west London suburb and spent 22 years there. In 1975 they sold that house and moved into their current house, a 'better class' property, in the same area. She thinks that to her grandmother, in her East End rented house with its backyard and outside lavatory, it would have represented riches she could never have imagined. To her mother it would probably have been a dream come true. She says: 'I find it gratifying that I live in a house she would have been proud of.' Her home is large, comfortable with a big garden, and she and her husband are very settled there. Our group has enjoyed summer parties in this garden which grows wonderful roses.

Jo

Jo recalls her father growing up in a house in Loughton. She knows nothing of her mother's family home apart from it being a rented flat. Her paternal grandmother had a large flat in Brighton full of solid furniture and good silver. She remembers other family members with a house full of chinoiserie, another flat with modern furniture, another with antique and modern plus a cocktail cabinet. All were rented. Her own family homes were often changed, she never had her own bedroom and shared a bed; all were flats, seldom with a bathroom; the only heating was from coal fires and furnishings were very basic, no radio but a rented 'relay box' tuned to three stations by the rentor. Jo describes her early homes as crowded and uncomfortable.

Her current home is in her words 'my very own personal space, fitted for my comfort and convenience'. She owns the downstairs of a semi, with one bedroom and has 'deliberately downsized' since retirement. She designed the conversion herself and made sure it fitted her needs. It is all very comfortable, she refuses to have valuable furniture or anything that needs looking after, her home has to serve her, not the other way round; there is no style other than eclectic. Jo comments: 'Perhaps my attitude is a reaction to my crowded, uncomfortable childhood homes, and also to years of sharing with a husband whose body clock was different. I am very aware of the privilege of having my own home and living alone in it.'

Elizabeth

Elizabeth's parents and grandparents lived in a small village in South Wales where, between the wars, housing of sorts was in plentiful supply, but often in poor condition. Homes were mainly rented, toilets were outside in a yard with the cold water tap.

In her maternal grandmother Mary's little house there was an open fireplace where cooking was done on a range, highly blackleaded to a wonderful polish. Furniture was sparse and linoleum covered the floors. Bedrooms were shared and often freezing cold, bedclothes had to last for years and beds were second-hand. Home was characterised by little privacy or space and she spent most of her time as a child playing out of doors with her friends. Her grandmother had a tiny house with a pleasant atmosphere as she collected bric-a-brac, pictures and photographs all round her. She had a large comfortable bed and a holy water container next to it which she used lavishly on herself and anyone nearby before retiring. She rented her house and put away her weekly rent in a bottom drawer with great care.

Elizabeth's paternal grandmother owned her own house and the one next door, which was very unusual in the village. The atmosphere there was dark and forbidding with an air of gloom. Elizabeth's parents left Wales for London in the 30s looking for work; they rented rooms but were evicted and obtained a three-bedroomed council house in 1932. Politically involved with socialism, they didn't believe in home ownership, and there was considerable discussion and snobbery about being a council tenant, or as on the other side of the street, owning your own home. There was sparse furniture and few pictures or mementoes in their London house. Elizabeth thinks this atmosphere mirrored their feelings of alienation from the home in Wales they had left behind.

Elizabeth says: 'Through the years I've lived in council housing, at college, in rooms, in a bedsitter, furnished and unfurnished flat; and finally, our own small terraced house, in North London. It's cosy, comfortable and cluttered, with a welcoming atmosphere. We have a small flat in Dorset with a similar atmosphere and enjoy moving between the two.'

Marj

Marj describes the council house in Middlesbrough which was her childhood home in the 1930s as having been adequate for her family. She had five brothers and sisters and they lived in a three-bedroomed house with a garden and a yard at the back and a 'stick house' where they stored wood, as well as a coal house and a wash house. She remembers being popped into the copper for a bath as a small child. She says: 'My mother was a resourceful woman. She didn't have a refrigerator, so when she needed a cool place for certain foods she would place a large bowl in the wash house and drip cold water into it from a hose-pipe, to keep the food cold in the bowl.'

Since she left home at the age of 23, Marj has lived in many different places. She was a Catholic in those days, and through the church she found a lovely Irish household. She says: 'My best friend lived on the top floor, another friend in the middle, and I shared the ground floor with the landlady and her family. I was called "the foreigner" because I was the only English person. I lived there for fifteen years and they were really nice people.' After that Marj lived in various insecure flats or houses with friends, but they never managed to buy a place and rents were very high.

Marj now lives in a housing association two-roomed flat on the first floor. She is in reach of good transport, in a leafy part of North London, has friendly neighbours, and considers herself lucky. The main drawbacks are that it has little sun and no garden though she has managed to plant arum lilies (blooming as she writes), and trailing ivy.outside the front window. She managed to be accepted by the housing association because she was living in a room in short-life housing (she says it is called that because it will either fall down or be pulled down). When the agent saw the cracks in the walls she immediately signed her on. She is sorry for single people now because it is much more difficult to find somewhere to live.

Conclusion

Reading through these accounts it is striking how vivid and detailed the history of our early homes is to most group members. The memories of where we and our families lived seems much more real and immediate than the descriptions of where we are all living now, perhaps because they are associated with our childhood.

One of the fascinations about exploring where we have lived is to see the way we have made the nests we want, despite the fact that outward events, wars and disasters, have so seriously affected the life-styles of our families and ourselves.

Housing has changed dramatically; what was run-down and declasse has now been done-up and 'gentrified'. Estella recently saw her childhood home in Bethnal Green on the market as a very fashionable residence at an astronomical price. These areas have been rediscovered, re-developed and re-allocated to the affluent and ambitious. But has the heart and spirit of the place been destroyed on the way? It may be just nostalgia but some of us think so.

> *'Home is where one starts from. As we grow older.*
> *The world becomes stranger, the pattern more complicated*
> *Of dead and living.'*

> T. S. Eliot, East Coker

Chapter 6

Clothes to Delight and Dismay

Patricia

Anyone interested in the changing styles of women's clothing during the twentieth century can easily find illustrations and descriptions in their local reference library. Our exploration has been personal rather than academic. We have discussed and reflected upon the differing lives of our grandmothers, our mothers and ourselves. Now we ask more light-heartedly: 'What did the three generations of women wear in those days?' Materials, styles and fashions have changed as the century has passed, just as women's lives, too, have changed.

Clothes arouse emotions as well as visual memories. This is no serious study aiming to link feminine clothing to an understanding of the perceived role of women in society. We seek rather to enjoy a few visual memories and feelings from the past; to look again at how it seemed to us then. The way we remember what our grandmothers and our mothers wore is an aspect of our personal relationship with our families. Scattered memories of what we ourselves wore link us with our past selves. A chord of memory may be struck in those of our readers who are our contemporaries; younger readers may be amazed or amused.

First to take the stage of memory come the grandmothers: with few exceptions they wore black (nowadays everyone seems to wear black). Our memories are vivid though scanty. A Dresden china granny in black silk and lace, too frail to touch, with a black velvet ribbon around her throat contrasts with one mainly remembered for her elegant habit of changing her dress each evening for dinner. A robust Welsh grandmother with hair parted in the middle and scraped back to form two plaits, comes striding back, with her flannelette petticoats, black stockings and her ample pinafore. There is a German grandmother too, clad in black from head to foot, with a high-necked blouse and no make-up. It is safe to assume that none of our grandmothers wore make-up. Most of our group have commented on the lack of jewellery worn, except for simple wedding rings. The scent of lavender water, mothballs, and carbolic soap stays in the nostrils. So our grandmothers stay alive in memory, even though many of us are now grandmothers ourselves. Those of us who never knew our grandmothers have family photographs, stiff and ghostly apparitions in black, linked to us by flashes of family likeness but not always people with whom we could easily communicate.

It might be thought that answers to the blunt question: 'What did your mother wear?' would come pouring out. Not a bit of it. What emerged seemed to be strong feelings and still pictures like excerpts from a film. One of us, Mary, still cannot bear the fact that her mother had no money of her own to buy clothes and had to ask her husband for everything. Another, Estella, remembers her mother as fashion conscious, wearing bright colours and 'flapper' style dresses. Renee has strong memories of a large family and great poverty, with mother wearing a sleeveless 'tube' dress. Irene remembers her mother in a white chiffon dress going to tea dances or wearing an enormous hat decorated with birds and flowers. The feelings that have etched those individual pictures on our memories may be forgotten; they are certainly more personal than the illustrations in a book on the history of fashion. The memories are mainly from our own childhood as if we ceased to register our mothers' appearance once we began to grow up ourselves. A glamorous house-coat, bright colours, and soft materials, a fawn tight-waisted dress with amber beads, these momentary snapshots spill out.

Self-evidently, each mother is unique, but almost all of them wore hats. Until 1939, it was extremely rare for a woman to go out without a hat. Another generalisation which comes through is that on the whole our mothers chose, if possible, quality rather than quantity. They may have had a 'clothes allowance' or they may have had to ask their husbands for money each time they wanted to buy clothes. If they worked outside the home, it was to provide absolute necessities for the family.

The third section of this Clothes Show pulses with greater excitement. What did we wear when we were young? Today's children, with their often bulging wardrobes, would be astonished at how little choice we had when we were young, how few clothes we had and how long they had to last. Our mothers decided these matters for us. We are the generation who wore vests and liberty bodices. When we were old enough to wear stockings, thick lisle leg-coverings were held up by suspenders, buttoned on to the liberty bodice or dangling from a suspender belt. In summer Charmian often wore boys' shorts and 'aertex' shirts. Dresses were mainly hand-made by mother, aunts or a local seamstress; some of us proudly wore coats tailored by a skilled father. Every neighbourhood had its dressmaker. Warmth came from knitted jumpers or cardigans. New clothes came to us for Passover, Easter or First Communion, and it would have been rare to have new clothes more than once a year, though there was always a clear distinction between everyday clothes and 'best clothes'. Rationing was in force during the childhood of some of our group, which was a further restriction on the quantity of clothes we could have. Marj passed easily through the era of clothes coupons because her mother bought material from Annie 'on the market'. When Annie disappeared to gaol for a time, suspicions of black market trading were rife but Annie was much admired and went on eventually to found a good business.

The clearest memories are of clothes we loved or hated. Thin leather gaiters, buttoned down the side with the help of a buttonhook, were tedious but warm in winter; an apricot-coloured silky dress was hated by the recipient though it was bought sacrificially as a Christmas treat. Hand-me-downs were common; we took it for granted that we should inherit clothes that our sisters had grown out of. Marj dearly loved a dress handed down to her when she was about eleven. It had a silky feel and the material was covered with purple and white squares. Other special memories of the clothes we wore as children include Estella's red sailor suit with white piping and Patricia's dark green velvet dress with gold flecks.

As childhood merged into early teens, the Deanna Durbin look (a pretty dress with pinched waist and white 'Peter Pan' collar), was loved by many in our group, no matter where we lived. Film stars and the Royal Family had an influence on fashion in the 1930s. The Joan Crawford wide-brimmed hat made us feel grown up and Princess Marina hats with an innocent turned-up brim were worn by less sophisticated members of our group.

Most of us wore school uniform: gym slips, alleged to suit all sizes and shapes, were worn over white or cream blouses, some with a tie and some having comfortable square necks. Knitted girdles completed the sack-like effect. Lisle stockings, green, fawn or black, and bulky knickers were compulsory. Headgear also figured in school rules. A panama hat in summer, a velour hat in winter, or a 'pudding basin' hat or a cap rather like today's baseball cap, all with the school badge on the front. Uniform was intended to blot out the difference between richer and poorer, but one of our group still remembers the shame and anger of having to wear black stockings with her heels showing white through undarned holes, and a blazer without a pocket badge because that was too expensive. Darning was a fact of life in those days before the invention of man-made fibres. Brownies had to pass a test in darning at the age of about nine and every home had a darning 'mushroom' in its mending box, often in use. Attitudes to school uniform varied: if you liked school, you generally liked school uniform. In the middle years of this century, uniform was sometimes worn at college as well as at school.

Charmian, who went to a physical education college, had to have different uniform for each individual activity she practised.

All of us remember the first time we went out to buy clothes of our own choice. Usually that coincided with our first job. Some of us reached this point earlier than others, with the help of expanded pocket money. Estella went to Harrods Sale in her lunch hour and with great daring bought a 'helmet' hat which was the very latest fashion. Hats were very important in our childhood and early adulthood. A hat was necessary to complete a special outfit and essential for job interviews. Both Elizabeth and Charmian's families, however, living hundreds of miles apart, had the habit of not wearing hats. Such family customs were not questioned, it was just the way things were.

Buying one's own clothes was not always easy. When Elizabeth left home a few years after the war she earned £5 a week and her rent took a big proportion of it. She loved clothes but she also had to eat. In contrast, Mary recalls that when she was posted to the USA as part of her war service in the army, the generous cost of living allowance she received enabled her to enjoy buying clothes with more freedom than she had known before. She chose loose-fitting dresses to celebrate the warm climate and the freedom from uniform.

Most of us remember the 'New Look' in the late 1940s, revelling in the almost ankle-length full skirts as a change from skimpy utility skirts that finished at our knees. One or two of us were still too young really to appreciate the 'New Look'. Joan was already wearing ankle-length nurses' uniform so did not enthuse.

The 60s are remembered as a time of loosening up in many areas of life. Clothes became less conventional, we wore what we felt like. For most of us that was the first time we wore trousers to work as well as for leisure activities. Hats had already been discarded except for weddings and funerals. Patricia had about eighteen hats mouldering on the top of the wardrobe, each one bought for a special function, never again to take the air. The knitted twin-set and the smart 'professional' skirt and jacket were blown away by winds of change. None of us has boasted of burning a bra but liberation was infectious. As individuals, we do not seem to have ever been excessively conventional but even so, all of us became during the 60s, more free to ignore the dress code if we wished.

Of all life's major occasions, a wedding most encourages female rebels to conform. Members of our group are made of sterner stuff. All but two of us have been married, but not one had a 'white' wedding in church or synagogue. We are a self-selected group drawn together by membership of U3A and an interest in women's history, so maybe some conclusions can be drawn from this. The year and the season of each marriage has not been researched, but to emphasise individuality and perhaps add a spot of extra colour to our life histories, this Clothes Show will end with a march of the wedding dresses.

For her elopement, Jo wore a pale yellow wool dress, a black corduroy coat with white lining, a small flower-strewn straw hat and sandals. She had worked in the fashion world and knew how to look dashing. For her wedding, Estella wore a dusty-pink wool jersey suit, an orchid buttonhole and a hat with a magnificent curled feather. Renee wore a green linen suit, the skirt reaching just below the knee, and a straw hat with black band. Joan was one of several who remembered the awesome expensiveness of her wedding outfit. She wore a blue-brown fine wool jersey two-piece from Liberty. Charmian, no lover of grand clothes, found it hard to choose, but eventually found exactly the right blue dress and jacket. Irene married only a year after she and her future husband arrived in UK as refugees. There was no money for fine clothes so she borrowed a green two-piece. Mary cares nothing for fuss; she had no special wedding dress as she and her partner married one day when they were out shopping. Elizabeth, ever a lover of style, wore a long dress of orange paisley with a feather boa. In earlier times the boa, a South African bird, provided long black soft and curling feathers, made into a long scarf, to be flung nonchalantly around the necks of rich ladies (Sima's mother worked as a feather curler for making boas). Elizabeth loved style, but not at the cost of South African birds, so her boa was made of nylon. For her January wedding in wartime, Sima found a remnant of beautiful wool, deep ruby red, and a friend made her dress, trimmed with light blue. Her black hat was borrowed and the fur coat that completed her wedding outfit was a gift from the States.

Today we dress as we please and enjoy what we wear. Our wardrobes are fuller than those of our mothers or our grandmothers. The seamstresses are all gone, or almost all. We have not lost our individual sense of style and we know how to dress for comfort as well as for celebration. Ready-to-wear, easy-care, the treasure trove of charity shops and all the other stores in town are there for us when we wish, according to the health of our pensions at the time. But oh, the bliss of one's favourite comfortable clothes, worn with individual panache!

Chapter 7

Food for Body and Soul

Patricia

Several times a year our U3A group feels the need for a party. We have been having regular book meetings for some years, but now and again a party breaks out. We meet in the house or garden of one or another of our members, according to season. We arrive clutching carrier bags full of tempting snacks which come together to form an appetising lunch. Sima's gefilter fish balls nestle up to Jo's outrageously wonderful gateau of jellied fruits on a bed of sponge, set in a chocolate basket. Those delights are backed up by all kinds of meat, cheese and salads nudged alongside crisp crusty bread rolls. Wine and fruit juice flow, and as always, interesting conversation seasons the occasion. Food definitely has its place in our project, so it was agreed we should explore a little bit of the way in which attitudes, traditions, likes and dislikes concerning food, have been part of the fabric of our families' lives.

The Jewish members of our group, coming from different geographical and social backgrounds, show a similarity in traditions concerning food. What is known of grandmothers demonstrates strict observance of food laws; in our mothers' generation there is a continuance of tradition (though not of religious observance). Chicken or fish still appeared on Fridays, when the whole family would sit down together to eat. As Estella says: 'Regardless of how rich or poor the family might be, it was chicken - rich roast or old boiler - and it was a treat.' Chicken soup was a constant. It nourished everyone, cured all complaints.

Shopping for food and the preparation of meals was clearly a major focus of a married woman's life in the first half of this century as it had been for generations before. In some families, such as Irene's, there were servants to do the cooking until the Hitler regime removed them. The poverty Irene experienced in her young adulthood in England did not stop her instinctive wish to provide good food for her family, just as Renee's mother went on providing for her family despite periods of extreme poverty. The explicit non-religious ethos of Sima's childhood did not deflect either Sima's mother or herself from the same Jewish tradition of the primacy of family meals. In the present generation they still maintain the tradition of skill and enjoyment in cooking and hospitality. Estella remembers special cakes for Purim.

'Haman's pockets' were a sort of jam puff, but filled with sultanas or apple, or maybe with poppy seeds and honey, instead of jam. At Chanukah there used to be a marvellous party for about a thousand children held at the People's Palace in the East End of London, when oranges and sweets were given to each child. The fact that Mary's father consciously rejected his Jewish roots at some stage, was perhaps one factor that denied her any resonance of celebration connected with food.

The interconnection of food and religion among Jews is well-known but we have found it in other faiths as well. The roots remain in the form of attitudes and values even if the shoots are no longer green. In Elizabeth's Catholic family in Wales, as in Marj's Catholic family in Yorkshire, there was fish on Fridays. Marj remembers that when she left home for a job in London, she and a friend would go to a restaurant on Fridays and wait for the chimes of midnight before ordering meat for a late dinner.

The tradition of simple home-cooked meals which Elizabeth knew in Wales would have been recognised in Charmian's family home. There, the ascetic Unitarian ethos, in which Charmian's mother gave lessons on the good life of kindness to others and no self-indulgence, meant that children were not to ask: 'What's for dinner?' as that would mean too much interest in food, or even dreaded gluttony. This clearly did not affect the enormous enjoyment of family meals shared with whoever happened to be around in their hospitable home. The roast dinner on Saturdays in Joan and Patricia's Methodist home was probably a way of not having to cook on Sundays. Jo's somewhat fluid family life did not lend itself to the building or keeping of traditions, but vestiges of Catholicism remained as a framework, even if a negative one in Jo's opinion.

Nearly half our group married partners of different faith backgrounds, which for some was a factor in broadening experience of food. Marriage, in any case, was a watershed. It was more fun to cook meals for another; eating with family or friends has remained for most of us a special pleasure. Estella has two sharp memories of early married life. She had no idea how to cook bacon and thought that when the fat became transparent the bacon was cooked. A leap of freedom from her childhood dislike of green vegetables led her to leave out such things entirely from their meals in the early days of her marriage. Not surprisingly, illness followed, but the advice of their family doctor put her on the right path to nutrition. Jo is realistic about the impact of female chores. She enjoyed cooking for her husband at first, but discovered it was labour-intensive, involving much more time in preparation than in enjoyable consumption. Charmian's husband was vegetarian when they married, which led her into new recipes and ways of cooking.

Wartime food has not evoked much comment from our group. Some of us mourned the absence of bananas, and some recalled the solid, stodgy food served in British Restaurants. Only Sima and Irene speak of ration books and Irene has kept hers as a souvenir. Dried eggs call up a murmur of distaste. Both Charmian and Joan have memories of the shortage of butter. At Charmian's college the ration was put out for each table of six, and the students used to draw lines on it with a knife to mark out exactly each student's share. Joan remembers how the ration of butter was given out to each nurse and kept in a screw-top jar for use at mid-morning or afternoon breaks with wedges of bread. One day when rushing to her ward she dropped the precious butter and burst into tears as she saw the shattered glass fragments and the irretrievable scrap of butter. Most of us were still at an age when someone else was feeding us, either at home, at college, or in the forces, so the extra calories of carbohydrate kept us from feeling too hungry. There were new discoveries in food. Patricia was introduced to Canadian breakfast while she was in the Women's Royal Naval Service. That delight consisted of bacon on a pancake doused with golden syrup. Mary sampled German food when she was in the Control Commission in Hamburg.

All the group were asked if they had ever gone hungry, in the sense of being too poor to eat. Patricia remembers her amazement at the confession of a girl in her form at school who, when asked by her teacher what she had eaten, said she had tea and bread and butter for breakfast, dinner and tea. Patricia herself, brought up to believe that the route to a healthy life was to eat up one's vegetables and go to bed early, had a glimpse into another world. Of course we were all hungry sometimes. Estella recalls gnawing hunger when she was evacuated to a school housed in two buildings. Cycling from one school to the other at change of lessons, she passed a bakery and bought a Madeira cake which she promptly stuffed into her mouth, juggling one-handed with books and handlebars as she sped on to the next lesson. Charmian found the helpings at college meals too small to quell the hunger roused by non-stop physical activity. On the whole, we continued the pattern of childhood at home and did not complain. Food was something taken for granted; it was the way things were.

In spite of the differences in our backgrounds, there was a regularity and similarity in the way those of us whose childhood was spent in Britain were fed as children. Most of us can remember a roast dinner on Saturday or Sunday, followed by cold meat the next day, mince the third day, and perhaps meatballs the fourth day. The remaining three days would probably bring offal, a vegetarian meal and fish. Pudding was for those who finished their first course. A nice clean plate was rewarded with steamed pudding, spotted dick, and golden sponge pudding or fruit pie with custard. Fresh or tinned fruit with cream or evaporated milk was definitely a treat and probably reserved for high tea. In Renee's home there were no puddings, in Joan and Patricia's home the toffee tin was produced after dinner and one sweet or chocolate each was allowed.

If there was pocket money it was mostly spent on food. There is space for only brief examples: Estella bought a pennyworth of pickled cabbage or two pennyworths of broken biscuits; Patricia bought sherbert, strings of licorice or chewing gum. Once she stole a bar of chocolate from the corner shop when her pocket money was all gone.

Irene's childhood and youth in Germany were very different from her life in England, not only because there were servants and large meals in her German home, but also because food and lifestyle in England and Germany were so different. English beef and lamb replaced the veal and venison of her childhood. For breakfast in childhood there were fresh baked rolls; frankfurters were a birthday treat. For teas there was stolle, a light raisin bread covered with powdered sugar.

What did we drink? In childhood tea and cocoa seem to have been almost universal though Charmian recalls drinking nothing but milk or water. Three of us can remember the delights of Corona cordials in violent colours which arrived in crates to be drunk with soda water. Sima's father insisted that she and her brothers should drink 'slops', a glass of milk and water guaranteed to flush out the system. Two of us reported that the male adults in the family went to the pub in the evening, two others have the perception that their fathers drank too much. The only memory of adult women drinking alcohol comes from Marj. Clearly there was more equality in Yorkshire, where the women enjoyed their Guinness or stout. In the 1950s Mary discovered Irish coffee, which she has cherished ever since.

In recent years, we have all enjoyed the extension of our experience of food provided by personal travel and the all-year-round variety of food on supermarket shelves. Joan, who remembers strawberries as her birthday treat in June, and raspberries as celebration of her mother's birthday in July, can if she wishes, have strawberries at any time of the year. Food is more cosmopolitan. Cookery programmes abound on TV. Ready-to-eat meals in cardboard boxes clutter the trolleys of supermarket shoppers and are very useful as meals for one, though not much used by those of us with others to cook for, unless the main cook of the family is unwell. We don't seem to eat in restaurants a great deal, but some of us enjoy pub meals.

Most of us have learned to take clever short cuts in our cooking. We have other things in our lives as well, although we have passed the age of paid employment. We are probably more adventurous in food than our parents were because we live in more prosperous times, and such a wide variety of food is available. Joan admits it is hard but enjoyable to give up habits of frugality. Food, as an ingredient of conviviality and celebration, is important. Soon we shall have another party.

Chapter 8

Lifelong Learning

Charmian and Patricia

Nothing illustrates so clearly the changes in British society in the 20th century as the educational experience of three generations, and particularly three generations of women. When our grandmothers were young, girls brought up in Britain were largely dependent on denominational or charity elementary schools. Small private 'dame' schools would have been used by some, and middle-class girls would have been educated by governesses at home, or a few in the pioneering girls' independent schools such as those founded by Miss Beale and Miss Buss. Except in these schools, the curriculum for girls was dominated by the three 'Rs' and domestic subjects.

We know very little about the education of our grandmothers; half of them were not in this country. Elizabeth, who knew her maternal grandmother well, thinks she attended a local Catholic school in Ireland long enough to become literate and numerate. Sima reckons her Romanian peasant grandmother was illiterate. Joan and Patricia's maternal grandmother probably went to a dame school. Irene remembers both her grandmothers in Germany as being well read. Although Charmian has no information about her grandmothers' education it is fairly certain her maternal grandmother was educated by a governess at home. She educated her own daughters in that way.

These sketchy bits of knowledge are in accordance with the social and geographical diversity of our grandmothers' families. We wish we had talked to them more about their childhood experiences while they were alive.

Our mothers
After the 1870 Education Act the haphazard distribution of schooling was supplemented by local Board elementary schools to fill the gaps left by church provision. These became free and supposedly compulsory up to the age of twelve by the turn of the century. The leaving age was not raised to fourteen until after the First World War and most children left at the minimum age, especially girls, whose help was needed at home. A slender ladder of opportunity was established by the provision of some free places in secondary schools after the 1902 Education Act; but these were built on a

foundation which assumed that boys and girls, and children from different social classes, should have different schooling.

It is not surprising to find, therefore, that the school experience of our mothers was mostly fragmented, short, and far from realising their potential. Sima's mother left elementary school at the age of twelve; although her teachers wanted her to stay on, her apprenticeship was needed for the family economy. Elizabeth's mother left the local Catholic school at thirteen to help in the nearby tavern. Both continued to educate themselves through their marriages, their reading and political interests. They were ambitious for their children's education as a route to secure employment.

Estella and Mary feel that their mothers became increasingly embarrassed by their own educational limitations compared with those of their daughters. Estella went some years ago to the GLC Record Office and found the admission roll of the school her mother attended in East London. She says: 'At least 95% of the entries were of Jewish immigrants. My mother told me that at the age of nine she stayed at home frequently in order to help her mother making men's caps. She also said that she left school at the age of thirteen. These facts may have contributed to her illiteracy, but she was desperately keen on her children receiving the best education they could.

'The fact that she was for many years able to conceal the extent of her illiteracy, points to her feelings of shame about it. When I was at grammar school, my notes to teachers were written by me and laboriously signed by my mother who would say that she didn't want to write them herself because her eyesight was so bad. It wasn't until I was about fifteen that my father told me the truth. I don't think it had any effect on my relationship with her - perhaps I already had, deep down, an inkling about her disability. But since recalling the matter in our group discussions, I feel a sense of sadness that my mother endured embarrassment and shame and was forced to hide these emotions. One rather touching anecdote: my father said that some time after my mother married him, her sister in a fit of pique blurted out that she had written the few letters purporting to have come from my mother.'

Mary's maternal grandmother died when she was very young and her mother was passed on from one set of kin to another throughout her childhood. She writes: 'Her education must have been very fragmented. This was borne out by her handwriting, which was badly formed, and her poor spelling. I think she realised, as my education went ahead, just how much she had missed, and she would never want to see my work or go to any parents' event. She was probably afraid of being shown up by her children and by the teachers.'

In contrast, Irene and Charmian's mothers were well educated for girls of their generation. Irene writes: 'My mother (in Germany), had private lessons in elocution because she wanted to be an actress. Later she went to a boarding school. They were very strict there because they wanted to make proper ladies of the girls. She was always a bit naughty. Opposite the school was a garrison with young soldiers. One night she and her friend sat in their nightdresses on the window sill, waving to the soldiers. One of the teachers came unexpectedly into their room and for punishment they were put on "house arrest" for several weeks. Apart from the strict discipline she loved the school and was very interested in her education, especially languages, reading and history.'

Charmian's father went to a public school, and her mother's brothers to a non-denominational fee-paying day school, but her mother was educated at home. 'She had lessons every morning, with her sisters and some neighbours' daughters. The little class of girls was taught by a governess who had herself been to "Miss Buss's school" and who remained a lifelong family friend. Of course school attendance officers never came to her home to find out if her parents were carrying out their duty to have her educated! She studied languages, history, geography and literature, art and music (singing, piano and viola), and played in a family quartet with her father and sisters. In her late teens she studied part-time at a music college for a while. Her arithmetic remained woeful and she knew no science. However, I think she was better educated than my dad who seemed to have only learnt to recite streams of Latin verse and skill with a cricket bat at his school.'

Ourselves

These educational experiences of our mothers are entirely predictable from their social and immigrant status. None of them became 'scholarship' girls through the free places offered by 'county secondary schools' after 1902. Sima's father did however, and Jo notes that her aunt was not allowed to take up a scholarship place she had won. It was different for our generation. We were all educated between the wars, or during the Second World War. Nearly half of us went to state or church elementary schools and won grammar school places. The existence of this opportunity was a major element in our occupational futures and our convergence from the diverse lives of our grandmothers. Though it was not all plain sailing as we shall see.

The Scholarship Girls

Mary went to the local girls' grammar school when she was ten. Her father had decided his children should be brought up without religion. She has never forgotten her innocent questions being rebuffed in her first scripture lesson and it set the tone for the rest of her education: 'I did not enjoy school, the teachers were mostly distant and discouraging, and seemed to parallel my father's attitude to me. I became depressed even though I did quite well. At the end of my first term in the fourth year my father announced I would leave school at Easter (when I would be fourteen), just like that, no warning or discussion. I was offered a choice between domestic science, which I loathed, and office work which I agreed to.' Mary seems to have satisfied her enquiring mind through reading all the volumes of the *Children's Encyclopaedia*, rather than at school. Her brother continued in grammar school to higher education.

Elizabeth won a place at the local grammar school in Bridgend and when her family moved to London in the Depression she attended (after pressure on the authorities from her father), a grammar school there. She enjoyed it, and matriculated, but left at seventeen in 1949 as her father decided she should start work and contribute to the family finances. She knew no one personally who stayed on to try for university which seemed a remote ideal.

Renee was brought up in the East End of London: 'I was born in 1924, the fourth in a family of nine children. The first big turning point in my education was when I won a London County Council scholarship at the age of ten and went to a grammar school in Spitalfields. It was quite a feather in my cap as I had been away a lot with illness. My aunts were against me taking up the scholarship but my mother was so proud of me, the first in the entire family to go to grammar school, that I was allowed to go, and stayed until I was seventeen. Joining the school made a great difference to my life. I was fitted out with new clothes (I had a grant of £27 for that purpose), and my mother bought me a leather satchel to hold my books. I was mixing with a completely different category of girls and from being the "clever" one, was now just one of lots of clever girls. The whole affair put me apart from my brothers and sisters, something which has more-or-less continued to this day.' This seems to confirm the fear her aunts may have had that her attendance at grammar school would threaten family cohesion.

Sima and Estella were two more East End Jewish girls who went to grammar school, Sima following her older siblings who had an academic reputation. She decided she wouldn't compete but would shine at drama having already been an 'Italia Conti kid'. She was in all the school plays, had several boy friends and one or two romances. She left at sixteen for the civil service.

136

Estella writes vividly of her schooling which made a great impression on her: 'In 1929 at the age of three I went to Virginia Road Infants' School. Miss Dibbs the headteacher, was always known as "Governess", and she sat on a dais in the hall, surrounded on three sides by classrooms. Children sat in rows, boy/girl together at iron-framed desks with tip-up seats. Boys did painting while girls were taught to knit. This caused the only problem I ever had (I was lucky enough to experience no difficulty with the three R's). I loved painting so I did my partner's painting while he tried to do my knitting. He was always congratulated on his pictures, I was always castigated for my tangled knitting. In those days classes were quite large, 40 or more, and silence was the rule. "Good" children were allowed to sit at the back of the class, those deemed troublesome sat near the front. I was considered "good".

'At seven we were marched round to the nearby junior elementary schools, the boys' school being on the ground floor, the girls' school on the first floor with its playground on the roof of the building. The interior lay-out was similar to that of the infants' school. The headmistress (no longer Governess), sat on a dais in the hall. Children lined up in silence outside their respective classrooms. My first teacher here, hair plaited in earphones, was very strict. Life in her class was minutely regimented. On her desk was a push-button bell, all commands were executed at the ping of that bell: e.g. pIng - enter classroom, stand behind desks; ping - sit down, register called, all present answer "Yes madam"; ping - open desk-lids noiselessly; ping - remove demanded book from desk, close lids noiselessly, place book on top; ping - whole class to commence work on particular page, as stated by teacher. Absolutely no talking amongst pupils.

'Whatever lesson the teacher presented, it was assumed that all the children would be able to learn it. Those who showed that they had learned little or nothing were reprimanded for not paying sufficient attention or for being downright naughty. I can remember pitying the poor girls who didn't know where to begin when it was their turn to read aloud, or for whom "sums" represented insurmountable problems. They suffered from the teacher's whiplash tongue. The three 'R's' ruled supreme in that class.'

As she moved up the school the regime became less rigid. Estelle describes it as being both 'serious and enlightened'. She found learning challenging and fun.

'In 1937 I won a Junior County Scholarship and went to Clapton County Secondary School (Laura Place). This was a turning point in my education. I entered a new and exciting world. School houses and house captains, games captains and form captains all contrasted with the teams and monitors of my elementary school. The loyalty we were expected to feel, and which I did feel, for my house, respect for prefects (even the odd 'crush'), the fact that the head was a *Dr*. Hunt, that we were taught in "forms" not classes and that these were designated by roman numerals, the caps and gowns the staff wore on certain occasions, the games; the vast array and connected paraphernalia of the uniform with its strict and various rules: these experiences which hitherto had been part of school stories had become my everyday life. It was all in sharp contrast to the life of the East End "street arab" that I had previously led.

'The interior of the school was as different as it could be from my elementary school. At Laura Place the entrance hall was always heavy with the smell of polish - polished parquet floor, polished panelled walls, polished brass fittings and a wide, curved, polished oak staircase that led up to the headmistress's room. This entrance was only used by pupils on the first and last days of the school year unless one was in real trouble and had to go and see the head. There was a tradition of academic excellence. When I arrived I felt I was living in a dream world, in spite of the fact that I was a new girl not yet allocated to a House, taking most of my lessons in hut classrooms outside the main building, and despisedly known as a "hut-kid". The following year I too would almost disregard the "hut-kids" when I became a part of main school life.'

Marj and Jo, the other two who were dependent on the state system, did not fare so well.

Marj was born in 1932 and went to a local Catholic school where she took the scholarship. She remembers having a terrible cold and trying not to sniff. 'Of course I failed the exam and went on to an elementary senior school. I stayed until I was fourteen. Lots of bad memories. I was good at English but I didn't get on with the teachers. No doors opened. I suppose I opened them myself through my reading.'

Jo says: 'I was a difficult, strong-willed child, resisting parental wishes and going on hunger strike.' She learnt to read at the age of three, but in spite of this early start Jo had a disastrous education, leaving school thankfully at fourteen after constantly moving from one school to another. She remembers 'very boring domestic science, learning to grate cakes of soap to make soap flakes, ironing with flat-irons heated on stoves and spitting on them to test for heat. Tiresome parsing in English. Boring kings and queens in history.'

Only four of us, two of whom are sisters, were educated outside the state system. Irene (born in 1917) went to school in Germany. She had a privileged education and enjoyed particularly, history, art, literature and languages. She had Jewish and non-Jewish friends. After 1932 'things began to change;' she was sent away to a boarding school near the Dutch border to escape anti-semitism. Irene was lucky enough to take her leaving exams, but her sister had to leave school at fourteen.

Patricia and Joan were privately educated in a Lancashire coastal town. Joan was the academic star in their small school and appreciated being allowed to continue alone into the sixth form even if it was as she says,'a bizarre kind of adolescence'.

Patricia (born in 1923 and a year younger than her sister), remembers how their father took them to school in the car and she used to scribble her homework on the way because she had been too wrapped up in her library book the night before. 'We had marks totalled each week and were placed in rank order in class. I was usually bottom in the weekly marks but did well in termly exams which must have infuriated the teachers. Little did I think then that fifty years later, the whole nation, egged on by the Government, would have a similar love affair with "lists of attainment", to similar limited effect. In 1938 we had to give up Latin because we made the teacher's life a misery with our bad behaviour. We struggled on with French, speaking in an anglicised way which has made spoken French impossible for me ever since. Games were important to me, and the annual school play. I specially remember December 1936 when the evening performance was interrupted so that we could listen to the abdication speech of Edward VIII broadcast by the BBC.'

Patricia left school for a civil service job her father had found for her, in the first year of the war.

Charmian, born the same year as Patricia, was lucky enough to attend the North London Collegiate School, one of Frances Mary Buss's pioneering girls' schools. She remembers it as an extension of her relaxed home life. Most of the time she was there the school was in wonderful premises on the edge of London with large grounds, plenty of trees to climb and playing fields. 'I spent a lot of time gazing out of the window of the classroom longing for the next games period or dinner break. School for me smells of newly cut grass, lime trees and wallflowers. It is always sunny. I enjoyed English and Art, and lots of extra-curricular activities, but never seemed to be under pressure to apply myself to less popular subjects. I loved to have lots of friends. It was indeed an enlightened kind of school for the period; no marks or rank orders as in Patricia's school, only broad categories of grades. The philosophy behind this was explained to us when I was quite little, and I was most impressed. I've remained cynical of rank orders ever since, specially when I see my much sought-after school nowadays coming near the top of the league tables.

'It seems to me my school life was idyllic. I was enormously happy and learnt a lot but left from the sixth form with only the glimmerings of academic interest, without matriculation exemption, and with little understanding of the extent of my privilege (in spite of the oft repeated prayer, "The Lord expects much from those to whom much is given").'

So the eleven of us left school after these contrasting experiences. We had very different schooling from our mothers because of the expansion of educational opportunity in the first half of the century, but no one could say we had fulfilled our potential, even in the formally defined terms of a universal education system. We were variously constrained by family economic needs or parental notions about a suitable future for a girl, and for several of us the Second World War disrupted our lives at a crucial time in our development. Very few of us continued to further education apart from shorthand and typing courses. Estella the successful grammar school girl started university but didn't finish. Joan applied for university but was too young and went into nursing instead. She finally got to university in 1949 with a mixture of self-financing and grant-aid. Charmian satisfied her urge to spend more time in the gymnasium and games field by training as a physical education teacher. Everybody else went into clerical or other work 'suitable for girls' but not satisfying their hunger for learning.

Some of the factors producing this frustrated potential are highlighted in the chapter on work.

Adult Learning
When we left school our lifelong education had only just begun. Jo, Mary and Marj all left at fourteen as we have seen. Here are their subsequent educational stories.

Jo describes how in the early 1960s she had fallen into a 'poor me, life hasn't given me a chance' mode. Discovering the opportunity for a grant-aided residential year of study enabled her to meet the problems of both her unsatisfactory marriage and her lack of promotion at work. She was scared of finding she wasn't worth educating after all, but continued to take a degree in history and politics at the age of 39, followed by an MA. Then she was fortunate enough to get a lectureship at the Open University, where she stayed until retirement, continuing until recently as a part-time teacher. 'My own educational experience is of course highly relevant to OU students, whom I greatly admire and enjoyed teaching.'

Mary (by this time in her 40s and married), found every really interesting job required at least five O levels. 'This gave me the idea that O levels could hardly be difficult as so many people were expected to have them; so I had better get them. I enquired at the local technical college and was told that five O levels at evening classes would take two years. I also discovered that one could put oneself in for the examinations and that past papers were available. "A pox on two years," I said to myself, and I bought past papers in five subjects and decided to sit them in six months time. This was a lot less self-important than it seems. As an adult who had read a broadsheet paper every day and worked in offices for years, I had learnt a lot without really trying. I duly sat the five O levels in the summer and got good grades. Of course my approach did not give me a thorough education but it did give me the desired qualifications.

'I got withdrawal symptoms and couldn't resist looking at past A level papers in some of the same subjects. I decided to carry on with British Constitution and history, and to add sociology. That autumn I took the first two, and sociology in the summer, a subject I enjoyed very much. By then I had already applied to some polytechnics and been accepted. All in eighteen months.'

After her degree Mary trained as a careers advisor and later she added a Diploma in Women's Studies to her qualifications. She says she still gets withdrawal symptoms if she is not studying.

After working in a factory and a shop, Marj qualified as a shorthand typist, but she didn't seem to get her career started until she reached the age of 40 in 1972. 'One evening when I was at a very low ebb I was sitting in my room listening to the radio when a female voice asked: "Are you unhappy in your job? Do you think your education was insufficient? Would you like a second chance?" I had spent many evenings throughout the years supplementing my education but still felt inadequate so I answered "yes" to all three questions. I rang the female at the City Literary Institute the very next day and made an appointment to see her. She was very interested in my story and said the course (complete with grant) was aimed at people like me. I spent a happy year as far as my education went but things continued to go wrong in my social life.' To help overcome her personal problems Marj did a counselling course which she records was 'enormously useful in helping me to move further on the road towards freedom (from fear)'.

Marj decided to apply next for a degree in English Literature, and enjoyed the interview, talking about the books she had read. The level of analysis needed on the degree course showed up the inadequacies of her education, but she managed to scrape through the final exam. She tried teacher training but was only happy in a one-to-one relationship so she returned to more counselling training. She takes a few clients, does voluntary work, is involved in feminism, and continues to work to enhance her development.

Even those of us who continued our schooling to seventeen or eighteen or went on to higher education did not leave it there.

Elizabeth, at the age of 33, and after the break-up of a relationship, exchanged a lively social life for what she describes as a 'more sober and productive way of life' by embarking on a one-year residential course at Hillcroft, an adult college for women. She describes it as a 'milestone and a challenging experience'. Although she failed to get a state scholarship to university afterwards it helped her to more socially oriented work and in 1971 she qualified as a probation officer.

Estella returned to education in her early 40s, when she was married with two children. She writes: 'In the early 60s when the children were in junior school, domesticity was a cushion that was beginning to suffocate me. In 1966 I saw an advert in the local paper about a college of education, and applied without telling anyone, to become a mature student there (I suppose I feared rejection again and could not face the fact that others would know). It was only when I was accepted that I told my family and friends. My husband was surprised that I wanted to give up my cosy domestic life and part-time jobs that I obviously enjoyed, to endure three years of study, but if that was what I wanted, then so be it. My parents too were somewhat puzzled, my mother remarking: "What on earth do you want to start doing this for at your time of life?" I was getting on for 41. 'Estella specialised in the junior age range and in art, and began her teaching career in 1969. 'Another new phase in my life had begun.'

Sima, also married and with two children and some onerous caring responsibilities, managed between leaving school in 1938 and retiring, to pick up an education in drama and elocution (with a scholarship to RADA), secondary teacher training in drama and English, and a Diploma in the Education of Handicapped Children; all of which she put to good use.

Joan, Patricia, and Charmian also educated themselves further as mature students. Patricia and Charmian graduated; Joan qualified in psychiatric social work and group dynamics and continued to learn by being involved in training other mid-career professionals.

At the end of the first year of our joint project we had a hunch that a number of us had 'changed direction' through our education as adults. We

142

recognised that we are a self-selected group, through our membership of the U3A and our interest in a participatory approach to women's history; but we were not prepared for the extent to which this 'hunch' was confirmed as we explored our life stories. Of the eleven of us, nine had acquired degrees or professional qualifications as adults, irrespective of our class backgrounds, school leaving age, or the type of school we had attended. We had also, nearly all of us, continued paid work, many in careers within or allied to education. (Details of this are in our chapter on work).

Compared with our grandmothers and mothers, our lives had converged. Progress through school was patchy, disrupted by parental decisions and war. Turning points in our personal lives significantly affected our decisions to pursue further education: the end of a relationship, a feeling that we were not 'getting anywhere' in our work or personal development. Of course the expansion of educational opportunity was crucial. We were all too old to be able to take advantage of 'free secondary education for all' after the 1944 Education Act, but were not slow to grasp the chances offered in the post-war period, for education in adulthood. The Robbins Report of 1963, which expanded higher education and grant-support for mature students, was important for several of us. The post-war Emergency Teacher Training Scheme offered the way forward for Patricia who continued to make a career in teaching and eventually became a headmistress. While preparing this chapter she and Charmian (who worked in teacher education) have been able to indulge in reminiscences about the early years of comprehensive schools from their contrasting perspectives; one shaping school policy, and the other trying, from a state of ignorance, to prepare new teachers to meet the challenges they offered.

Earlier studies of changes in job status between generations have confirmed the link between education and occupation by comparing career patterns of fathers and sons. It is only recently that the more complicated effects of expanding educational opportunities on different generations of women have become a focus of study. Previously they were assumed to take their status from their husbands if they had them! Certainly many of our grandmothers would be amazed if they could see what their granddaughters have achieved; and if we only consider our own generation, the status and satisfaction of our work has been transformed through our determined pursuit of education as adults. Jobs and education were interwoven in our lives. Our foremothers' schooling was mostly brief, and entirely determined by social class. We on the other hand have become a group of well-qualified women able to pursue professional careers.

But to consider only formal educational qualifications and their significance for a better job is too narrow. Patricia distinguishes different kinds of learning: the plain acquisition of knowledge from those who know to those who want to know; the acquisition of skills, or learning by doing, from someone more skilled than oneself; the exploration of experience, drawing out from oneself what is essentially there but not recognised or understood.

Learning also takes place in other settings than educational institutions, and has outcomes other than qualifications. Renee, writing about turning points in her education, follows her account of achieving her grammar school place, with a discussion of how her paid employment educated her. She learnt shorthand and typing at school, and changed jobs within the Air Ministry during the war several times. 'My educational horizons widened each time.' She moved to Norway in 1952 and married a Norwegian she had met in London. 'This constituted a turning point as I was partly working in another language, and participating in another culture. Later, when I joined a bank, I was being educated in another field.' She progressed to more and more responsible work, handling large sums of money and taking a lot of responsibility, working entirely in the Norwegian language. 'Another turning point was that I was elected leader of the union in the bank, and took part in wage negotiations, decided who got various jobs, and was consulted on any problems arising with the work force. I attended many courses in this connection, thus again widening my education.' In this account Renee seems to encompass all three of Patricia's kinds of learning.

Irene had an education in adapting to another culture when she arrived in this country as a refugee just before the war. She has always had a full cultural life with her husband, reading, theatre going, and doing charity work. She attends several classes at the U3A and in spite of health problems is an active member of our group.

Learning takes place in families too, and some of us have been lucky enough to have come from families which not only provided informal learning through reading, discussion, and encouragement of our interests, but also supported our ambitions. Elizabeth writes: 'My mother could read and write, she never lost her enjoyment in books, she also studied newspapers closely. Both she and my father were politically active in the Labour Party, and despite their limited formal education they would discuss social issues together and with us and their friends. My mother believed in education and was happy for all her three children to attend the local grammar school. She saw the end-result of this as a route to security of employment which for her was the goal in life, as her own had been so precarious, with many long periods of economic hardship over the years.'

Patricia remembers the joys she and Joan had from books. 'A.A. Milne, Lewis Carroll, my mother's Sunday School prizes; improving stories about the evils of the Klu Klux Klan, and impossibly good white people with their black servants who were faithful and devoted. I read them all many times. Mrs. Williams across the road invited Joan and me to go whenever we liked to borrow the *Children's Encyclopedia*, a mine of information. Every Thursday we had the *Children's Newspaper*, rather dull, but anything in print was worth having. A sense of unlimited riches came to me from the public library, and from the school library which was housed in two cupboards, open for borrowing every Friday.'

Some of the group were not so lucky in their family backgrounds. Education became a way of breaking away from the limitations imposed by families or circumstances. In every case the urge to continue learning has been central to our lives.

Conclusion

The notion of 'lifelong learning' which has become popular today is certainly appropriate to our educational histories. After all we are still at it! In its narrower sense lifelong learning recognises that education is not rigidly divisible into school, further and higher education, but people need the opportunity to move flexibly in and out of it as their circumstances, needs, and personal readiness allow. In its wider sense it recognises that learning does not happen only in formal educational institutions, but informally through families, workplaces, and an increasing variety of media. It is not just individual but socially interactive, not just rational but emotional. In fact it is closely interwoven with all aspects of life and crucial to our sense of self-worth. Our educational identity is a significant part of our personal identity and our ability to shape an acceptable story about ourselves. Theoretical learning becomes incorporated, shakily, into our understanding of the world. Whether it affects the way we act is another matter, but we hope so!

Chapter 9

A Woman's Work is Never Done!

Jo

In terms of opportunity and choices of work, defined as paid employment, we are the fortunate generation. We didn't all start with a full range of choices; acceptable choices for girls were limited when we left school and some of us did not have the opportunity to take advantage of what there were. Nevertheless at times during our working lives, particularly during the 1960s, we were able to use the opportunities then made available and either rectify earlier educational limitations or retrain for more interesting careers. So our work became important to us, personally rewarding as it has traditionally been for professional men.

Estella tells how she first sought work and then further education and training after some years at home as a wife and mother. First she took part-time jobs that fitted in with her children's schooling 'When the chance came to to attend a college of education I gave up paid work and qualified to teach at the age of 43.'

Neither our grandmothers nor our mothers were able to make such choices. For our grandmothers, class was the main determinant as to whether or not they worked after marriage, and together with gender, governed what they did before marrying. Where we have sought and found identity and independence through our careers, our grandmothers and our mothers looked for fulfilment in family life. The definition of work as 'paid employment' shows the extent of the undervaluation of the skilled and important work that women have traditionally performed at home.

Our grandmothers' work

As we saw in the chapter on the family, not all our grandmothers had paid employment, but four of them were widowed while still young women and had to earn their living in any way they could, before the days of state benefits. Jo's middle class paternal grandmother was widowed in 1909 and left with five children. Whether for that reason or another, she left South Yorkshire where the family lived and opened an exclusive 'ladies' dress shop in a suburb on the edge of London. This was the second bereavement in her life, her parents having both been killed in a train crash after which she was made a ward of court. This resulted in money being available, and it could be that that was what she used to open her dress shop.

Another widow, of more working-class origin, was Elizabeth's grandmother, Mary. She was widowed when she was 30 and had three small children. She didn't have the option of opening a shop, and had already moved from her native Ireland to South Wales. She earned the family living by taking in washing, cleaning, home brewing, and selling home-baked bread. 'She was the fastest chicken plucker in the village.' In these ways Mary supplemented her clearly inadequate parish grant. Later on she rented a small house and took in lodgers to help with the costs.

Both Estella's grandmothers were widowed in their 30s, and left with young families. Rebecca, her paternal grandmother, left with four children when her husband died of lung disease, moved from Swansea to London and worked as a cap maker in the tailoring trade, putting two of her children temporarily in an orphanage.

Marj's grandmother worked from home selling vegetables, while Renee's had a market stall. Jo's maternal grandmother, Bertha, somehow acquired training as a tailoress, which she used informally taking orders from neighbours. The more middle-class non-working grandmothers (Patricia and Joan's, and Charmian's), employed domestic help in the home. Jo's paternal grandmother probably also had help with her five children while she ran her shop.

Thus, although there are class differences, especially evident in the paid employment of the widowed grandmothers, gender is also important. The clothing trade was largely the realm of women, whether at the more privileged level of running your own dress shop, or in more lowly ways, as tailoresses or cap makers in small workshops in the Jewish East End of London. Nearly half of our working grandmothers were in the clothing trade at some time or another. Elizabeth's grandmother was engaged in the typical women's work of domestic service, even though she did so as an outworker. Less typical were the traders, whether at home or at a market stall.

Our mothers' work

Diversity continues to be apparent in considering how our mothers earned their living. Even after the First World War when conditions for women supposedly improved, the range of occupations available for women, especially working-class women, was still limited. Marj's mother left home to go into residential domestic service. The son of the house slept next to her bedroom only separated by a thin partition; he threatened to share her bed. 'She was terrified of this, and knew that if she complained she would be blamed or disbelieved and that if he carried out his threat she'd be even further blamed and would lose both her job and her character, so that she would not receive a reference for further jobs.'

The traditional areas of women's work (domestic service, the clothing industry, catering) were also well-represented in the occupations followed by our mothers. Sima's mother was apprenticed to a feather curler at twelve and a half pence a week, Estella's mother was a felling hand. She was very proud of her appearance, Estella recalls: 'She used to boast that she always dressed very smartly, saying that when she took the tram to work she looked more like an office girl than someone who worked in a sweatshop.'

Elizabeth's mother left school at thirteen: 'She worked in a local tavern which the landlady kept open all day to deal with the miners and steel workers coming off shift, and later worked in households and helped with the lodgers her mother took in.' Renee's mother was a cashier in a Lyons tea shop.

This was a generation that saw great changes in the labour market. The general introduction of the newer technologies of the day - typewriters, telephones, cash registers - led to the replacement of male clerks and secretaries with women; Jo's aunt was the first female secretary of the editor of a national newspaper. This replacement while opening up wider areas of employment for women, at the same time downgraded the status of these occupations. The households of male clerks had often employed domestic help, but in our mothers' generation only the more middle-class families among us continued to do so. We trust none of their servants suffered the humiliation described by Marj's mother!

Our work

It is with our own generation's careers that the process of convergence into the middle class started, although our first jobs were still very much influenced by class. It is also at this stage that the age difference between us became significant, affecting whether or not we were still at school or already working at the outbreak of the Second World War; and whether we served in the forces. But for most of us what is striking is the extent to which the decisions about leaving school and about what work we did were made by our families - usually our fathers.

The way we went into our first jobs was very similar to that of our grandmothers and our mothers, although the nature of the jobs was different. That is to say, we made the best we could of what was on offer at the time. The emphasis was on having a job and earning a living rather than on looking for fulfilling careers as such. This was so whether we started work before, during, or soon after the war. Charmian and Joan are exceptions to this. Joan went into nursing, influenced by the needs of war, at far below a living wage. Charmian also made her own decision and trained as a physical education teacher. 'I had a crush on my games teacher and thought all that admiration was just the thing for me - swanning about in shorts and physically active too. Being called up and ordered about was definitely to be avoided.'

Marj also decided for herself, but under the limitation of lack of qualifications and self-confidence. She was very afraid when she left school at fourteen and this fear influenced her choice of job. 'I still felt like a child and was too shy to stand face-to-face and serve people in a shop. I had no skills so I started work in a factory that made brushes and tiny Christmas trees.'

By now, the transformation of offices into largely female domains had made great progress, and for more than half of us the first job was, with varying degrees of willingness, clerical and/or secretarial. Neither Sima nor Elizabeth had been happy to finish studying when they left school. Family pressure was put on Elizabeth after she gained her school certificate: 'I was asked by the school to stay on, but my parents were in conflict about this. My father was the breadwinner and thought it was time I went to work and contributed financially.' Her first job was as a clerical officer in the LCC.

Sima was also frustrated by not being able to study further after she matriculated: 'My brother was a medical student, my sister had just graduated, and I had to enter the civil service and hated it.'

Mary's brother was allowed to continue at school but she, like Patricia, was told without any warning or discussion that she must go out to work. Mary later worked in the careers service and she points out how typical these patterns of girls' transition from school to work were for the period before the service was established. Most of us followed the path dictated by gender, decisions being heavily influenced by fathers, by local opportunities, and by current ideas of respectable work for girls. As the chapter on war shows, the Second World War was also an important factor, even for those of us who continued to higher education.

Renee describes the boredom of her first job doing clerical work at an estate agent's in Ely. Estella, too, was bored with her work in the German Section of the Foreign Office, and Patricia had to leave the happy security of school and plunge into the dreariness of civil service work. Jo's first job was in the office of an aircraft repair factory, manually writing clock cards for the personnel. But she had not enjoyed school, left at fourteen, and was too excited with her perceived adult status in the world of work to be bored. Anyway, she knew that her real ambition was to leave home and get a job in fashion in London.

When she succeeded, and was serving in an Oxford Street store and living in a hostel, she had so little to live on her only pair of shoes became unwearable. 'Having no money for new ones I stole a pair from Marks and Spencers. I was very frightened of getting caught.' She describes how the environment of work in London's West End stores was shaped by class and gender. The conditions and relationships in Marshall and Snellgrove in the 1940s are reminiscent of H.G.Wells *Kipps*.

'The war was still on, so the staff were women and a few older men. The clientele - customers would *not* be an appropriate term - were met at the door by a floor walker in a formal suit with striped trousers who was rather like the person who seats one at posh restaurants these days. He would escort them to the lift or the department if it was on the ground floor. The assistants were quite servile in their attitudes and proud of the eminence of the people they served, as though it somehow reflected glory on them. We juniors were referred to as "little girls" and when we were sent on errands it was "I'll send my little girl over." I was in the haberdashery department and every evening before leaving had to cover the counters and stock with dust sheets; taking them off was my first job in the morning. I was allowed to address and serve customers only when the older assistants were too busy. There was a sort of pecking order about serving customers, the most senior assistant having first pick. I was last.' (Jo was fifteen).

'C&A, my next job, was quite different. The customers were working/lower middle-class women. The assistants were not interested in the customers' status but were very interested in their appearance and smartness, as well as their own. There was still the same sort of pecking order among the assistants but not nearly so sharply defined. The Brook Street hat shop, part of Claridges Hotel, was different from either. The hats were "creations" and largely made to order. I was earning £1 a week and the hats cost twelve or fifteen guineas. When one woman who had had a hat virtually made on her head exclaimed at the cost of a little ribbon, a few feathers and some net, the milliner unpinned it all and gave it to her, saying he would make her a present of them. The customers were society women doing "the season" and we would make hats for Ascot and for royal garden parties. Mothers would bring in their debutante daughters. I was often sorry for them, they seemed so subdued and such little puddings. There was a stock of models which were seldom sold until the end of the season, but were copied in the colours the customers wanted and often with variations on the trimmings. I used to model the models, run up and downstairs to the workroom, brush all the hats every day. I had to wear very high heels and at about eleven in the morning would go into the lavatory and take my shoes off for a while to rest my feet on the tiled floor. Twice a year we would combine with Hardy Amies and hold a fashion show in Claridges' ballroom, which would be set out with fragile gilt chairs.'

Jo was thrilled with the sense of adventure in wartime and post-war London. 'I remember hearing that the Labour victory in the General Election was "a revolution" only to be be disappointed when the tumbrils didn't roll down Oxford Street.'

Others of us who started work in London were quick to take advantage of the excitement it offered. Friendships made at work were also an important counter to the boredom of the actual tasks. Elizabeth comments: 'The work was tedious and gave no opportunity for creativity as it was largely filing records and keeping track of vehicle registrations, changes of address and so on. However the company of others was far from dull. Working in central London and travelling from home every day I felt liberated and part of an exciting new social life, which after school life seemed very sophisticated. The work was easy to manage, leaving time for lively conversation. I frequently stayed on with other colleagues after working hours. I made friends and enjoyed myself during those early years.'

Sima found a way out of her frustration through drama, enrolling in the Unity theatre, which she stayed with even after going to RADA in 1939. In May 1940. with France overrun, she left RADA. As her war work she was sent to learn law costing, to replace one of the men who had hitherto monopolised that profession. Mary and Patricia both escaped into the women's forces where they were able to develop their confidence and interests. Mary had the opportunity to travel to the United States and Germany, and Patricia enjoyed her time in the WRNS. Their experiences are described in the chapter on war.

The end of the war was a period of optimism in Britain: yes, there was a vast task of reconstruction both here and in Europe, but there was the first-ever Labour government with an overall majority. Not quite the revolution Jo expected, but with a clear commitment to solve many outstanding social problems. Importantly, there was a commitment to a policy of full employment. Patricia and Mary left the forces: Mary to a secretarial job and Patricia to train as a teacher. Renee had come back to London and after a spell in the typing pool of the Air Ministry, found a responsible secretarial job in a manufacturing company. Joan moved from nursing to psychiatric social work and later to child guidance. Sima's teaching career continued in spite of onerous family responsibilities.

We nearly all experienced different forms of breakthrough from the 1950s until the early 70s, that marvellous, much maligned time. Patricia, by now working in a girls' school in Southampton, had been asked to take over careers. She explains that: 'Girls careers were taking off. No longer was it a question of only teaching, nursing or office jobs for girls with GCEs. My filing cabinet grew fuller and fuller of brochures and prospectuses.'

In this expanding world after the austerity of the immediate post war period, there was no longer a feeling that simply earning a living was enough; jobs were to be fulfilling and give personal satisfaction. For some of us this involved retraining and for others the resumption of education, helped by the generous grant arrangements of the time. There were also other personal factors involved: Jo's marriage was in trouble and Elizabeth had finished an important relationship. We were from now on converging towards middle class professional careers. The qualifications we achieved and the way we achieved them have been chronicled in the chapter on education.

Elizabeth worked with the Family Welfare Association and from 1971 the probation service. 'It was completely different from my previous experience. The job was demanding, never the same, involving face-to-face contact with people from all walks of life who had problems ranging from the trivial to the desperately serious. Many were socially disadvantaged. The work called for patience, good communication skills, the ability to find and absorb information quickly, and clarity of thought. There was nothing like the mechanical day-to-day experience of my previous work. I found it absorbing, stimulating and rewarding. In short I loved it.'

Estella, as we have already seen, went into teaching. Sima also became a teacher, first in a 'sink' school, then in remedial work and later to work with so-called 'educationally subnormal' and 'maladjusted' children. Renee differed from the rest of us in that she had gone to live in Norway, where, after a period at home with her children, she, too resumed work. She was trained by her employers - a trade union bank - to be a loan consultant.

The important thing about these moves is that they were not only economically driven. We had mostly moved on from just earning our living, in fact some of us were financially secure and could have stayed at home devoting ourselves to our families. But for a variety of reasons we decided to take advantage of the expanding opportunities of the time. The same circumstances that gave us the opportunity to retrain and/or complete our education, also provided jobs for us to take up when we were qualified. Thus, Mary went into the recently established careers service and Jo was able to work in the Open University, which hadn't existed during the earlier part of her working life. This atmosphere of expansion, the grants, and the new opportunities, no longer exist in the same way. The development of electronic communications has brought new careers such as those in information technology, but working conditions have hardened into insecurity. We have been fortunate in the timing of our working lives. A combination of social and economic factors has given us opportunities that were not available to our grandmothers or our mothers, enabling us to consider issues that were not on their agendas: the issues of personal satisfaction and fulfilment through our work.

Our experiences of women's work in the post-war period
For those who were married and had children there was a price to pay for these opportunities. Charmian says 'I felt thankful to be in a job with flexible hours (teaching in higher education) that could be fitted round children and the limited hours of au pair girls. I should have hated the sort of way career women with families now have to juggle expensive nannies, children's commitments and so on - and not being there in school holidays; though of course I suffered the usual guilt about not doing my work properly. The children came first and I doubt if I would have survived the present competitive and insecure academic environment.'

Joan met this problem by taking eight years off work when her children were small and was then able to start back part-time and build up gradually. She was married to an academic who had already established his reputation and was able to arrange his hours to be at home when her children arrived from school. Child guidance is not a male dominated field, her hours were flexible, and her clinic within walking distance of her home. These circumstances illustrate the importance of favourable conditions for women to develop a successful career.

It has been said that the 1950s was a low point for women. Perhaps this view is based on the fact that there was so much pressure for them to return to the home as men left the forces. Also traditional attitudes to girls' careers had not changed much even by the 1970s, as Mary found when she worked in the careers service. She writes: 'I had had no previous experience of dealing with teenagers since I had no children of my own and had never been a teacher. So I had a lot to learn. I brought to my work my own interest in feminism, and I was keen to find out what the new generation of girl school leavers was thinking about.

'I found in general that the girls were both more mature and more realistic than the boys, and sometimes than their parents, who might have aspirations beyond their daughters' achievements, or alternatively under-estimate them. The problems of Asian girls always worried me a great deal. If they couldn't continue in full-time education they were frequently faced with a marriage arranged by their parents with a man they had never met, so it was doubly important to find them a college place if possible.

'I always tried hard to encourage bright girls to be ambitious and would often suggest an occupation which might suit them very well, if only they would take a training scheme first. Girls were more willing to consider this than boys, and at the time, Crawley where I worked, was among the highest employment areas in the country so that successful training would almost always lead to a job. I often had to persuade the parents of clever children that they should be looking towards A levels and higher education, especially if everyone in the family had left education at sixteen or younger. Some of them were particularly doubtful with regard to their daughters because they had come to the interview sure that they didn't want a career, "just a nice little job until she gets married and starts a family". I could hardly bear those parents who saw their daughters as "walking wombs" rather than as individuals with real choices available to them.

'Of course most of the girls finished up in offices or shops or catering, just as most of the boys started their working lives in engineering or building or warehousing. Work was very gender segregated then, and even after the Sexual Discrimination Act of 1975 some employers were determined to discriminate. If one quoted the law to them they would say things like "I will interview as many girls as you send for the job but I shall take a boy". That left the careers service in a very invidious position because if we sent girls we were wasting their time and their hopes; if we only sent boys we were colluding with the employers against the law. We usually refused to accept such vacancies.

'I did as much as I could in the cause of equal opportunities, and sometimes got into hot water with the head of the County Careers Service, but gender segregation was mostly accepted by parents, employers and young people alike, and the law was meanwhile being ignored.'

154

Work place attitudes to women did not change either. Jo found the Open University which she joined in the early 1970s, a complete contrast to working in shops, but there were still gender issues around. Here is her perspective on this experience: 'There are no students on campus so staff relationships could be very intense. It was a largely male environment. Academic women tended to be invisible, secretaries were treated without any respect, their rooms were barged into, their conversations interrupted. There was a contractual obligation to attend summer school, but I commuted mine to unpaid tutoring on the courses I'd been involved with. Summer school was quite difficult for female staff. The male staff were often concerned to use their status to sleep with the more attractive female students. They wanted to be polite to female colleagues but not too friendly as they didn't want us to cramp their style - especially if we were not interested in sleeping with them.'

Patricia was appointed in the 1960s as deputy head of a mixed secondary school. 'In those days there were separate staff rooms for men and women and at first the men's staff room was a no-go area for me. Mostly they were good colleagues, but if I got across one of them the cry would be "You only got the job because you are a woman!" I found that in teaching mixed classes I had to be careful to include the girls as they tended to sit back and let the boys answer all the questions. I was always able to make decisions I knew my male head would honour, but I came across a woman head of a mixed school who prefaced all her remarks with "I'll have to consult the men". It struck me that in her job you had to be either very peculiar or very brilliant. I didn't see myself as either of those things so I decided to restrict my applications for headships to girls' schools.'

It is also true that women were still employed on far from equal terms with men. Equal pay for teachers and civil servants was not agreed until 1955 and even then it came in stages over seven years. Patricia remembers: 'Each April when the pay slips arrived we did a spontaneous dance in the staff room, celebrating the news that we were worth yet another seventh of a man.' The Sex Discrimination Act and the Equal Opportunites Commission were not established until 1975, and most of us now we are retired, suffer from diminished pension entitlement because of the way we have moved in and out of work. It is also true that we have all worked in areas regarded as women's work or that have become women's work: the caring professions: counselling, probation, education, dealing with 'difficult' children. Perhaps now we would have chosen a wider range; but how far would we find attitudes at work changed?

Conclusion

The enormous changes in women's work opportunities between our three generations is illustrated by the cases where we know the paid work of our grandmothers and mothers as well as ourselves. Our grandmothers and mothers, if they worked at all, took whatever was at hand to supplement the family income, and often there was no clear division between their domestic and paid work. The situation for our mothers was similar to that of our grandmothers, and the contrast is between our mothers and ourselves, and again between our first jobs and our final ones.

Nearly all of us have had fulfilling working lives, and some have managed to reach senior positions in our professions although our careers were not started until we were quite mature. So in the long term we feel we were the fortunate generation. We were lucky to develop our working lives in the interlude between the hardships and lack of opportunity of our foremothers, and the new insecurity of short-term contracts and inadequately supported higher education suffered by many of the current working population.

Chapter 10

The Experience of War

Mary and Sima

Modern war is a major disruption in our expected patterns of life. It casts a shadow of anxiety and disaster but has also opened up opportunities, particularly for women. Historians have debated the long-term effects of war on women's lives, but however much opportunities are curtailed after war is finished, a legacy persists. Memories of war continue to colour our outlook on life, particularly if we suffer it at a crucial time in our development, which was the case for our grandmothers, our mothers, and ourselves. Our family life, education and paid work were all cut across by the disruption of war; sadness and death, and the expansion of experience are all apparent in our stories.

THE FIRST WORLD WAR
.
Jo remembers her mother telling how she was on a seaside holiday as a child in August 1914. They watched the fleet sail by, and her father said: 'This means war'.

Although women became involved in many aspects of the war effort, at first the government had been reluctant to accept their offers to help. This changed because of the demand for munitions and the shortage of labour created by the conscription of men, which was introduced in 1916. Women were not actually conscripted for any form of war service, but many began work in munitions and other factories as the men were called up, often leaving women's traditional low paid occupations, such as domestic service. Married women, especially those with children, were not expected to do war work, though some did.

During the course of the war women worked on buses, trams and the railways, in munitions and in engineering. They became bank and civil service clerks, they joined the Women's Land Army, and the women's auxiliary services of the Army and the Navy; they went to France as nurses or in Voluntary Aid Detachments (VADs) and drove ambulances as members of the First Aid Nursing Yeomanry (FANY). The number of women in these uniformed forces was small, around 60,000 altogether, according to the *Statistical Digest of the War* (HMSO), and fears were expressed of a rising tide of immorality because of women working long hours alongside men, travelling to and from work at night and mixing with soldiers in barracks. Women in uniform were suspected of every kind of sexual transgression, from vampishness and sluttishness to lesbianism.

The majority of our group have little or no knowledge of our parents' experiences or activities during the First World War. Mary says that her parents lived in London throughout. Her father's occupation was reserved by his employers, so he was never called up. She believes he was given white feathers in the street because he was not in uniform. Elizabeth's mother lived with her family in the Welsh village which was their home, while her father, who was only sixteen, volunteered for the army and lied about his age; she believes he wanted to escape a harsh and unaffectionate home. He spent four years in the trenches and survived despite the terrible casualties. By the end of the war he was one of only a very small number left in the Welsh Fusiliers. His experiences damaged him emotionally for years after. Jo's father, similarly lied about his age in order to enlist in 1918, was sent to Archangel in terrible conditions and this ruined his health without qualifying him for a pension. Both Elizabeth's and Jo's mothers must have suffered the long-term burden of their husbands' shattered lives.

Irene was born in 1917, her parents having married the year before. Her father served in the German army as a Hussar and her mother followed him with her baby to be near his training camp, working as a Red Cross nurse. It is strange to think how similar is this wartime life to that of Charmian's parents in England. Charmian's father served in the Navy and spent some time based in Dover where her mother lived in lodgings to be near him. Like Irene's mother she nursed, as a VAD.

The only extensive account we have of First World War domestic life comes from the archives of Charmian's family letters. Charmian herself has selected those quoted and written a linking commentary. They give a vivid picture of middle-class wartime life on the edge of London, and of the voluntary work of various kinds done as contributions to the war effort. The writer is Charmian's maternal grandmother Margaret, nick-named Peg, and the letters were to her brothers and sisters.

Peg's family letters

In *1914* she wrote: 'It is no use writing about the war. It is a nightmare upsetting the whole world and all one's previous ideas about the Germans. I cannot but believe they will be beaten in the end, but they are proud and determined and it will be a bitter struggle. But I must get on with the socks!

January 1915. Tea and bring your knitting is the new formula. I boldly took mine to Mrs. Hicks' At Home Day. The other people hadn't; perhaps they will next time. A certain young lady who took hers to the Village Hall tea said: "Oh! I couldn't waste all this time; I have three regiments to provide with socks." Apparently there was such an outbreak of patriotic knitting that the War Office stated it had enough socks, in an attempt to regulate the supply.

Early 1915. 'Gallipoli may be pleasanter than Flanders but the fighting is very stiff there now. Our (family) boys have been fortunate so far. I can hardly hope they will all come through safely so I will not think of it. One must always be prepared for bad news. It will be a doleful winter for them if they remain in exposed Gallipoli. The winds are cutting. We've just received a telegram to say that Ray has landed. He and Evelyn [Charmian's aunt] are thinking of getting married. He would like a happy time with her before going off again. And everyone is doing it. There's the rub. They meant to wait till after the war.'

The weddings in the family were part of a national trend. As the casualty lists mounted, so did the marriage rate. According to the Tatler, the attitude was: 'Better to be married a minute than die an old maid.' Some didn't wait to be married; there was controversy in 1915 because of record numbers of illegitimate births. Many condemned the mothers, others praised them for their contribution to the welfare of the troops.

The work of middle-class women is recorded in Peg's letters in several ways besides the mania for sock knitting. In *August 1914* a war refugee committee had been formed and found accommodation for 100,000 Belgian refugees. Peg and other women in Potters Bar raised money and helped to settle a family of Belgians in an empty post office building. Peg writes: 'There are now 60 people contributing in some way, mostly one shilling a week, some five shillings, a few sixpence. The cottages were ready ten days after the meeting. The landlady had them repapered and repaired and we made curtains, had linoleum laid in the living rooms, and on a certain day all the promised furniture was fetched by a coal cart and by Boy Scouts with their handcart.'

Daisy, Charmian's mother, and Peg's other two daughters, enrolled to help in a new local hospital in a private house. Peg writes: 'For a long time they have been going to practices of bedmaking, bandaging, etc. and lessons on invalid cookery. It will be a wonderful band of inexperienced nurses, so we'll hope the patients will be good and not have relapses while here.'

Peg reports on *2 May 1915*: 'One of the most interesting events at the council meeting was an address by a policewoman. Two of them came. They looked like naval officers, dressed in neat navy blue with a few brass buttons and peaked caps. Their bearing was grave and they saluted the Chair as they reached the platform. It was a Miss Dawson, who spoke, like a college girl, fluently and to the point. They are not in patrols, but are another movement, at present voluntary, hoping to prove their usefulness and get Government recognition later on. Miss Dawson said there are 30 or 40 of them, who have been trained in London and are scattered round various towns. She spoke earnestly of the need for more women to join.'

As domestic servants left their jobs for factory and other war work, often better paid and offering more freedom, Peg's family found themselves doing unaccustomed tasks in the home: 'I make beds, dust and sweep. There are only three of us at home and we live very simply'.

Three Zeppelins were shot down in the area in 1916 and these seem to have been viewed by the family as a kind of firework display. 'It was a still night, clear to the north but misty towards London. Poking my head out of the window I beheld to the left a golden Zep being peppered with shells. We congregated in the dining room and watched from behind the thick curtains. The Zep was turning about, trying to escape. It looked like a great shining fish in the air. At one time it seemed perpendicular. Then it began to come our way and dropped a bomb that shook the house and made the air hit our faces. So we adjourned to the back passage, where the walls are thick and no glass could hurt us. No sooner had we done so when a glare shone through the back door glass panels. "Its burning!" we cried, and hurried back to the window to see it falling in flames. It looked as if it might fall on to the house but really fell in a field behind the church. Next morning we saw its crumpled remains hanging on a tree. The field, where the Zep is, is guarded by lots of soldiers and policemen. Strangers are coming in from round about. They say the commander was nearly saved; he was holding on and hanging down till within some way off the ground he let go and was killed. What a horrible fate the Germans send the Zep crews to! Busy searchlights continued to examine the sky till after three in the morning.'

In *February 1917*, in a letter written after the death of her eldest son, Peg writes: 'You won't expect much of a letter from me this month, but we mustn't forget the living in thinking of our dead. Daisy had gone to Dover to find new rooms, leaving baby in my care when the dreaded telegram came. The helpless little life needing our care was really a blessing though it seemed impossible at first to think of it.'

160

Food shortages affected this family, as all others. In *January 1918*, Peg wrote: 'We are not yet reduced to dormouse pie or cockroach stew. Butter has been unobtainable since Christmas, but as Roy [her son-in-law] is living on a farm he has been able to send half a pound most weeks. We have had our first experience of standing in a queue for meat for one hour. The wind was very cold. Ration cards have produced queues, there never used to be any before. The butcher will no longer deliver or send for orders.'

And after the death of her second son on *28 April 1918* she wrote: 'He had a soldier's funeral. The cemetery is on a sunny hill where larks sing. I feel a bit stupefied, after the unexpected blow. Marjorie (his widow) hopes to become a nurse. All her dreams are shattered.'

Four months later Peg's son-in-law was killed.' The old times have gone, leaving sweet memories. Hardly one of the young men who were happy here is left. Now we must draw close to those of us that remain and give thanks for the babies that promise a new life.'

So this family was denuded of nearly all its young men as were so many other families. But Peg kept on writing her monthly letters, maintaining continuity in spite of catastrophe. She describes how difficult it was to rejoice at the Armistice in November 1918 when they had 'no one to come home.'

Although the war transformed (temporarily) traditional attitudes to women's work, many trade unions were opposed to women's involvement in skilled jobs, hitherto the preserve of men. Socialist feminists predicted that after the war there would be an adverse reaction to the advances made by women, and this in fact, came about. However, more opportunities were opened up for middle-class women, and one of these was political. Peg qualified to vote for the first time, under the 1918 Representation of the People Act, which enfranchised most women over 30. On *31 March 1918* she wrote: 'Miss Cameron told us our duty as voters and incidentally that we must see that we are in the register by 15th April, otherwise we mightn't get down.'

Her voting intentions were largely determined by her active involvement in the British Women's Temperance Association. 'Now the elections are coming. If my vote is really registered it will be given to Mrs. McEwen. She will support the coalition, still keeping her Liberal principles, and believes in dealing with the liquor trade by local option. Apparently state purchase is expected by the Trade because all the pubs are being done up and repainted. So it behoves us to know our candidate's standpoint. I shall therefore vote for the lady. She is a good one and her election address is business-like and clear. She has worked at baby welfare and is President of the Women's Liberal Association at Enfield.'

Even before the war ended, women began to be dismissed from the labour force. As early as February 1918 some 8,000 women munitions workers had been dismissed, and the National Federation of Women Workers began to think that so far as women were concerned something like demobilisation had begun. By March, the *New Statesman* spoke of 10-20,000 sacked women, though at this stage there were still openings for them in the auxiliary service and the Women's Land Army. But by November 1919, three-quarters of a million women war workers had been laid off, and there was exceptionally high female unemployment. In spite of improved political rights most women were expected and pressed to return to their homes and domestic life. Very quickly, praise for wartime women workers gave way to attacks on women who persisted in working or tried to claim dole money. The workings of the national insurance acts and of the dole offices drove many women out of the work force altogether, and marriage bars in the professions made sure that only single women could engage in them. This marriage bar continued until after the Second World War, when many of us were embarking on working life.

THE SECOND WORLD WAR

When the war started in September 1939 the call up of men began almost immediately, and a little later of women too. For women, being called up did not necessarily mean joining the women's services, as Sima's experience shows. Women were conscripted to do all kinds of essential work, and there was some scope for choice between for instance the services, munition and other factories, nursing, or the Women's Land Army. Some women were sent reluctantly to join the women's services, but for others, such as Mary and Patricia, it was a liberation from the restrictions of their lives.

Evacuation of children from areas judged at risk from bombing also began immediately, and was often traumatic for both evacuees and host families. Renee and Estella who were evacuated at the outbreak of war, give vivid descriptions of their experiences.

Food rationing was introduced at once, and our mothers were faced with the problems of adapting recipes and finding alternatives to ingredients no longer available. Charmian developed an aversion to margarine which has remained with her ever since! Shopping involved much queuing for scarce items and taking advantage of local grapevines about availability. Clothing coupons were introduced and some brilliantly creative redesigning and sewing had to be done, making use of parachute silk as Patricia describes.

The blackout was strict and even a glimmer of light brought the street wardens to the door. Going out after dark was difficult and at first much public entertainment was discontinued especially in heavily populated areas, but as the expected heavy bombing did not happen immediately (1939-1940 was the period of the 'phony war'), it was gradually restored. Sima describes how small theatres such as Unity managed to keep going.

As was to be expected, everyone in our group experienced some disruption from the war but our experiences varied according to our age at the time. In 1939 Elizabeth and Marj were still primary school children whereas Irene had just arrived from Germany as a refugee in her early 20s. The majority of us were in our late teens, a crucially formative time when decisions about the future have to be made. Apart from Irene, only two of us, Mary and Sima had already left school and were established in jobs, and they were still living with their families. The rest of us were still at school.

For Jo, the immediate impact of the war was the employment of both her parents. Her father managed a newspaper shop and when he was called up to an 'essential' job her mother took it over so that they could stay in the attached flat. They lived near Woking in Surrey which was on the bombers' flight path so they slept under the stairs. This was an evacuation area and Jo became friendly with evacuees who came to her school. Eventually her mother couldn't retain the job and they were billeted on an old countryman in a very primitive cottage. 'I don't think he knew what had hit him! I guess it was the chaos of evacuees and wartime that enabled my mother to shuffle us around between different schools the way she did.' She goes on: 'When I left school the war was still on and I went to the Labour Exchange for work, and was sent to an aircraft repair factory. I was thrilled to be doing war work. The actual task was quite boring. I had to write out the weekly clock cards of the staff, keep them sorted into sections, and see that they were distributed at the end of each week to the part of the aerodrome where they would be needed.'

Estella vividly remembers the night of the fire raids that lit up the centre of London on December 19th 1941: 'The night sky was red and the pungent smell of burning pervaded the house. The next morning the front path was an inch deep in ashes even though we lived quite a long way from Central London.'

Charmian lived in a 'neutral' zone, which meant evacuees were neither sent away nor received. She recalls that the war put a huge burden on her mother. 'We had a large house in which every room was occupied by essential workers billeted on us; nurses in the local hospital and a member of the Intelligence Service. My sister and her baby came home while her husband was away in the Navy, and friends of my brother came on leave. A Jewish refugee boy also lived with us. There were usually about twelve people living in the house and my mother juggled with all the ration books and the cooking. There were mass washing-up sessions when we all sang songs. The house was a focus for friends, relations and those needing a home. I was never aware of this at the time, but my mother must have been haunted by the fear that she would lose her two sons and her son-in-law as she had lost her two brothers and a brother-in-law in the First World War.'

She adds: 'The war was the context for the coming together of sections of the population who had never had any contact before: country and city dwellers, different social classes. While I was in the sixth form I went fruit picking to help the war effort. We spent hours crouching down picking, and hours on a fruit canning production line in a factory, steering cans along a conveyor belt. I was bored stiff, found it very tiring and the conditions bad. I was shocked to discover that some people did this sort of work for a living. I later found potato picking in Cornwall an equally painful experience.'

Estella's family lived in South Tottenham, London. Their father worked in the clothing trade, and he also became a street warden, and various items of equipment were stored in their tiny hall. Their front room contained a large Morrison shelter in which her parents slept during air raids. One night in September 1940, her heavily pregnant mother decided that they would be better off sheltering in the crypt of a local church. During that time she went into labour, but the air raid warden was able to stop an ambulance and she was taken to the Salvation Army Mothers' Hospital in Clapton, where her youngest son was born. Her mother received food supplements for the baby, concentrated orange juice, cod liver oil, the occasional fresh egg, and the even rarer orange.

Evacuation

Four of us were evacuated. Elizabeth, still a little girl of seven, was the most fortunate. She was sent to live with her grandmother in the village in South Wales from which her parents had come. She says: 'I spent seven happy years with my grandmother and we became very close. My mother's sister lived nearby with her large family and I was seen as a member of this family as well as enjoying the privilege of having my grandmother all to myself. My parents and sister visited me regularly throughout. I attended a local Catholic school and from there obtained a scholarship to the nearby grammar school.

'Life in the village was relatively peaceful after London, but the war touched many lives, often tragically. There were several nearby munitions factories and these transformed local women's lives in a liberating way. My aunt's daughters worked in the factories, and two were sent to High Wycombe to do munitions there. One of my male cousins was taken prisoner in Germany; another deserted from the army and was on the run for some time before capture and imprisonment.

'On the whole we were well fed as the local farms helped out with extra butter, eggs and milk (at a price). Looking back, I think the war years were a good turning point for me as I enjoyed living with my grandmother and having her complete attention. We lived a peaceful life with no friction, which was not the case in my own home in London. I believe this gave another dimension to my life, which proved enriching and stabilising.'

Renee aged fifteen, was evacuated with her brothers and sisters to a small town near Cambridge at the beginning of the war. She was placed in a large house with servants: 'the two ladies kept to their part of the house and we had to live with the servants.' She got her first typing job in the same town, but after nine weeks of boredom she returned to London, and got a job with chartered accountants. Her year was not called up but she felt she should be doing something for the war effort so she joined the Air Ministry, only to sit in a typing pool for the rest of the war. The Air Ministry staff were forced to stay on after the war, but Renee told them she was going abroad and so was able to leave.

Estella, at the age of thirteen, was also evacuated with her brother. By the end of the war she had lived in eight different billets: 'A day or two after the declaration of war we were all transported to the market town of Bishops Stortford, where we were deposited in a large church hall. We were on show to local townsfolk, and people came in and chose their evacuees to take home with them. A few children, mostly those with siblings of the other sex, were left unchosen at the end of this exercise. My younger brother and I were taken off by car and during the journey I heard the driver say: "I'm taking children who don't want to go to people who don't want to have them." No truer words were ever spoken!

'We arrived at a typical thirties house on the outskirts of the town. it looked like those houses so beautifully advertised by the estate agents of the day. Inside, the house was immaculately furnished. The occupants' hearts must have sunk when they saw us, not with pity, but with dismay. We had been thrust upon them because they had a three-bedroom house and only one baby daughter. I had no idea how to look after myself, let alone a young brother, and I think the couple's experience with children only extended to their little daughter.

'My brother and I became scruffier and possibly dirtier. The few clothes we had in our rucksacks may (or may not) have been washed and ironed. I know that I certainly did nothing about them. My mother and father visited us at the beginning of our stay and were probably much impressed by that house, so spick and span. Eventually we were discovered to have nits - I can't remember ever washing my hair - and no doubt this was the final straw for our foster parents. Who can really blame them? We had to leave.

'Had I been a spoilt child? I had always relied completely on my mother to keep me cleanly clothed and washed. I felt ashamed and humiliated by my condition, as well as bewildered. Anyway, I wrote home saying that I could no longer look after my brother, and my father came to take him back to London. I said nothing about the nits.

'I was then sent to what was known as a half-way house. The weather was particularly severe that winter and the house was dilapidated, with no lights (candles only) scarcely furnished and with no heating. There was a small number of children there, together with a couple of mothers. We slept on makeshift palliasses and camp-beds, and I slept in my clothes; I have never felt so cold in my life. Luckily this accommodation was only for one night, and the next day I was sent, together with five other girls from my school, to live in a large house near the centre of the town.

'Our new foster-mother (Miss S.) had been in service with some local gentry, and on leaving their employ she had rented this house. With the help of the local billeting officer she had managed to furnish it with second-hand furniture. She received 7s.6d per child for our upkeep. She was a maiden lady in her early 50s and very religious. She had a cheerful personality and was a real country woman growing as many vegetables and fruits in her small garden as possible. We girls enjoyed living there, in spite of having to attend church three times every Sunday.'

When Miss S. let one of the rooms to two young soldiers, Estella and her friends had to move yet again, this time to a Miss W. who was 'very aware of a person's place in society, and the evacuees were definitely on a low level. We were not allowed to sit on the good chairs and when her family came we had to sit at the lower end of the table. We never had our butter ration; margarine was good enough for us, and we were always given only two slices of bread each (it wasn't rationed). Thank goodness for our midday meals at the local British Restaurant.

'One day, one of us rashly left an unsealed letter to her mother on the sideboard. Mrs. W. just peeped inside to make sure who it was for and happened to notice that she herself was described as "the old dragon" amongst other uncomplimentary references. Naturally, she found it impossible to give houseroom to such ungrateful low lives as us; so off we went again.'

After she had matriculated Estella found herself in another billet with a Mrs. H. 'She was a well-provided-for widow who lived in a "nice" house in one of the "nicer" parts of the town. She was a stickler for right and proper behaviour; a place for everything and everything in its place. She was frugal but fair. We always got our proper rations plus little extras when she did some baking, and she was a keen needlewoman, making us small items like embroidered face flannels; she could get four out of a new terry towelling nappy. She was houseproud and I was once told off quite harshly for not putting the wet bathmat over the edge of the bath after I'd finished using it, especially as she had discovered a few small puddles on the floor. Our bedtime (homework finished or not) was 9.30 pm except for one day a week when we went to the cinema. On rare occasions she would invite us into her lounge to listen to some of her collection of Gilbert and Sullivan records.

'My friend and I were aged seventeen and eighteen by then, and we stayed with her for two years while studying for and taking the higher schools certificate. Maybe she was a bit of a martinet but she looked after us, and provided ideal conditions for us to study. At the end of our stay with Mrs. H. we returned home to London, where we learned that our exam results were OK and both of us went to University College, London.'

Estella seems to have survived these varied living conditions with her usual resilience.

Charmian was evacuated when she went to college. She says: 'I spent one year in the sixth form but if I had stayed longer I would have been called up for the women's forces. The prospect of this was a liberation for some of our group but for me it was a fate to be avoided at all costs: all that regimentation and communal living! I went instead to a physical education college.

'The college was evacuated to Cornwall and so no longer had the advantage of purpose-built facilities. We lived in summer hotels on a windy headland outside Newquay. There was no winter heating and I remember writing essays in my room wrapped in a rug, wearing gloves and with a hot water bottle on my knees. We did gymnastics in a converted garage, danced in an orphanage hall, and swam in the freezing cold harbour. We played hockey on the golf course, and did teaching practice in village schools and evacuated schools, cycling between different venues.

'We needed a lot of specialist clothing and we were allowed to wear our old school uniforms at the beginning because rationing made it difficult to get a lot of new clothes. However, gradually we acquired dance tunics, gym wear, games shorts, and big blue cloaks to fling over them in between sessions. We were constantly changing from gym gear to dance wear to games shorts, and woe betide anyone who turned up in the wrong uniform. It was a much more regimented life than I had experienced before, a bit like being in the forces after all! The war conditions added a lot of pressure to what would have been a rigorous training anyway.

'We students helped with the reception of evacuees arriving in Newquay. Some of the children and babies were inadequately dressed and suffered from skin complaints like impetigo. They seemed undernourished, smelt of urine, and their mothers were bewildered after the long journey to a strange place. It was my first encounter with the inner city poor.

'This experience and that of fruit picking while I was still at school, were significant for my slowly developing realisation that Britain was a socially divided society and I was a privileged member of it. No tragedy affected my family as it did my mother's in the first war, but seeing the condition of some evacuees, hearing and reading about the occupation of Europe and the deaths of millions in concentration camps, helped me to realise I had been living a charmed and sheltered life.'

Patricia, the same age as Charmian, had her education abruptly terminated. She was already in the sixth form when she was suddenly told to go straight home as her father had found her a job. This turned out to be in the civil service, which she had previously considered as a career, but now found was much too boring. She remembers that her family (like Elizabeth's) were able to get extra food by driving out to country farms and buying eggs for storage in waterglass. The problem of clothes rationing was partly solved by making underclothes out of parachute silk.

Several of us had personal experience of bombing, though none of us was seriously injured. Sima who stayed in London throughout the war, had two bad experiences. First the block of flats where she lived had a direct hit from a doodle-bug. She was very shaken and covered with glass and plaster, but otherwise all right. She says others were not so lucky and two residents were killed. When the V2s started she had another narrow escape. 'Our office was only about 100 yards from Smithfield market and a friend and I would meet there before work to buy some offal as this was not on ration. On that particular morning as we met, a bomb fell and my friend was sucked into the blast and I was blown in the other direction. She was very badly hurt and was in hospital for many weeks; I was bruised and battered and shocked but in one piece.'

Mary's office in central Birmingham was completely destroyed one night when the bombers were particularly active. She arrived for work the next morning to find the place was unrecognisable and all the staff were sent home. New premises were quickly found but involved a long and difficult journey by bus. Because she suffered from travel sickness Mary decided to cycle to work even though it was an hour's ride. Her parents disapproved because they thought it might be dangerous in the blackout, but she had no problems.

Estella says that towards the end of the war when her middle brother had returned to live at home, a rocket bomb landed very close to his primary school. He was in the school hall with the other second dinner service children and they were blown about by the blast and most of them suffered cuts and bruises. But the first dinner service children were in the playground and some of them were killed.

Other changes in our lives

Two of our group gave up opportunities for higher education in order to work for the war effort. Joan had hoped to go to university but the war had caused a reduction in the number of places. She decided to do something constructive in the face of all the destruction and enrolled as a student nurse at the Liverpool Children's Hospital. Bombing of Liverpool was severe and they had to move patients to the cellars and sleep there themselves. After a bad night, she would find her way through debris and fire hoses to let her sister know that she was all right. Joan says: 'After qualifying I moved on in 1943 to do general training at the Radcliffe Infirmary in Oxford. We had D-day casualties flown direct to us in 1944. I remember a colleague who lost all her possessions when a fire-bomb hit the nurses' home. She told me how liberating it was to lose one's possessions but to survive oneself! Nursing was a protected occupation, so I was not allowed to change from it.'

Sima was 21 when the war started. She had just left the civil service which she hated, to attend the Royal Academy of Dramatic Art. She was a member of Unity Theatre, often working there in the evenings. She writes: 'With the rise of fascism and the Spanish Civil War, the voice of protest was sounded in many parts of the world. In England in 1935 Unity Theatre was founded by a group of left wing people in the arts. First shows were put on in various halls; but in 1936 the theatre acquired its own premises. We had the support of many well-known people in the fields of drama and music, although no-one was paid for their work. Later, with public support, we built our own real theatre very near the Working Men's College where our branch of the U3A has its home. For one play we put on, Paul Robeson turned down a West End part to play with us amateurs. The theatre grew from strength to strength, always having a show on at the theatre as well as having a large mobile outside show group. The theatre never closed during the war.

'My work in the theatre at night and RADA complemented each other, but by the time France had been overrun I became very uncomfortable as a student and felt I must do something else, so I left RADA and was called up. I said I did not want to leave London, but would do whatever was wanted there.

'The first job I was sent to was a new office set up to deal with air raid casualty figures. Each day we would get reports of the number of bodies, or bits of bodies, that had been found and where and when. It all had to be listed and added up. Casualty figures were published, but far less than our figures showed. However, after two weeks the director discovered that I knew no shorthand or typing, and I was released.'

Shortly after, Sima was sent to a big firm of solicitors in Thaivies Inn, to learn law costing in order to replace their law coster who was being called up. She had to read solidly for six months to learn the job, and faced initial suspicion because she was a woman, but presented many bills before the war ended. She was the first woman ever to do the job of law costing.

'19 December 1941 was the date of the big fire raid on central London. Thaivies Inn went up in flames, together with most of the Inns of Court. Only St. Pauls still stood there proudly, but it was really heartbreaking to see what had happened. Our building had stood for many centuries and we lost documents going back hundreds of years.

'At this time at Unity Theatre, we were in trouble because we were losing our casts almost as soon as they had been rehearsed. So I approached the London County Council and they agreed we could run a school for our theatre under their auspices. Each term we sent newly trained players to Unity Theatre and to the outside show groups which took shows to air raid shelters, factories, and the Underground. We would perform until two or three in the morning and then go to Lyons Corner House basement on the corner of Tottenham Court Road and have soup, rolls and tea until the first tube trains ran. Then we'd go home for a wash and change, short rest, and back to work. Travelling by bus during the blitz was an adventure, as we never knew if the bus would get there. Roads were closed as craters opened up, and passengers often directed the drivers down side roads to rejoin their routes. Bus drivers were real heroes during the blitz.

'And so we survived. We worked very hard: nine till five in the office, then a rush to prepare whatever meal we could manage, and then back in the evening, either to run a class or work in the theatre. We slept when we could, ate when we could, and still managed to have good times and many laughs.'

When Irene's future husband arrived in England, he immediately put his name down for the army in case of war. He was called up to the Pioneer Corps, as were so many refugees, but later transferred to the Intelligence Service. He survived Dunkirk, and after he returned they got married at 48 hours notice on his first leave. Irene says: 'I was able to join my husband and travelled wherever his company went. Wherever we went I did some kind of war work. Amongst other jobs, I ironed pilot's gloves and inspected mosquito nets. I always found my fellow workers very friendly in all the different jobs, and staff very helpful. I managed very well with rationing, as there was usually a nearby British Restaurant (these were specially set up to provide cheap meals and meant one could save one's rations), and I got occasional parcels from my mother and sister in America.

'I had lots of funny experiences. In one village in Wales my husband was not allowed into the house as I alone had rented the room. In another, whenever the landlady left the house, her brother and I had to leave as well. Once she went out for the whole day and it was pouring with rain and there was nowhere to go in that small place.'

Serving in the forces

Only two of us actually served in the women's services. Three of us were too young, two were in higher education, and others found suitable 'reserved' work. Patricia and Mary however were both pleased to escape from their boring office jobs.

Patricia joined the Women's Royal Naval Service which she chose because she thought it the most glamorous. She describes the WRNS as a very small service, with one central reception point in North London. New recruits were sent there for four weeks. Their tasks included washing up, scrubbing decks and polishing floors (for the first time in her life). The induction was like going to a new school, with lectures on uniform differences in the whole Royal Navy. There was lots of squad drill. They had a drum and fife band, the only one in the country, in which Patricia played the fife; the band accompanied them on church parades.

They were given some choice of trades and she chose to be a wireless telegrapher, a small secret group. The training took six months after which she was posted to Scarborough, where she served for the rest of the war. They worked underground, and were divided into four watches rotating through the day and night. The pay was fourteen shillings a fortnight. Patricia remembers the night she came off watch to find the street lights were on. The war was over.

Mary had a wonderful war. She was seventeen when the war started and working as a junior secretary in a big electrical engineering company, which immediately switched to war work. She was employed in the lamp sales section. Mary was happy in the job; she says electric lamps are more interesting and varied than one might expect, and she was also the teleprinter operator for the whole branch. Partly because of the call up of men, she received promotion. However, she was keen to join the forces, and in 1942 signed the papers for the ATS (Auxiliary Territorial Service, the women's army corps) without telling her employer or her parents. 'They all raised the roof for their different reasons.'

After basic training she managed to be accepted for training as a cipher operator and later to move to Whitehall and be promoted first to serjeant and then to company serjeant- major. 'I hasten to say that these promotions were automatic. They went with the job provided you did your work well and behaved properly, they involved no leadership responsibilities whatsoever.'

Life at the War Office was very different. 'We worked in Whitehall, two floors underground. The work was real cipher work, traffic in and out and to and from the war zones and all sorts of other places, so it was very revealing. We never discussed it, but something big was obviously developing. It turned out to be D Day.

'After about twelve months we were told that cipher operators were needed in Washington DC and those of us already on the overseas list were asked if we wanted to go. There was one snag; we were asked to reduce in rank to corporal. That was too much to ask, but we accepted a reduction to serjeant. I never knew why this was required - in both the other women's services, all high grade cipher operators were commissioned officers, while we were only warrant officers anyway.

'Fifteen of us assembled in London and were sent off by army truck to a suburban station. We were a comic sight; we looked as if we were going to the war front, with standard issue impedimenta such as water bottles and tin mugs tied about our person with pieces of string, boxes of emergency rations, and all our possessions in kitbags, and of course tin hats. We did not know where we were heading for. We waited for ages at the station. It was already dark when the troop train arrived, full of soldiers, with some of them hanging out of the windows and making hopeful suggestions when they saw us on the platform. In fact, we had the two front carriages to ourselves, with the door to the rest of the train firmly locked. The train stopped fairly often as groups of soldiers were being dropped off or several carriages being unhitched at junctions. Eventually we arrived at Greenock on the Clyde, by which time only our two carriages were left on the train.

'And there in the distance, moored in the river, was the Queen Elizabeth. She had been launched before the war but had been used as a troop-ship ever since. The public rooms of the ship had been fitted out for civilian use and they were very opulent. But the cabins were just empty spaces and so we lived in primitive conditions, though we ate in the officers' mess and shared the beautiful saloon with them. Apart from one or two women officers, we were the only females on the ship, and the rest of the accommodation was filled with a variety of servicemen, probably on their way to the Far East. I assume our privileges were the result of fear that we would be assaulted by the squaddies, whereas the officers were expected to be gentlemen!

'Because of the possibility of attack by submarine, the ship had to zig-zag across the Atlantic making a 90 degree turn in her own length all the way, so the passage was not as smooth as it might have been. We had to wear our uniforms, and we had our serjeant's stripes on by then and a few of the women felt their demotion keenly. I didn't mind, it was worth it for the adventure. The most memorable feature of the crossing was the food in the officers' mess. The ship took on all its stores in the USA where of course there was no rationing. The menus for our meals were high luxury, and the amount of food served was unbelievable to our rationed eyes. Soon the waiters got used to serving us one meal between four, which worked out about right.

'On arrival in New York Harbour we were put on a train to Washington DC, where we were met by a British army truck - very much a case of from the sublime to the gorblimey - and taken to the hotel where we were to be billeted. It was large, fairly old and rather grotty, particularly with regard to cockroaches.

'The work was much the same as in London, but conditions of service were totally different. They were treated more like civilians and received a weekly allowance to pay for everything. It was a very good deal. Our allowance was enough for us to live on and most of us saved the whole of our pay for when we went on leave. We could afford to buy civilian clothes, which were less expensive than in England, and food was also cheaper.'

They were able to save up their leave allowance and during the eighteen months she was there Mary travelled to California and the Grand Canyon; to Florida and Cuba and New England; and to Canada, with a stop-off at Niagara Falls. She had short breaks riding in Virginia and in New York. Although they were interested in the American way of life, at the end of the eighteen month tour of duty, they were all looking forward to going home. This came as a big surprise to their officers in Washington, because they had decided to offer an extension of a year and promotion to commissioned rank.

'So in the autumn of 1945, with the war just over we were once again crossing the Atlantic on the Queen Elizabeth, but this time without the zig-zags. I was posted back to the War Office until I was demobbed. I was never unhappy in the Service or homesick, and I must say to Charmian that the ATS was never as rigorous or regimented as her physical education training!'

Conclusion

Mary's exhilaration at the life of travel and responsibility opened up for her by the ATS is obvious. Sima, Joan and Patricia also took opportunities which would not have been available to them as women but for the exigencies of war; and from these they gained in self-confidence, knowledge and independence. Our mothers, on the other hand, were much more constrained. They had to worry about their children and husbands in air raids or on active service, struggle with food and clothes rationing, and go without many of the pleasures of life. The greatest tragedy in our group was in Irene's family. Irene's mother left her family behind to try to establish a life for them in USA; her father who had fought for Germany in the first war was gassed in Auschwitz at the end of the second. Irene herself had had to abandon her adolescent hopes of a career and rebuild her life from scratch in England.

There was one outcome of war from which we all benefited. The centralised planning developed to meet the welfare and survival needs of the population in wartime was built upon in the development of the welfare state by the 1945 Labour government. As the chapters on education and work show, we were not slow to make the most of the opportunities it offered for our further personal development.

Wartime

*Patricia WRNS
about 1944*

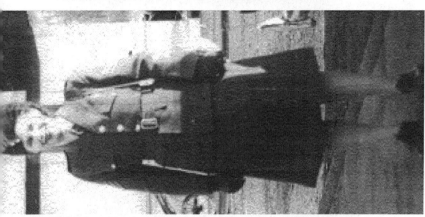

Mary ATS in 1942

*Charmian's mother and aunts
as VADs in 1915*

Charmian's family 'nursery' 1944
drawn by her sister and called 'The Nurse's billet'

Chapter 11

Growing Old at the Turn of the Century

Joan

> *'You are old Mother William the young woman said*
> *And your hair has become very white.*
> *And yet you persistently stand on your head,*
> *Do you think at your age it is right?'*

With apologies to Lewis Carroll

Within our lifetimes, but perhaps particularly in the last twenty years, social and technological changes have happened so fast that few people have anticipated their consequences. Some of these changes have particularly affected relations between the generations. According to a *Guardian* newspaper article in January 1998 soon almost half the population of Europe will be over 60. We have discussed some of the effects of family planning and of women starting careers before having children; as a result, the age gap between the generations has widened. Mobility in work and globalisation of trade have encouraged economic migration in addition to the migrations caused by war and persecution, making it more difficult for members of the wider family to help care for each other.

There has also been a change in employment patterns from full-time life-long work to short-term, casual and part-time jobs for an increasing number of those of normal working age. This means political assumptions about the funding of universal welfare services have to be re-examined.

It has never been easy to forecast the future but we face a social situation in which the pace of change is so fast, the way forward so uncertain, and the relationship between the past and the possible futures so tenuous it is difficult to find a thread of continuity between them. Senior citizens have a contribution to make, and from the reception we have had from younger people who hear of our work we think this is increasingly recognised.

There have certainly never been so many older people, particularly women, living active and independent lives. In the 1960s care homes for the aged were largely filled with 65-75 year olds. In the 1990s the average age of old people in such homes is 80. If that can happen over 30 years, who knows what can happen in the next 30 years? Polly Toynbee writing in *The*

Guardian in February 1998 points out that the electoral power of the retired has never been so great. Rather condescendingly, however, she sees the benefit of the third age movement in terms of increased happiness rather than political power or economic and social value. Of course happiness is important to everyone, but how is it achieved? A look at the life histories of members of our group, aged between the mid-60s and early 80s, shows that our satisfaction results from carrying out a range of activities, including paid and voluntary work, political involvement, and family care. The passing on of accumulated wisdom to the next generations has traditionally been seen as the prerogative of old age. But when change is happening so fast, our accumulated wisdom may not be as relevant as we think! It is easy to get caught out in yesterday's thinking.

Fear of ageing and the process of dying may be the reason why people tend to wax so prescriptive about the needs of the old. Listening to what older people themselves have to say about what is important to their quality of life, may be the way to keep up with the changing scene. We, as older people, need imagination to see the opportunities for a full life in spite of the handicaps that may come with age, and our solutions will affect other people as well as ourselves. Judging by the number of requests for volunteers from U3A members to take part in research projects, there must be a growing body of knowledge about ageing which is relevant not only to the possibility of reducing the need for expensive welfare services, but also indicating the variety of useful roles that can be filled by senior citizens.

In spite of travelling problems, older people may still be found minding grandchildren when both parents are working, a meeting of generations which may be beneficial to both; helping with literacy projects; telephone networking; preserving and recording the traditional skills of cooking and gardening. They are also confronting the challenges of computer technology and web-surfing. They may even be writing a book. The common cry of the 'retired' is: 'I don't know how I ever found time to work!'

We find it invigorating to be old at a time when it is beginning to be accepted that anything can be legitimately attempted. We all behave at times as though nobody else has had the experience of ageing. There is a sense in which this is not as absurd as it sounds, because ageing at the end of the twentieth century is so different from at any previous time It is our privilege to monitor, record and reflect on this.

PART THREE: REFLECTIONS

Charmian

'the past experience revived in the meaning
Is not the experience of one life only
But of many generations –'

T.S.Eliot, The Dry Salvages

When we meet for a social gathering or a discussion about the progress of the book, we no longer see each other just as a group of women sharing a common interest. Stretching back into the end of the 19th century we see Estella's grandmother selling produce in Vilna and acting as midwife in her village; Sima's is travelling by boat from Romania to Palestine with her four children to join her husband on a kibbutz. Elizabeth's grandmother, a widow, is taking in washing in her cottage in Wales; Joan and Patricia's, photographed in old age, is looking shrivelled, sitting in a bath chair wearing a feather boa and a hat.

Superimposed on these images are their daughters, our mothers. One is living in cramped accommodation in East London helping her husband in the tailoring workshop in the yard; another lives a protected life where girls are expected to cultivate their talents, but not to earn money. The First World War alters the lives of one or two irrevocably and has no respect for class. Our mothers bring up their daughters as best they can, some struggling greatly in the 1930s Depression, and some as members of large families in crowded homes involving much domestic drudgery. The daughters of these women are ourselves, irretrievably linked yet so different from them.

Many of our grandmothers could never have met, except as mistress and servant or buyer and seller of goods. If their paths had crossed they would have had nothing to say to each other. We on the other hand, never stop talking, and certainly know much more about one another than would be expected from an adult education class. Even if we have male partners we 'know' each other differently; women in a group who trust one another have a shared perspective which changes when men are present. We have described how we came to recognise the extent of our diverse origins, and traced the steps of our convergence in three generations through the experience of family life, education and work, and changes in social status. We have outlined our geographical moves, from Europe, Scotland, Wales, different parts of England, to come together in London. Each of us, needing continued stimulation after 'retirement' decided to enrol in the U3A. What happened then has already been described.

It is clear from the material we have analysed that much of this convergence of our lives is the result of increased opportunities; the recognition of women's rights, expressed through changes in the law, and making possible our schooling and our careers. Although some of us may feel there are many gender issues still to be addressed, our stories are a reminder of what has been achieved. We are not just passive recipients of these changes. Women themselves, in various feminist pressure groups, have pushed them forward.

The history of women is not just the history of changes in the law and in attitudes, fought for by well-known feminists. It is also the history of women's private lives. It is Charmian's grandmother considering earnestly how to cast her first vote in 1918. It is Jo demonstrating about Greenham Common, and Mary encouraging young women to raise their aspirations.

Although two or three of us are active feminists we have no evidence that any of our grandmothers or mothers were (a bit disappointing really!). Some of them were completely preoccupied with family life; Joan, writing about her mother, comments on the amount of frustrated ability that must have hidden behind her 'correct' behaviour. The history of women is about the everday lives of these women, as well as those like Irene's mother, travelling to Cuba alone as a strategy to try and save her family from persecution. It is about those of us who left school at fourteen and made up for their inadequate schooling in adult life.

We come from different cultural backgrounds, but cultures are not monolithic; they are interpreted by families, and within families sometimes by one strong individual. If the family culture is adaptive and flexible it makes it easier for open choices to be made by members; or alternatively decisions may be taken by individuals in rebellion against a rigid or disintegrated family life. The narration of biography can help to unravel the tangled skein of social and individual strands determining the course of a life. We find in our stories that although we have shaped our own histories 'under circumstances directly given..and...transmitted from the past', we have been less constrained by them than were our mothers and grandmothers. Joan said in one of our discussions: 'It's not what happens to you but what you do with it that counts.' But there were more choices open to us in the middle of the century than for our foremothers at the beginning.

The tracing of our life histories and those of our mothers and grandmothers shows how these choices were made, how they affected later choices, what inhibited our foremothers and the consequences for us; the opportunities we missed and those we grasped, as we tried to change our lives.

The chapter on the family draws attention to the differences between us in the continuity between generations. Continuity is particularly important during childhood, in building up a sense of identity. We develop a stable notion of 'who we are' through our place in the family, among friends, at school, in the work place. We can do this because as humans we can reflect on ourselves; we constantly tell and retell our own story inside our own heads, making sense of new experiences, modifying first impressions, interpreting the world in a way which we can acknowledge. It is made easier if we can root it in a sense of the past, and see ourselves as part of a chain reaching backwards and forwards through the generations. This gives us a sense of immortality, a feeling that we don't just crumble to dust.

A stable sense of identity makes it easier to face the ups and downs of life and to feel in control. The theoretical writings about developing a sense of oneself in a fragmented, individualistic modern society, stress the importance of keeping a narrative going; of telling, modifying one's story, and filling the gaps in it. We, between us, have shared this process, made it conscious, modified it through listening to each other and finding we are not alone. We have done this much more than is apparent in the text written for publication.

A sense of continuity is much easier if there is communication between generations. We have seen what a difference it has made to our sense of the past to have letters and documents, or a fund of stories handed down. Estella's image of her grandmother being the midwife in her village may be apocryphal but it is true in essence. She has lots of loving family photographs; Sima has a rather blurred picture of her grandfather's life on the first kibbutz in Palestine. Photographs can evoke the past more immediately than words. As so often happens it is the women who have preserved these memories. These are not limited to any one class though the form they take depends on literacy, leisure, and a sense that such details are significant.

Those from families with no such traditions cannot picture their grandmothers because they know so little about them. Many of our families have suffered disruption. Starting again in new countries makes the need to preserve continuity even stronger; treasures laden with meaning - christening robes, wedding dresses, photographs - were brought all the way from Europe to Ellis Island by early immigrants to America. Irene's mother's life story acted as a bridge across the generations after the family had been so grievously split up. Charmian's grandmother used letters to hold the family together in the First World War. All of us suffered some disruption in the last war; but as we have seen, for some it offered wider horizons and the chance to reassess one's capabilities.

So perhaps we should not make too much of the significance of continuity. It can lead to complacency or be oppressive. Discontinuity on the other hand forces one to re-tell one's story, to face the past and the question 'Who am I?' directly. Disruption can be overcome through luck and enterprise and we have seen how this has happened in several of our families.

Our project was a success because of the way it enabled us to face the past and the present, tell our stories, and reach a new understanding of how we came to be the way we are. For some of us it was the first time this had been possible. Sima said: 'Out of a tiny acorn an oak tree has grown.' She was referring both to the three generations of women, and to the development of our project. It may not look like an oak tree to others but it does to us, strong and with many branches.

It hasn't taken quite as long as an oak tree to grow but it has taken several years during which we who started it as old women in the world's terms have become older. But we don't think of ourselves as old, it's only other people who do. 'I feel about 35,' says Mary, 'though my body doesn't.'

Whatever we feel about ourselves most of us have become used to being the oldest generation of our families, which is sobering when it happens. We accept as a blessing the right to travel free within London which makes our active lives possible. One or two of the group are involved in a feminist pressure group representing the concerns of older women. Several spend time visiting friends or siblings who are recovering, or not recovering from illness or operations. We try to come to terms with varying physical disabilities, and the effects of one of these is described by Patricia in her life story.

None of our burdens or responsibilities prevents us from following our interests. Will our generation still be seen as old when more of us are caring for parents as Estella does when she visits her 94-year-old father every week? She writes of him: 'His bedroom is a confusing mess of present and past - a jumble of memorabilia - and he says that it represents his whole life and it must be on view to him so that he doesn't forget.' Maybe we shall feel the same at his age.

What will happen to traditional ideas of three-generational families when there are more and more people living into their 90s and there are four generations or even five to consider? Joan has written about the ways older people contribute to society and in the face of these changes the traditional notion of old age seems irrelevant.

Why has the spreading oak tree of our work flourished so well? During the years we have been together we have seen initial wariness and occasional irritation at each others foibles, give way to tolerance and appreciation of differences. We have written a lot about the social factors in our convergence. But when we discussed what we thought held us together we mostly came up with a rather self-congratulatory list of personal characteristics, such as openness, curiosity about the world and ourselves, an independent spirit.

These qualities are expressed in our lifelong pursuit of education in the broadest sense; the acquisition of knowledge and skills, and the exploration of experience. This was what made us come together in the U3A as a place for learning, and focus on women's history. We have appreciated the co-operative learning involved in both the way we conducted the group, and in preparing our work for publication. Education is central to our lives and to this project. Because the U3A is not concerned with qualifications we have been free to develop it as we wish, sharing our skills and insights in a relaxed way.

Here are some of our reflections on the experience.

Jo: 'The project has brought great pleasure in the company; it has illustrated, made real and added depth to what I had already known about the strength of women, and the rich variety of London's population.'

Marj: 'The project has contributed to my emotional education. I found talking about my early life really harrowing. I was practically in tears most of the time even though I wasn't relating traumatic or dramatic things. It gradually got easier and I realised I felt better about what we were doing and began to appreciate the group much more. The experience seems to have cleared away some confusions in my mind'.

Charmian: 'At first I had more academic ambitions for the way I thought the group should develop. However I came to appreciate the informal learning we were all doing through shaping our own stories and appreciating each others. For myself, participation in the group has been the incentive to study the theoretical approaches to life history and the problems of group writing.'

Estella: 'The project has made me explore my own and my family's history in great depth, and enabled me to find reasons for my own and my family's behaviour. In many ways compassion and understanding have replaced blame and guilt. The fact that this sort of detailed exploration has been carried out by each individual member of our group and our findings have been expressed orally and in writing, openly and frankly to one another, has given our project a certain poignancy as well as uniquness.'

In the chapter on education, Patricia distinguishes between the acquisition of knowledge and skills from others, and learning from the exploration of experience. She continues: 'An account of the education of our grandmothers, our mothers and ourselves includes the gaining of knowledge; subjective facts emerge as we tug the thread of memory and look at it in the context of history. It involves learning new skills as we (relatively unskilled in writing, not to mention the mysteries of incompatible floppy discs) seek to organise and reflect on the wealth of material we have uncovered. It involves learning through experience as we come to share insights and memories without pressure and with respect for privacy. Increased understanding of oneself and one another grows imperceptibly in a climate of undemanding relationship.'

> *'We shall not cease from exploration*
> *And the end of all our exploring*
> *Will be to arrive at where we started*
> *And know the place for the first time.'*

> T.S. Eliot, Little Gidding

Chapter 12

Using Life Histories

Charmian

We didn't realise it at the outset of our work, but the gathering of life histories has become increasingly popular, and has been used in many different ways. One development has been 'reminiscence work,' often with our age group. Of course 'reminiscence' means remembering the feelings and experiences of the past, which can happen in a number of situations and for a number of reasons; it is often used in documentary programmes on television and in local history groups, particularly fuelled at present by millenium fever. In the professional world of 'life history' it has come to be associated with remembering in groups about the size of ours, encouraged by skilled facilitators, and often in residential or day-care settings. It aims not only to record, but also to stimulate those who are understimulated, often unused to being listened to or unused to writing; to help them to feel positive about the value of their own experience and to enhance their sense of self-identity.

So are we engaged in reminiscence work? To the pupils of the international school who share the building with the U3A we must seem like just another group of the old people who go more slowly up and down the stairs or prefer to use the lift. Most of us would agree with Patricia, who said 'I've never thought of myself as elderly'. But we must be, as the students of the U3A are by definition members of 'the third age'.

It will be obvious to any one reading this book that the experience has been beneficial for us in personal ways. We have all attended meetings regularly, often travelling considerable distances. The project has given us permission to talk about ourselves, and some of us who have had traumatic experiences have felt able to speak of them for the first time. One of the benefits has been the realisation of shared triumphs and difficulties in spite of our extemely varied family backgrounds.

But older women are not all in residential homes, nor do they all suffer from lack of stimulation nor a feeling that their lives have no value. We are in a sense at the opposite pole from the people with whom reminiscence work is often practised; life has not been a bed of roses for us all but we lead active lives, and are lucky enough to have considerable personal autonomy. The institution of the U3A is not at all like a residential home, and we make claims for our project other than the personal therapy often associated with reminiscence work. It is only in the last few months that we have realised that as our three-generational history spans the century, and the year 2000 is upon us, it is admirably suited to be part of the millennial jamboree!

The academic underpinning of a life history approach crosses the boundaries of sociology, anthropology and history as well as literature. Oral history was of course the first kind of history, but life history embraces all sources of life narrative from oral accounts to written autobiography; personal documents such as diaries, letters and Mass Observation archives; and official documents such as registers of births, deaths and marriages. Samuel Pepys' diaries of life in seventeenth century London are a record of his everyday life, just as the diary of the project's development kept by one of us has been a valuable source for writing about its 'life history'.

Henry Mayhew's investigation of the lives of the London poor in 1851 was a pioneer in the use of verbatim accounts such as that of the rat-killer who had all his life 'been a-dealing a little in rats...my father had a notion of the same'. Mayhew writes a page on this man's account of his life.

Most of his respondents were men, but here is his report of the life of a coster girl: 'My mother has been in the streets selling all her lifetime. Her uncle learnt her the markets and she learnt me... the gals begins working very early at our work, the parents makes them go out when a'most babies. There's a little gal, I'm sure she ain't more than half-past seven, that stands selling watercresses next my stall, and mother was saying: "Only look there, how that little one has to get her living afore she a'most knows what a penn'orth means".' These wonderfully authentic accounts were all recorded by a stenographer he took with him round the streets of London.

The use of the personal in-depth interview, and the careful observation of everyday life while participating in it, has continued and been made much easier with modern ways of recording what people say. As we discovered during our own work, the distinction between 'facts' and personal responses is not clear. We interpret everything we know about the world through the medium of language and ideas, which we develop and which in turn shape the way we think and behave. This is particularly so of the social world. In other words all history is a matter of interpretation from different perspectives. Official history has been dominated by the interpretations of academic men; but there are perspectives to be found from the oppressed and the poor as well as those of women.

In Britain in the 1950s sociologists began to look at 'deviant' young people through their own accounts of their lives and the processes which led them into rebellion. But this was usually from the top down, or the outside in. The sympathetic investigator got the confidence of the deprived teenager, recorded his point of view and then interpreted it from within his particular theoretical framework. And it was usually 'his'.

Early approaches to the women's perspective came with the Co-operative Women's Guild *Letters from Working Women*, published in 1915 about their experience of maternity. This was followed later by a similar volume, *Life As We Have Known It*, containing first-hand accounts of the lives of Co-operative women. The first essay in this collection begins: 'I was born in Bethnal Green, April 9th 1855, a tiny scrap of humanity. I was my mother's seventh child, and seven more were born after me - fourteen in all which made my mother a perfect slave. Generally speaking she was either expecting a baby to be born or had one at the breast. At the time there were eight of us the eldest was not big enough to get ready for school without help.'

These books were edited by a woman from another class, Margaret Llewelyn Davies, educated at Girton and general secretary of the Women's Co-operative Guild for over thirty years. The second of them begins with a letter from her friend Virginia Woolf, always conscious of the unbridgeable gulf between herself and the writers. She could not be one of them because she had never stood at the washtub; her hands had never 'wrung and scrubbed and chopped up whatever the meat might be that made a miner's supper'. She ends her letter: 'These voices are beginning only now to emerge from silence...the writing has been done in kitchens, at odds and ends of leisure, in the midst of distractions and obstacles.'

The Women's Co-operative collections are fascinating precursors to the developments described below, which aim to break down the barriers between women and replace them by a sense of what they have in common.

Life history and feminism

It is only with new developments in the women's movement of the 1970s and 80s that 'she' really begins to have a say. The life history approach has been influential in women's consciousness-raising groups; these were groups of women who discussed all aspects of their experience as female children and adults. The aim was to develop enough insight to challenge preconceptions both personally and collectively, and to become aware of previously unrecognised similarities in their lives.

187

Life history has also been used by academic women historians and anthropologists in the burgeoning women's studies and women's history courses of the same period. They wished to challenge the male-dominated nature of most interpretations of history, and also to question the whole idea of research as an enterprise engaged in by an academic with particular expertise, on 'ignorant' subjects who are therefore open to exploitation. Some women researchers have tried to replace this conventional idea with one in which research findings are shared between all participants at every stage, and the views of the researched are given as much value as those of the researcher. A notion rather uncritically used in a feminist approach has been that of 'empowerment'; the idea that women should feel able to take their own initiatives to understand and change their lives, and that participatory research could give them the insight and confidence to do it. This is a similar moral position to that of the consciousness-raising groups already mentioned. It also underlies some reminiscence work which may encourage people to write as well as talk, and to discover that they can even publish their work and so bring it to a wider audience.

So are we a group of feminists doing feminist history? It depends what is meant by 'feminist'. Three of us are politically active in women's organisations. Two of us have been involved academically in the history of women and gender in society. Others in the group would repudiate the label 'feminist' as not representing their idea of themselves.

However, we feel that we have all been influenced by the ideas of feminism which have become part of the culture in our adult years. As our life histories show, the majority of us have been, or still are married. But have not been conventional in our relationships and several of us have lived with partners outside marriage. All of us have earned our living and nearly all of us have continued to work after marriage and having children. Four of us have worked professionally well after retirement age.

We also chose to come to the women's history group which was a new and minority interest at our branch of the U3A. This choice was sometimes for pragmatic reasons such as time-tabling; and Joan says she chose the topic originally because it was in a small room which meant there would be a group small enough to make full participation possible. However, it also says something about our awareness that history when we were at school was written by and for men, with a few queens and suffragettes thrown in. Women's contribution to history is not just that. They have a different perspective on the past, and this was something we were keen to know more about.

Although our group consists only of women, we never excluded men from the class, though there have only ever been two men interested enough to attend. One came for a term in the early days when we were still doing a formal taught course, and never said a word. The other came when we were in full flood on our own histories. We welcomed him, and talked to him about the value of a man's perspective. We explained what we were doing and he sat through to the end of the session, then left quickly saying he had learnt a lot. It was not the best moment for a new arrival and probably quite unlike any history he had met before. Shortly after that we closed the group to newcomers because continuity had become so important to our work.

So we have varying attitudes to feminism, and definitions of it. We are doing history by, with, and for women, though we are delighted if men take an interest in it, as some of our partners do. Why should they not? Women have been studying men's history for years.

To conclude:

With the developments indicated above, and others in working class and local history, the value of a life history approach using oral history as a source has come to be increasingly recognised in this country. It is now possible to study its methods and applications in academic courses such as those at Sussex University. But even before we knew of these developments the approach of sociologists such as the American C. Wright Mills in the 1950s had been an inspiration for our work. For him the 'sociological imagination' consisted of the ability to grasp the relationship between history and biography in society. Public issues such as unemployment, war, marriage, the nature of urban life, are also the personal troubles of individuals and the sociologist must understand both the public and the personal, and the links between them. We are not just pawns in a game though the rules of society impose limits on our actions. Social change occurs through individuals and groups pushing against these limits.

Through recording the processes of our lives and our responses to war, economic depression, persecution, and educational opportunity, we can begin to understand cultural and economic change. Life histories are a vital link between the individual and society, and a bit of personal therapy too. And we stumbled into all this unexpectedly.

Chapter 13

The University of the Third Age

Joan

The U3A is less than twenty years old, yet already some of the thinking which led to its inception sounds dated. The fact that most of the literature written about it at the time is no longer in print and available in only a very few libraries, is evidence of this. The movement started in France and a small group of academics felt moved to explore its relevance in the UK. The historian Peter Laslett wrote an article: *All Our Futures: The Education of the Elderly in Britain*. Michael Young brought to the idea a passion for accessibility, and Eric Midwinter made a brief broadcast on Radio Four's *You and Yours* programme in 1981, after which 400 listeners wrote in excitedly. Dianne Norton joined the original committee as administrator, and became executive secretary to the first National Committee. Grants were sought to develop the project and by 1986 the organisation was able to envisage further development being self-financed by modest subscriptions: a model for the independence of spirit that is so highly valued by the elderly.

The Eight Objects and Twenty Principles on which the U3A was founded in 1981 were amended in 1984 and have remained unchallenged since. They acknowledged that for the first time in history lengthy retirement was commonplace, and that such an institution was appropriate in order to make the possibility of intellectual and aesthetic satisfaction available, affordable and reproduceable throughout the country. They are characterised by liberal idealism, expressing a perhaps naive belief that, if the will is there, it is possible to create a better society through education. Nevertheless, the vision of a community of learners helping each other without financial reward, without reference to standards and qualifications, has proved a fruitful and versatile one. It has endorsed learning as a proper activity for everyone, removing blocks which many have carried forward from an unsuccessful or unhappy early education. This has been no condescending blue-print for the less fortunate, but rather the mutual enrichment of members with different educational backgrounds.

Our own experience of the U3A in action has been characterised by the pleasures of shared activity; of independent reflections on our family histories and explorations into the changing customs of the society in which we, our mothers and our grandmothers, have lived. The process of examining our own experience is doubly rewarding when we can stand back and relate that experience to all that is going on in the world around. Our project has developed within the enabling context of the U3A, to culminate in our book.

This level of participation does not happen automatically in every U3A class. Sometimes previous experience of education perpetuates a distinction between teacher and taught so that passive dependence replaces interaction and frustrates mutual learning.

However, accommodation also influences the degree of participation. In the central London U3A large lecture halls get filled with large groups, so there is competition for airspace and retiring violets do not thrive. In smaller branches, the cosiness of private house venues may deter serious effort. The poor aesthetic quality of affordable premises may also discourage those who are not yet committed. As with all services it is not enough to have a right-sounding policy. What actually goes on will vary through time and circumstance and needs constant monitoring.

14. Sources and Further Reading

These are the books we have consulted for the different sections:

Part One
Marx, Karl (1852) *The 18th Brumaire of Louis Bonaparte*, Marx/Engels Collected Works, Lawrence and Wishart 1968 edition. p.97
Rousseau, J.(1781) *Confessions*. Several translations exist, one being Penguin Books 1953. The quotation is from the beginning of Book 7

Part Two
There's no place like home
Burnett, John (1978) *A Social History of Housing 1815-1970*, David and Charles p.252
Eliot, T.S. (1944) *Four Quartets*, Faber and Faber Ltd. pp. 15 & 22

What is a family?
Purvis, June ed. (1995) *Women's History: Britain 1850-1945*, UCL Press, particularly chapter by Harrison on Women and Health

Lifelong learning
Young, M.F.D. (1998) *The Curriculum of the Future*, Falmer Press

The experience of war
Beddoe, Deirdre (1998) *Back to Home and Duty*, Pandora
Turner, E.S (1980) *Dear Old Blighty*, Michael Joseph

Part Three
Eliot, T.S. (1944) op.cit pp. 28 & 43
Giddens, A. (1991) *Modernity and Self-Identity - Self and Society in the Modern Age*, Polity Press

Part Four
Using life histories
Llewelyn Davies, M. ed. (1931) *Life as We Have Known It -*
 by Co-operative Women, Virago 1977 pp.xxiii, xxxxi & 1
Mayhew, Henry (1851) *London Labour and the London Poor*, in Mayhew's London Quennell ed. Polity Press 1949 pp. 87 & 400
Wright Mills, Charles (1959) *The Sociological Imagination*, OUP

The University of the Third Age
Laslett, Peter (1980) *All our Futures: The Education of the Elderly in Britain*, Elmgate Trust and National Extension College

To find out more
About using life histories:
Plummer, K. (1990) *Documents of Life: an Introduction to the Problems and Literature of a Humanistic Method*, Unwin Hyman 2nd edition

A Resource for Women's Studies, The Mass-Observation Archive, University of Sussex, Brighton

Samuel, R. & Thompson, Paul (1990) *The Myths We Live By*, Routledge History Workshop

Thompson, Paul (1978) *The Voice from the Past: Oral History*, OUP 2nd edition 1988

About women's history:
Beddoe, Deirdre (1993) *Discovering Women's History: A Practical Guide to Researching the Lives of Women since 1800*, Longman 3rd edition

Caine, Barbara (1997) *English Feminism 1780-1980*, OUP

Holdsworth, Angela (1988) *Out of the Doll's House - The Story of Women in the 20th century*, BBC Books

Oldfield, S. ed.(1994) *This Working-Day World: Women's Lives and Cultures in Britain 1914-1945,* Taylor & Francis

Some studies of women's lives:
Forster, Margaret (1996) *Hidden Lives*, Penguin

Llewelyn Davies, M. ed. (1915) *Maternity: Letters from Working Women*, Women's Co-operative Guild, Virago 1978

Schweitzer, P., Hilton, I., Mosa, J. eds. (1985) *What Did You Do in the War Mum? Women recall their Wartime Work*, Age Exchange, new edition 1993

Ideas for writing about your own life:
Stanley, Jo (1998) *Writing Out Your Life*, Scarlet Press

[Midwinter, Eric (New edition 2001) *A Voyage of Rediscovery: a guide to writing your life story*, Third Age Press (see following pages for details)]

Useful Addresses

Age Exchange Reminiscence Centre,
11 Blackheath Village, London SE3 9LA. Tel: 020 8318 9105.
Website: www.age-exchange.org.uk. Has an extensive list of publications
and reminiscence resources. A hands-on reminiscence museum.

Growing Old Disgracefully Network,
102 Grosvenor Avenue, Carshalton, Surrey SM5 3EP. Tel: 020 8647 1860.
A national network of women with groups throughout the country.

National Life Story Collection,
British Library National Sound Archive, 96 Euston Road, London NW1 2DB.
Tel: 020 7412 7404.
Publications and advice on recording life stories.

Older Feminists Network, c/o Astra, 54 Gordon Road, London N3 1EP.

Oral History Society (as for National Life Story Collection above).

University of the Third Age (U3A),
26 Harrison Street, London WC1H 8JG. Tel: 020 7837 8838.
Website: www.u3a.org.uk. Send an SAE for contact details of your nearest
U3A. Many U3As have study groups on local and personal history.

Women's History Network c/o The Institute of Women's Studies, Lancaster
University, Lancaster LA1 4YL